THE QUAKERS

THE QUAKERS

THEIR STORY AND MESSAGE

by

A. NEAVE BRAYSHAW

B.A., LL.B.

> *As ye dwell in that which is of God,*
> *it guides you up out of the element-*
> *ary life, and out of the mortal into*
> *the immortal.*
>
> GEORGE FOX

LONDON: GEORGE ALLEN & UNWIN LTD
NEW YORK: THE MACMILLAN COMPANY

First Edition *1921*
Second Edition, Revised . *1927*
Third Edition, Revised . . *1938*

Always feel a growing in the power of the Lord God that is universal and everlasting.

GEORGE FOX

Take heed of the earth, and keep a-top of that which will cumber the mind.

Ibid.

ERRATA

Page 55, line 6: *For* Boehe *read* Boehme.

,, 121. The paragraph printed in small type commencing "Conceive, now, of a Church composed . . ." is not a quotation from another work, but is the author's own material. The footnote on Harvey and Brown's book refers solely to the passage "Forgiveness [which] does not truly . . . passive a word." (The addition of a footnote reference after ". . . *in one another*" is an error.)

,, 248, line 21: *For* (p. 129) *read* (p. 119).

Index: Henson, Hensley, *the references should read* 23 n., 27 n.

Fox, quoted: *To the references given add* 158.

Fry, Eliz. : *To the references given add* 178.

(*The Quakers*)

PREFACE TO THE THIRD EDITION

IN pursuance of my object, as stated in the Prefaces to
the earlier editions of this book, of setting forth the past
history of the Society of Friends so as to give understanding of its present work and condition, I have ex-
panded Chapters XIV, XV, and XVI, which tell of the
changes that came about in the middle of the nineteenth
century, when it emerged from its long seclusion within
its own borders, apart from the rest of the community.

For some of the additional matter contained in Chapter
I, and for a criticism of the whole chapter, I am indebted
to Dr. Albert Peel and to Geoffrey F. Nuttall; for the
sketch at the beginning of Chapter VI of early Quakerism
in Ireland, to Miss Isabel Grubb; for a revision of Chapter
XIX, telling of the work of Friends in and after the war
of 1914–18, to Miss A. Ruth Fry; and for the account at
the end of that chapter of certain Quaker work abroad,
to Carl Heath. To each of them I express my thanks for
their respective contributions, which I myself should have
found difficult or impossible to make. To Percy Stanger
my thanks are due for his help in seeing this edition
through the press.

A. N. B.

PREFACE TO THE SECOND EDITION

FOR this edition the statement of early Quaker teaching and the account of the religious thought of the time have been rewritten, a chapter on early American Quakerism has been added, and many other changes have been made. Throughout, my object in telling of the past has been to give understanding of the present. To Dr. J. Vernon Bartlet and to Edward Grubb I am grateful for help in the writing of Chapters III and IV, and to Stephen Hobhouse for his reading of the proofs and for various suggestions.

A. N. B.

P.S.—Attention is drawn to *The Faith and Practice of the Quakers*, by Dr. Rufus M. Jones, a work which is to appear about the same time as this present one.

PREFACE TO THE FIRST EDITION

IN setting forth this historical sketch of the Society of Friends in England, I have wished to portray the Society and its message at the present time rather than to compile a chronicle of past events. Inasmuch, however, as the present is not to be understood apart from the past, I have indicated the lines of thought which have gone to the shaping of present-day Quakerism both in its weakness and its strength. For this a knowledge of history is necessary, first of early days when Friends found themselves in a position of isolation; then of their century and a half of voluntary and, in fact, studied seclusion; and then of the years of bewilderment at finding themselves open to the world, no longer protected from it by visible barriers. I have also spoken of the strands that have run continuously through the history, the emphasis laid on Divine guidance, variously as this has been understood, and the philanthropic concern for the outward well-being of mankind. My aim throughout has been to tell enquirers what they may expect to find among us, and it may be that the historical information will be useful to our own members also.

I am at the mercy of any critic who points out that I have overmuch indulged in quotation; I cannot rebut the charge, and I have no wish to do so; I can only say that when I have wanted to confirm my statements or make good my points I have found it impossible to summarize in my own words the language, often quaint and beautiful, in which our fathers in the faith still speak for themselves.

For the help of those who would follow up what they here read I have given full references. Particularly am I glad in this way continually to draw attention to the two books, *The Beginnings of Quakerism* and *The Second Period of Quakerism*, written by William Charles Braithwaite. In my treatment of the seventeenth century I am indebted to these two works, as will be obvious to everyone who knows them; but, in fact, every future Quaker historian of that time will find himself bound to make similar acknowledgment. Furthermore, I am grateful to the author of them for a careful reading of the manuscript of this book in one of its later stages and for certain suggestions which I have incorporated. My thanks are also due to Ernest E. Taylor and Robert Davis for their suggestions and other help, and to Rachel B. Braithwaite, who, more than once, has read over my account of Friends' relief work carried on during the late war and after it.

To those who wish to know more about the Society of Friends at the present day, I commend *The Faith of a Quaker*, by John William Graham; and I would also draw attention to the forthcoming work written by Dr. Rufus M. Jones in continuation of the two volumes by Braithwaite, already mentioned, bringing the history of Quakerism to the end of the nineteenth century.

Like everyone else who writes Quaker history, I have good cause to acknowledge the services rendered by Norman Penney, F.S.A., Librarian of the Friends' Reference Library, and by the Assistant Librarians, M. Ethel Crawshaw and Grace Yewdall.

A. NEAVE BRAYSHAW

CONTENTS

Chapter I

THE CENTURY PRECEDING GEORGE FOX

THE year 1647 witnessed the first recorded success of George Fox in persuading his hearers to receive his message. He was then twenty-three years old and before this he had, in his search for light, conversed with many in the midland counties and in London. Being attracted into Lancashire by the report of a woman who had fasted for twenty-two days and finding her to be "under a temptation," he spoke to her what he "had from the Lord," and passed on to Dukinfield and Manchester, where, as his *Journal* records, he "stayed a while and declared truth. There were some convinced who received the Lord's teaching by which they were confirmed and stood in the truth."

A hundred years before this, in 1547, Henry VIII had died and the succeeding century of English religious life had been marked by continual change. Less than fifteen years before his death, Henry, in his quarrel with the Pope concerning his marriage with Katharine of Aragon, had cast off the Papal rule, announcing that he himself was the supreme head on earth of the Church in England. As soon, however, as the Church found itself freed from an alien yoke, it showed itself to be divided on matters of a more properly religious nature, and, under the influence of the Continental Reformers, from the successors of the Lollards there arose a Protestant party which stood far from Rome.[1] The King and most of the bishops and

[1] Concerning the spiritual ancestry of this party from Wyclif downward, see Rufus M. Jones *Studies in Mystical Religion*, ch. xv, "The Pre-Reformation in England," and "The Lollard movement after 1384" by Geoffrey F. Nuttall, "Congregational Historical Society's Transactions," September 1935.

clergy, as well as of the laity who took sides with him against the Pope, contemplated little change either in doctrine or practice beyond the abolition of certain extremes of Roman Catholic practice. Thomas Fuller speaks of Henry's religion as a "medley religion"; and describes what he calls a "motley execution," on the same day and at the same place, of three clergymen on account of their Protestant views and of three Roman Catholics because of their denial of the King's spiritual supremacy. He adds that "a stranger standing by did wonder (as well he might) what religion the King was of." It was in 1546, twelve years after the "Reformation," that Ann Askew was burned for denying Transubstantiation, the doctrine that, on consecration by the priest, the "substance" of the bread and wine is turned into the very body and blood of Christ.[1] During the short reign of Edward VI (1547–53) the extreme Protestant party was in the ascendant; and this was followed by the Roman Catholic reaction under Mary. In the latter half of her five years' reign about 280 people were burned for their faith.

The settlement of the Church of England under Elizabeth (1558–1603) is the one which, with comparatively small modifications, has lasted to the present day. It was more distinctly Protestant than that of her father, Henry VIII, the Thirty-nine Articles being Calvinistic in wording and spirit, but she set up a rigid order of discipline and procedure from which not the slightest deviation was to be allowed. She knew her position to be insecure and while she professed probably in all sincerity, that she had no wish to enquire into the private belief of anyone, she insisted on uniformity in the conduct of

[1] The maiden name of George Fox's wife (*post*, p. 73) was Askew, but the often-repeated statement that she was a descendant of Ann Askew is incorrect (Braithwaite, *Beginnings of Quakerism*, p. 99, Crosfield, *Margaret Fox of Swarthmoor Hall*, pp. 2–4).

worship, holding that any breach of such uniformity was a disintegrating element in the life of the state. "The right of free belief was granted; the right of the free expression of that belief was denied."[1] This, as far as it went, was an advance on the claim of the Church to a right to take the initiative in enquiring into a man's belief and punishing him if he were found to be heretical. The extreme party in the Church, Puritan, as it came to be called, wished to hold meetings, "prophesyings," as they said, in addition to the ordinary Church services and, in their determination to stand as far from Rome as possible, they protested against all ceremonies and vestments that savoured of Catholic practice. With a fine sense of progress in spiritual reformation they also protested against the rigidity that was fastened on them, holding that "the tieing of ministers to the whole form so precisely . . . makes the people think that the very reading or hearing of all or a part of the service appointed is a sufficient serving of God."[2]

Isaac Penington, the Quaker, writing in 1660, says that in the Puritan days the most eminent Christians were those men "who were most against the form and persecuted for their conscientious stumbling at it"; and that the greatest persecutors were those "who were most zealous for the form, both of the government and worship of the Church of England."[3] The Puritans also protested against the shameless scrambles of the clergy for preferment and against the evil of a non-resident ministry due,

[1] Jordan, *The Development of Religious Toleration in England*, p. 128, and see 174. "No windows, Elizabeth claimed, were made into men's souls; they might think what they liked provided that no expression incompatible with public order was given to their opinion." Pollard, vol. iv of the series, *The Political History of England*, p. 356.

[2] *The Seconde Parte of a Register* (i. 96) edited by Peel.

[3] *Answer to that Common Objection to the Quakers, Works* (edn. of 1761), i. 427.

in many cases, to the fact of one incumbent holding several livings at once. A picture put forth in 1642 shows a clergyman carrying a church in each hand and one on his back and saying to another, "I would I had thee too." Of the Puritans it has been said:

> They were learned men, and large numbers of the clergy were extremely ignorant. They were earnest and eloquent preachers; and the enormous majority of the clergy were unable to preach. They were moral men and too many of the clergy were living in notorious vice.[1]

Nevertheless, it was this party, disturbers of the uniformity deemed to be essential to the safety of the State, that Elizabeth was determined to suppress. Grindal, Archbishop of Canterbury, whom she rightly suspected of being favourable to them, was for some years suspended from the exercises of most of his official functions and for part, at least, of this time he was forbidden to leave his house. He was succeeded by Whitgift, who was to a large extent responsible for increasing the power of the Court of High Commission to enable him the more easily to persecute the Puritans. This he did with great cruelty. The cleft in the Church which was apparent at the beginning of the English Reformation became a chasm in the days of Elizabeth; from her reign there went forth the streams of High Church, Low Church, and Non-conformity which are still flowing.[2]

The other disturbers of outward religious uniformity were the Roman Catholics. For the first few years of the Queen's reign her wish to avoid conflict with their Church and to secure a broad religious settlement in which they would be included led to a practical suspension of

---

[1] Dale, *History of English Congregationalism*, p. 117.
[2] The terms High and Low Church did not come in till the reign of Anne, but they may be used here to describe the situation.

the penal laws directed against them, but this position of existence on sufferance was humiliating and was calculated to weaken the Catholic fibre. In 1570, Pope Pius V issued a Bull of Excommunication against Elizabeth absolving her subjects from allegiance to her and anathematizing those who obeyed her. "As far as a Pope could do he rendered treason a necessary part of the religious duties of every English Romanist."[1] Many Catholics, however, were also loyal subjects of the Queen, and they viewed with disfavour the activities, bringing trouble on them all, of foreign Jesuits, who descended on the country stirring up plots in every direction.[2] Many of them centred round Mary Queen of Scots. Certain of the invasions of Ireland were carried on in the Pope's name, and the attack of the Spanish Armada was part of the Catholic assault. The penal laws were now rigorously enforced and in the last twenty-eight years of the reign nearly 190 Roman Catholics were hanged, most of them after being tortured. Some of them were martyrs for their faith in the usual sense of the word, others were rebels against the Crown, and in the general confusion accurate discrimination was not always made. The widespread belief that Catholics were officially permitted to show outward marks of loyalty to the Queen[3] while

[1] A. F. Pollard, *Political History of England, 1547–1603,* pp. 77 and 429 *note.* "The papacy . . . had made it virtually impossible for an English Catholic to be at once a loyal subject and a devout son of the Church." Jordan, *The Development of Religious Toleration in England,* p. 118.

[2] See Jordan, *Development of Religious Toleration in England* (edn. of 1931) particularly ch. vi. For the Roman Catholic contention that this mission had no political aim whatever (except, of course, indirectly) but that its immediate concern was wholly the cure of souls, see Meyer, *England and the Catholic Church Under Queen Elizabeth* (translated from the Italian by McKee), pp. 134 ff.

[3] Many historians on the strength of a document that came into the possession of Lord Burleigh have stated that this permission was given by Pope Gregory XIII; for the Roman Catholic contention that the

waiting their time to strike deepened the atmosphere of terror and suspicion. Other sufferers under the penal laws were a company of Dutch Anabaptists,[1] two of whom were burned in 1575. John Foxe, the author of *The Book of Martyrs*, and others, made earnest appeals for mercy, but Elizabeth was pitiless. Eight years later John Lewes was burned at Norwich "for denying the Godhead of Christ, and other detestable heresies."[2] Throughout these turbulent years not only the people at large, but the bulk of the clergy, with deplorable ease, adapted both practice and profession to each new change that was imposed upon them. Of this uneasy time William Penn gives a satirical description:

> King Henry voids the Pope's supremacy and assumes it himself. Comes Edward VI and enacts Protestancy with an oath to maintain it. [By the Act] 1 Queen Mary chapter 1 this is abrogated; Popery solemnly restored and an oath enforced to defend it; and this queen repeals also all laws her father made against the Pope since the 12th of Henry VIII. Next follows Queen Elizabeth and repeals *her* laws, calls back Protestancy, ordains a new oath to un-oath Queen Mary's oath; and all this under the penalty of losing estate, liberty and sometimes life itself which thousands to avoid lamentably perjured themselves four or five times over within the space of twenty years. In which sin the clergy transcended; not an hundred for every thousand but left their principles for their parishes.[3]

document was the work of an "unknown theologian" which never received the desired approbation, see Meyer's work (named in preceding footnote) pp. 235 ff.

[1] An Anabaptist is strictly one who has been baptized *over again;* that is, in adult life, notwithstanding his baptism in infancy. For some time the word was used as equivalent to Baptist, and later as a term of contempt.   [2] Fuller, *Church History.*

[3] *England's Present Interest Considered,* 1675. Further on in the same work there is a similar passage, bringing the history down to a later date. Fox in 1689 wrote in the same strain: "And how often have the priests generally turned within this hundred years, to Queen Mary and from Queen Mary to Queen Elizabeth, and to King

More than fifty years before this Quaker summary of history, Robert Burton, a clergyman, had said the same thing. Near the beginning of his *Anatomy of Melancholy*, published in 1621, three years before the birth of George Fox, he writes:

> Formalists, out of fear and base flattery, like so many weathercocks, turn round, a rout of temporisers, ready to embrace and maintain all that is or shall be proposed, in hope of preferment.[1]

Thomas Fuller, who also was a clergyman, writing shortly after the middle of the seventeenth century, tells of a vicar who, under Henry VIII, Edward VI, Mary and Elizabeth, was

> first a Papist, then a Protestant, then a Papist, and then a Protestant again. He had seen some marytyrs burnt at Windsor, and found this fire too hot for his tender temper.

James, and then to Oliver and Richard Cromwell, and called them Caleb and Joshua that led them into the Promised Land. But was it not in the tithes, offerings, augmentations, and glebe lands? And then when King Charles II came in, did not they most of them turn to Common Prayer and persecute them that did not? And when King James came to the throne, what did many of the priests and bishops do then with their passive obedience and non-resistance? Were not many of them posting to Rome, their mother church as they call it? Let all the sober judge" (*Gospel Truth Demonstrated* (*Doctrinals*), pp. 1066–67). Also on the pliability of many clergy and others see Humphrey Smith, *Works*, p. 235, George Fox the younger (*post* p. 252 n), *A Noble Salutation . . . unto Charles Stuart* (1660), pp. 11–12; Caton, *Truth's Caracter of Professors and their Teachers* (1660); and *Memoirs of Benjamin Bangs*, p. 3, edn. of 1798, often bound up with the *Journal of John Banks*. In the reign of Elizabeth there comes similar testimony from George Withers, Archdeacon of Colchester: he describes many of the clergy as "servants of men who can do nothing according to the principles of the Word, but are obliged to act in every respect at the nod of the Queen and the bishops . . . most of them are Popish priests . . . and the far greater number of the remainder are most ignorant persons." Davids, *Annals of Evangelical Non-Conformity in Essex*, p. 74. For this reference I am indebted to Geoffrey F. Nuttall. See also Whitehead, *Truth Prevalent* (1701), pp. 154, 162, 167.

[1] From the Introduction, "Democritus Junior to the Reader," in the 1845 edn., p. 27.

This vicar taxed by one with being a turncoat and an uncon-stant changeling: "Not so," said he, "for I have always kept my principle, which is this, to live and die the vicar of Bray." Such many, nowadays, who, though they cannot turn the wind, turn their mills, and set them so that where-soever it bloweth, their grist shall certainly be grinded.[1]

The well-known song transfers the vicar to the days of Charles II and his successors, a time when again changes of profession were lightly made.

Naturally, as a result of all this, sincerity in religion was to a large extent destroyed and replaced by a more or less hypocritical conformity. Over the mass of the people the Church came to have less hold than it had in the days of even weakened Catholicism. Unhappily there is much evidence to support the charges brought by the Puritans against the clergy in general, and even against some of the bishops, of shameful neglect of duties and of a low standard of life. The fury of the attack is seen at its height in the *Marprelate Tracts*, which, in 1588–89, kept appear-ing in audacious defiance of authority. The authorship is not certainly known but it is most highly probable that John Penry, one of the Independent martyrs, was largely concerned in the writing of them. When the printing press was run to earth at Manchester certain of the printers and others were seized and put to the torture to compel them to reveal the secret.[2] Spenser, in his satirical poem, *Mother Hubbard's Tale*, published in 1591, gives

[1] *History of the Worthies of England*, pp. 82–83, edn. of 1662. I am indebted to Charles I. Evans for pointing this out to me, quoted in Ditchfield's *Byways in Berkshire and the Cotswolds*. Matthew Prior (1664–1721), in his *Dialogues of the Dead*, invents an amusing con-versation between the pliable vicar and the unpliable Sir Thomas More. The vicar begins: "Farewell, then, to the dear vicarage, 'tis gone at last. I held it bravely out, however. Let me see, from the twentieth of Henry VIII, and I died in the twenty-ninth of Elizabeth, just seven and fifty years." Bray is on the Thames, near Maidenhead.
[2] *An Historical Introduction to the Marprelate Tracts* (Pierce), c. iv.

"a description of the clergy which could hardly be sur-
passed in point of severity by the avowed enemies of the
English Church."[1] It describes how the priest seeking a
benefice must ingratiate himself with those who had the
power to confer one upon him, and to this end he must
put on a pious demeanour and be ready to lie, forge,
cringe and bribe.

The year 1581 saw the rise of the Independents, the
beginning of Nonconformity in the present-day sense of
the word. Robert Browne, about to publish (in the
following year) his tract, *Reformation Without Tarrying
for Any*, gathered round him a small company who, as a
consequence of the positive principle of church fellowship which they professed, adopted the congregational
form of church organization, setting up their first regular
assembly for worship at Norwich.[2] They held that a true
Church is composed of Christians, willingly (however
few), by mutual covenant with God and with one another,
gathered out of or separated from the world; and that in
such a Church with Christ in its midst, there is true
fellowship, ability to govern itself and right preaching
pure worship and discipline.

> The Lord's people [says Browne] is of the willing sort.
> They shall come unto Zion and enquire the way to Jerusa-
> lem, not by force nor compulsion, but with their faces
> thitherward.

[1] *English Religion in the Seventeenth Century*, p. 14, by H. Hensley
Henson (afterwards Bishop of Durham). He adds, "there can be no
reasonable doubt that these accusations contained a large element of
truth," pp. 15–16.

[2] This act of Browne, generally taken as the first definite step of
Nonconformity, was part of a movement that had already set in, and
it may be that there had been earlier Separatist congregations not
simply meeting "under stress of temporary necessity" as some had
done in Mary's reign with the intention or hope of returning to the
Anglican Church. See *The First Congregational Churches*, by Albert
Peel. On the main question see a pamphlet by the same writer, *The
Congregational Principle: Positive and Inevitable*.

Nevertheless, even he was not prepared to go the whole way of complete toleration of religion on the part of the State; this service was, as will be seen immediately, reserved for certain Baptist teachers. In the course of the next twelve years Greenwood, Barrow, Penry and other leaders were hanged. For the time the persecution was successful. Francis Bacon, then rising into eminence as a lawyer and politician, makes record:

> As for those which we call Brownists, being when they were at the most a very small number of very silly and base people here and there in corners dispersed, they are now (thanks be to God) by the good remedies that have been used, suppressed and worn out so as there is scarce any news of them.[1]

The wisdom of the wise man was foolishness.

In 1603 James I succeeded Elizabeth, and nine years later the first settled Baptist congregation was established in England. It was formed by a group of men who, along with others, had fled to Holland and who now, impelled by a sense of duty, under the leadership of Thomas Helwys returned to London and there suffered persecution. Helwys and other leaders continued to proclaim the principle of complete religious toleration first enunciated by John Smyth, who had died in Holland. Among the early Baptists are found certain principles and practices which afterwards were permanently adopted by the Society of Friends.[2]

A number of Separatist congregations now led a precarious existence and for some years there was but little sound of religious strife in England. In the eyes of the

---

[1] Taken from Masson's *Life of Milton*, ii. 538.
[2] Tallack, *George Fox, the Friends and the Early Baptists*; and "The General Baptists and the Friends," by Sir William J. Collins, *Transactions of the Baptist Historical Society*, v. (1916–17), p. 65.

world these Dissenters were no more than "a company of rude, illiterate capricious, base fellows."[1] In 1625, however, Charles I became king, and a few years later William Laud became successively Bishop of London and Archbishop of Canterbury, and both king and ecclesiastic set themselves to suppress the Puritanism that was again becoming strong within the English Church, as well as the Separatism that was growing up outside it. In the course of the eleven years, 1629 to 1640, in which they governed England without a parliament they attempted to prevent the emigration of Puritans to America in order to crush them at home; and in 1639 the two Archbishops and the Lords of the Council were considering the question of burning a Dissenter. The plan, however, was not carried out.[2]

To the corruption which was at this time lowering the vitality of the national Church, Milton makes reference in *Lycidas* which appeared in 1638. He speaks of those who sought office and preferment:

> . . . such as for their bellies' sake
> Creep and intrude and climb into the fold:
>
> .   .   .   .   .
>
> The hungry sheep look up and are not fed.
>
> .   .   .   .   .
>
> Besides what the grim wolf with privy paw
> Daily devours apace and nothing said.

These last lines refer to inroads of the Roman Catholic faith which, under the influence of the Queen, Henrietta Maria of France, was becoming fashionable at Court and was receiving converts from many quarters. She had

---

[1] Burton, *Anatomy of Melancholy* (1621), Pt. iii. § 4, mem. 1, subs. 2; in the 1845 edn., p. 679.
[2] *Transactions of the Congregational Historical Society* (1902), i. 195. See my *Personality of George Fox*, pp. 2–3 (edn. of 1933).

come to England avowedly to forward the Catholic cause.

And now, to the growing confusion of the country another element was added. The upholders of despotic kingly rule were challenged by those who stood for constitutional parliamentary government, and in 1642, two years after the Long Parliament had been forced upon the King, civil war broke out. On the King's side were the High Churchmen, the Roman Catholics and the greater part of the aristocracy of England; on the side of the Parliament was the greater part of the Puritan element of the Church ("thousands that wished for good bishops were on the Parliament's side")[1] together with the Independents and other Separatists. The contest had thus a twofold aspect, the cleavage caused by the religious issue coinciding with that which was caused by the political or constitutional issue as the Puritan and Parliamentary movements coalesced. "The spear of Parliamentarianism was tipped with Puritanism." For the first year the war went in favour of the King; and in desperation the Parliament called in the aid of the Scots, who were eager to give it on their own terms. The Long Parliament, though strongly Puritan, had at first resisted a proposal to abolish the office of bishop, desiring rather to end the monarchical power and other abuses (affecting the secular as well as the religious life of the community) which had gathered round it and to "make the bishops such as they were in primitive times," namely, "first among equals," that is, among the Presbyters.[2] Of the need for some reformation we have evidence from certain of the Royalist leaders, who advocated moderate and not

[1] Baxter, *Reliquiae Baxterianae*, Sylvester, Pt. i. 31.
[2] There were some who took up a position less extreme than this and would have been content to see Episcopacy stripped of Laudian accretions and restored to the Edwardian or Elizabethan pattern.

extreme measures. Two months before he was killed at Edgehill defending the Royal Standard, Sir Edmund Verney had written, "I have no reverence for bishops, for whom this quarrel subsists."[1] It became clear, however, that nothing short of a "Root and Branch" revolution was to be attained, and Parliament was compelled to pay the price exacted by the Scots, the establishment of Presbyterianism as the official form of church government in England. Episcopacy, the government by bishops in any form, and the use of the Prayer Book were made illegal, but the latter of these prohibitions was not always strictly enforced.[2] This agreement was set out in the Solemn League and Covenant of 1643 in order, as it says, "that we and our posterity after us may as brethren live in faith and love, and the Lord may delight to dwell in the midst of us."[3] The Scots also obtained as part of their price the execution of Archbishop Laud in revenge for his attempt to force Episcopacy on their country. It was not, however, mainly by them that the military victory of the Parliament was finally won, but by the army trained and

---

[1] This occurs in a letter written to Hyde in which Verney expresses his wish that the King would grant the concessions demanded of him, Gardiner, *History of the Great Civil War*, i. 4. From other Royalists there comes similar testimony: Lord Digby in 1641 said in the House of Commons, "I do not think that any people hath been ever more provoked than the generality of England of late years by the insolencies and exorbitances of the prelates" (*English Religion in the Seventeenth Century*, Henson, p. 80). He was followed by Lord Falkland (afterwards killed at Newbury) also advocating moderate measures but saying that the bishops were more eager that men should conform to ceremonies than that they should conform to Christianity and while men had been ruined for scruples they [the bishops] had been only admonished for the grossest vices. (From the summary of the speech as given in *History of English Congregationalism*, Dale, p. 240). The debate is, in part, reported in Shaw's *History of the English Church During the Civil Wars*, i. 29 ff.

[2] Dale, *History of English Congregationalism*, pp. 339–40 (edn. of 1907).

[3] *Constitutional Documents of the Puritan Revolution*, edited by Gardiner, p. 268, edn. of 1906.

led into the field by Oliver Cromwell. In 1649 Charles I
was brought to the scaffold, but, earlier than this, strife
had broken out between the different parties on the victorious side, on the one hand the Presbyterians, and on the
other the Independents who had, by this time, attracted
to themselves some of the best elements of the Puritan
party. Only in London and in South Lancashire and the
adjacent district, and there only to a limited extent, was
the Presbyterian system carried out on any considerable
scale; in fact, from the very hour of its triumph the cause
began to fade down. "As for the Presbyterial Government . . . we know that everywhere it is spoken against"
wrote a number of its own ministers and elders in a tract
issued as early as 1650.[1] Even before this, Milton in his
poem, *On the New Forcers of Conscience Under the Long
Parliament*, had upbraided the Presbyterians for their
tyrannical intolerance as bitter as that of Archbishop
Laud whose death they had brought about only a short
time previously. Obvious is the twofold meaning of the
concluding line:

New PRESBYTER is but old PRIEST writ large.

At this time all manner of strange doctrines were being
put forth on all hands, and although the newly won freedom may in some ways have stimulated spiritual life, a
deterioration was already setting in. Men on each side had
entered upon the war with high motives, but in the con-

---

[1] *A Vindication of the Presbyteriall Government and Ministry.* See
Shaw, *History of the English Church Under the Commonwealth,* ii. c. 3.
The Puritans within the English Church, though becoming increasingly strong against Prelacy, never wished for the rigid Scottish form
of Presbyterian government; they leaned toward an episcopacy
strictly limited by Parliamentary supervision. Hence the "ordinances"
for the establishment of the Presbyterian machinery met with much
passive and active resistance even in London, Lancashire and Cheshire
where the Presbyterian clergy were most numerous and zealous. For
this information I am indebted to the late F. J. Powicke.

fusion these gave way to the lust for victory by whatsoever means it might be won. It was a true testimony
that was borne by Richard Baxter, who was a chaplain in
Cromwell's army but who always disapproved of extreme
measures and opinions:

> O what abundance of excellent, hopeful fruits of godliness
> have I seen blown down before they were ripe by the
> impetuous winds of war and other contentions. . . . I
> never yet saw the work of the Gospel go on well in wars nor
> the business of men's salvation succeed among dissensions,
> but if one have in such times proved a gainer, multitudes
> have been losers.[1]

The evil tree of war brought forth evil fruit. A number
of the Episcopal clergy, estimated at about two thousand,[2]
were deprived of their livings on the ground of unfitness
for their office, and though in some instances their ejection
was due to political reasons, in others it was amply justified. Baxter says that, as far as his knowledge went, six
out of every seven of the ejected ministers were "proved
insufficient or scandalous or both," and that but few were
cast out merely on account of their opinions.[3] In the
bitterness engendered by the strife these proceedings were
often conducted with harshness and great suffering

[1] *Saints' Rest* (1649), Pt. iii. c. 14. § 10.
[2] *Encyclopaedia Britannica*, eleventh edn., ix. 450, Article "Church
of England." The number is disputed, the estimates varying from
1,200 or 1,700 (Dale, *English Congregationalism*, 341–43; Neal,
Puritans, ii. 261–62, edn. of 1837; Masson, *Milton*, iii. 30) to 3,000
or 3,500 (Tatham, *Dr. Walker and the Sufferings of the Clergy*,
pp. 124-32, and *Puritans in Power*, pp. 88–91). There were about
8,500 livings in England; at that time more than one could be held by
the same clergyman. "Whether it exceeded or fell short of 2,000 is of
no historical importance. The real significance of the ejectment is that
it rendered permanent the eccelsiastical disruption of the English
Church" (Gardiner, *History of the Great Civil War*, iii. 200). Of
course, this 2,000 will not be confused with the ministers, nearly
2,000 in number, ejected in 1662, after the Restoration.
[3] *Reliquiae Baxterianae* (Sylvester), Pt. i. 74.

ensued. Moreover, many of the preachers who succeeded to the vacant places did not worthily fill them and some of the noblest of the victorious religious leaders mourned over the moral declension of their own people. John Owen, Vice-Chancellor of the University of Oxford, one of the foremost of Independent leaders, laments that those ("a colony of Puritans" brought from a low place) who were enjoying the positions and emoluments of ejected Royalists had "by sin shifted spirits with them," "what," he asks, "were those before us that we are not? What did they that we do not? Prosperity hath slain the foolish and wounded the wise."[1] (Milton in *Eikonoklastes* (1649) had accused the episcopal clergy of vice and ignorance, "learned in nothing but the antiquity of their pride, their covetousness and superstition.") Richard Baxter closes a fierce tirade against the ministry of his day with the words, "Those that are not able to speak sense or reason are made the ambassadors of the Most High God,"[2] but a few years later he sounds a more cheerful note. In 1653, Parliament, in order to complete the work which it had begun in its early days, appointed a number of Commissioners, "Triers," as they were called, to enquire into the suitability of preachers for their office, and Baxter, writing in 1656, says, "they did abundance of good in the Church in removing drunken preachers, etc." In his rejoicing at the completeness of their success in this direction he professes himself highly satisfied with the ministry so far reformed, and speaks of his happiness in seeing the change that had come about in the preceding twelve years.[3]

[1] *On Temptation* (1658) c. 3 and see *The Mortification of Sin in Believers* (1656) c. 2, § 6 (Goold's edition) and also *The Christian Progress of George Whitehead*, pp. 235–37, and *Letters of Isaac Penington* (1828), p. 271.   [2] *Saints' Rest* (1649), Pt. iii. c. 14, § 8.
[3] *Reliquiae Baxterianae* (Sylvester) i. 72 and *The Practical Works of the Rev. Richard Baxter* (Orme) xiv. 152–53 (Reference due to G. F. Nuttall).

Nevertheless, although the most glaring scandals were thus removed, we still hear of others which remained. In 1659 Milton published a small treatise entitled *Consideration Touching the Likeliest Means to Remove Hirelings out of the Church*, repeating the charge of self-seeking which more than twenty years earlier he had made in *Lycidas*. From it the following passage is taken:

> Now commonly he who desires to be a minister looks not at the work but at the wages, and by that lure or lowbell[1] may be tolled from parish to parish all the town over.

In *Paradise Lost* which appeared eight years later he again sounds the same note. In his telling of the intrusion of Satan into the Garden of Eden, he writes:

> So clomb this first grand thief into God's fold,
> So since into his Church lewd hirelings climb.

In reading the controversial writings of the early Friends we often wish that they were free from the abusive language which disfigured seventeenth-century polemic, but their strictures on the "hireling ministry" of their time receive abundant confirmation from beyond their own borders.

This, however, must not be taken as a complete picture of the religious life of the country. Sending forth spiritual influence were Lancelot Andrews, Bishop of Winchester, George Herbert, writer of sacred verse, and Nicholas Ferrar, pastor of the company at Little Gidding; in Worcestershire Baxter was the pastor of multitudes of men and women, the Churches counted among their leaders men of piety and learning; among the ministers were hundreds who, after the Restoration, would go out

---

[1] *Lowbell*, "a small bell, *especially* a cow-bell or sheep-bell; jocularly, a bell generally," *Oxford English Dictionary*, quoting as illustration the above passage.

into the wilderness, refusing to violate their consciences in order to retain their livings. In many places there were groups of earnest-minded "seekers" meeting apart from the national worship, bewildered in the mist but seeking for the light. And now, from out of the turmoil of sectarian bitterness and outward warfare, a new voice was to be heard in England.

It is desirable to note the changes of meaning of the words "Puritan" and "Nonconformist" as applied to political and religious parties (not to a way of thought or doctrine). "Puritan," according to Fuller (*Church History*), came into use in 1564, being applied to those members of the Church of England who wished to move as far as possible from Romish doctrine and practice, seeking to carry the Reformation further than it had gone. They repudiated the idea of separation from the Church, but since it was this party that supplied the non-episcopal sects, Presbyterians, Independents, and Baptists, the name "Puritan" continued to be applied to those who definitely came out of the Church of England and to be less used of those who stayed in it. The essential element common to the various types was the rejection of the Papal doctrine as to the way of salvation which centred in the Mass and the priesthood, and of all that in their eyes was associated with it. The word "Puritan" (as a party name) began to be superseded by "Roundhead" about 1640. In the seventeenth century the word "Protestant" was sometimes used exclusively of members of the Established Church in contradistinction to Presbyterians and other Dissenters, and in this sense it continued to be known in Ireland after the usage had died out in England. The Independents who broke away from the Established Church were at first called "Brownists" (a section of them "Barrowists"), and they and other separators were called "Separatists," the equivalent of "Nonconformist" or "Dissenter" as these words are now used. "Nonconformist" at first had a meaning similar to that of "Puritan" at the first, one who, in the main, adhered to the doctrine of the Church of England, but refused conformity to certain points of discipline and (particularly) ceremonial. After the eviction of 1662 the word acquired its present-day meaning—one who stands outside the Established Church. Toward the middle of the seventeenth century the word "Dissenter," also, came to have this meaning; it had never been used of members of the Established Church, and neither it nor "Nonconformist" has ever been used of Roman Catholics. In 1843 a number of seceders from the Established (Presbyterian) Church of Scotland gave to their organization the name of The Free Church of Scotland (i.e. free from State control), and a number of years later the English Nonconformist bodies began to call themselves the Free Churches.

Chapter II

GEORGE FOX: THE NAME "QUAKER"

IN 1624, the year before Charles I came to the throne, George Fox was born at Drayton-in-the-Clay, Fenny Drayton as it is now called, in Leicestershire. He was one of several children; their father, a weaver, was known as "Righteous Christer" and their mother, "accomplished above most of her degree in the place where she lived," was "of the stock of the martyrs." The family, certainly raised above poverty, was of good standing in the village.

The boy as he grew up was employed by a shoemaker who also dealt in cattle and sheep, and it was in the sheep that he took most interest, being very skilful in the management of them. By contemporary writers, both hostile and friendly, he is spoken of as a shoemaker. Nevertheless it was to his open-air shepherd life that his thoughts in later years turned. Reminiscence of his shearing days is seen in his repeated counsel to Friends not to be in overmuch fear of imprisonment and the spoiling of their goods: "Fear not the loss of the fleece, for it will grow again."[1] And in the following passage and others like it we see his joy in the life of the country, fresh and green under the heavenly watering:

> Be subject in the power and life and wisdom of God to God and to one another, that in it ye may be as a pleasant field to the Lord God, and as the lilies and the flowers and

[1] *Epistles*, p. 199, and for the same illustration see pp. 151, 312, 339, 352, 394; for the shepherd and country life see pp. 9, 58, 146, 307; and of this book, pp. 40, 113; also my *Personality of George Fox*, pp. 8–13, edn. of 1933.

C

the buds, feeling the pleasant showers and the streams of life from the Living God flowing upon you.[1]

As Fox grew toward manhood he knew spiritual longings which were not satisfied; and from the "priests," the ministers of the state-established Church, he could get no help. Far and wide he wandered in his search, sometimes in "heavenly joy," sometimes in misery "great and heavy," speaking little of yielding to temptation but much of temptation itself in his quest for the principle that would overcome it. When all hope in man was gone he testifies:

> Then, O then, I heard a voice which said, "There is one, even Christ Jesus, that can speak to thy condition," and when I heard it my heart did leap for joy (*Journal*, bi-cent. edn., i. 11).

Yet even after this experience a sense of evil in many forms still oppressed him:

> I cried to the Lord saying, "Why should I be thus, seeing I was never addicted to commit these evils?" And the Lord answered that it was needful I should have a sense of all conditions, how else should I speak to all conditions? And in this I saw the infinite love of God. I saw also that there was an ocean of darkness and death; but an infinite ocean of light and love which flowed over the ocean of darkness. In that also I saw the infinite love of God, and I had great openings (*ibid.* i. 19–20).

In a word, he had reached what has been called "a first-hand knowledge of God," a knowledge *ultimately* grounded on his own personal conviction and not on outward authority. He found it useless to "start in" with a

[1] *Epistles*, p. 140, and see pp. 22, 24, 39, 58, 120, 199, 212–13, 235, 318, 410; and *Journal*, bi-cent. edn., i. 391; ii. 239, 243. Some of these passages are quoted in my *Personality of George Fox*, pp. 55, 80 (edn. of 1918–19); pp. 111, 158, 159 (edn. of 1933).

profession of "belief" in something which he had heard of only from outside, but he came to understand that his personal experience of the highest he knew was a revelation of that which he sought. Writing to "All Friends," he says, *Mind that which is pure in you to guide you to God.*[1] The Church or the Bible might put into his mind ideas which otherwise would never have come there, but his own assurance of their truth was the rock on which he took his stand. In the two chapters next after this we will follow up the consequences of his discovery; for the present we continue the story of himself.

From 1647 to 1652, except for such times as he was in prison, Fox continued to give forth his message in the midland counties and in Yorkshire, the earliest settled congregation of his followers being formed at Mansfield in 1648. His first fellow-worker was Elizabeth Hooton, a Nottinghamshire woman. In a marked degree he possessed the qualities of leadership, his striking personality, compelling attention in whatever company he found himself, being enhanced by his big frame, his powerful voice and his piercing eyes. "He was," writes one who knew him, "a goodly person and of an amiable countenance"; and another, describing his manner of life, says that few men were more abstemious and temperate. His great bodily strength enabled him to survive the attacks of the mob and the horrors of seventeenth-century prisons which carried away many a younger man, so that he reached the age of nearly sixty-seven. Early in his life he performed three or four acts which had the appearance of madness or fanati-

[1] *Epistles*, p. 9; for other passages expressing this thought of being guided to God along the way of obedience to whatever of good we know see *Epistles*, pp. 14, (*ante*, title page), 20, 27, 51 (twice), 52, 58, 59, 70, 71, 72, 83, 91, 94, 97, 108, 115, 154; *Gospel Truth Demonstrated*, pp. 11, 96, 101. Almost all of these passages were written when Fox was 27–33 years old. Note the similar experience of Penington, *post*, p. 64.

cism, but apart from these he showed throughout a sobriety of conduct and a sound judgment in his organization and guidance of the religious Society which he founded.[1] He possessed shrewd common sense and business ability together with a ready humour, bewildering his opponents by his apt replies; and, along with all this, a sense of God's presence opening up within him regions of personality, "psychic," as we call them, unknown to most men. But he never ceased to be a citizen of this world; alive to its friendships and material needs, he was no dreamer of another life as if this one were of small account; he showed himself heedful of the iniquities of the penal laws and of other abuses of the time, offering practical suggestions for their remedy; he saw that wasteful luxury of the few brought hurt to the many; he called on Friends to be honest in business,[2] on innkeepers to conduct their houses properly, on Cornishmen to cease their practice of plundering wrecked ships; he took thought for the relief of the poor and the insane, for the education of children, of girls as well as of boys,[3] for the apprenticing of boys to suitable trades, and the raising of funds for the purpose, and for the right way of settling "differences" among Friends. In the management of property, in the defence of himself in courts of law and in the organization of the Quaker Church he showed great ability; to certain settlers in America he gave counsel to get into some business as soon as possible, to hold their markets regularly, to build market-halls for the purpose, and to see to it that there was no infringement of their liberties in any direc-

[1] For these few acts, particularly his crying "Woe to the bloody city," through the streets of Lichfield, see my *Personality of George Fox*, pp. 8–9, and footnote to p. 8 (edn. of 1918–19); p. 23 of 1933. The *Short Journal*, stated in the said footnote to exist in manuscript, has now been printed.

[2] *Post*, p. 139.   [3] *Post*, p. 210.

tion.[1] His concern for outward affairs and his practice of
the presence of God were not different or ill-fitting parts
of life lying in different layers or strata; the fusion of the
two, in their bearing one upon the other, resulted in a life
rightly unified as to its different sides or parts.

Speaking now of Fox's psychic nature, we recall the
fact that on his mother and others he wrought cures that
were counted as miracles, and the research of Professor
Henry J. Cadbury, of America, has shown that of these
there were more than one hundred and fifty.[2] Some insight
into this side of his mind is given us by his story of recovery
from the attack of an Ulverston mob when he was twenty-
eight years old. After being beaten senseless, he recovered
to find himself "lying on a watery common" with people
standing about him. He says: "The power of the Lord
sprang through me and the eternal refreshings refreshed
me that I stood up again in the eternal power of God." "A
mason, a rude fellow," with a stick gave him a terrific blow
on the back of his outstretched hand so that he could not

---

[1] *The Friend* (Philadelphia) vol. vii. (1834), p. 55. Fox was
addressing the Governors of Rhode Island, not a settlement of
Friends as I have elsewhere stated.

[2] See Cadbury's note contributed to my *Personality of George Fox*,
as a supplement to Appendix B (edn. of 1933). (The edition of 1918–19
appeared before his discovery.) For further information see Cadbury's
forthcoming work. In the said Appendix B to the list of references on
pp. 173–74 dealing with the attitude of Friends to the challenge often
made to them to work miracles as a guarantee of their message *add*
G. Whitehead, *Truth Prevalent*, pp. 81–82, and Barclay, *Truth
Cleared of Calumnies*, Collected *Works* (1692), p. 37. For the account
of Fox's healing his mother of "a dead palsy," see *Journal of the
Friends' Historical Society*, xvi. (1919), p. 61. See also his account of
his inducing a company of Friends to set themselves, successfully as
it turned out, to the healing of a distracted woman at Skegby, Nottinghamshire, *Cambridge Journal Supplement* (the *Short Journal*), pp. 2–3;
also Braithwaite on spiritual healing, *Second Period*, p. 368, footnote
continued on p. 369; and Grubb, in *The Venturer*, 1916, pp. 212
and 236, and in *The Friend*, 1924, p. 600. Concerning the psychic
element in Fox's personality, see R. M. Jones, pp. xxviii.–xxxii. of
his *Introduction* to Braithwaite's *Beginnings of Quakerism*.

draw it in again. "But [he continues] I looked at it in the love of God and I was in the love of God to them all that had persecuted me. And after a while the Lord's power sprang through me again, and through my hand and arm, that in a minute I recovered my hand and arm and strength in the face and sight of them all."[1]

Though he knew little of school education, he had in him, says William Penn, "the foundation of useful and commendable knowledge"; others testify to his courtesy and his sympathy; and some of those who were nearest to him bear witness,

> . . . though of no great literature nor seeming much learned as to the outward . . . yet he had the tongue of the learned and could speak a word in due season to the conditions and capacities of most, especially to them that were weary and wanted soul's rest (*Journal*, bi-cent. edn., ii. 520).

This was part of the "testimony" given forth after his death by his six surviving step-daughters, the children of his wife Margaret Fell, and by their husbands. In the extraordinarily close affection between them and Fox, so far different from themselves in social standing and education, we have evidence, abundantly confirmed elsewhere, of a charm of personality that went with him. Penn, the aristocrat and courtier, admitting that in some ways he might be accounted uncouth, bears witness that he was "civil beyond all forms of breeding."

> But above all [says Penn] he excelled in prayer. The inwardness and weight of his spirit, the reverence and solemnity of his address and behaviour, and the fewness and fullness of his words, have often struck even strangers

---

[1] *Journal*, Camb. edn., i. 58, and (wording slightly different) bi-cent. edn., i. 133. See *post*, p. 41.

with admiration[1] as they used to reach others with consolation. The most awful, living, reverent frame I ever felt or beheld I must say was his in prayer (*Journal*, bi-cent. edn., i. p. xlvii.).

Furthermore, an understanding of Fox and of the influence which he exercised is not to be reached apart from knowledge of his wonderful tenderness. Hard in judgment as he might sometimes be, not toward his persecutors but toward those whom he counted as false brethren or as sinners against light and knowledge, very deep was his love for children, for all who were young either in years or in the Christian life, for the young minister, for all seeking souls, and for those who had slipped on their way.

> No man [he wrote] after he hath beaten his child hateth him ever afterwards, but loveth him (if he repent and amend, so doth the Eternal Father), and if the child be fallen down into the dirt, he doth not go and tumble him more into the dirt or into the ditch and there let him lie in the dirt and ditch, but takes him out and washes him; and so doth the heavenly Father which leads His children by His hand and dandles them upon His knee. And so all that be called fathers in the truth or mothers, their tenderness should be the same to all little children in the Truth that can hardly go without leading, that sometimes may fall into the dirt and ditch, and slip aside and then be troubled and cry. To such there should be tenderness shown, and to wash them and help them, and love to such should be manifest; for there is a difference betwixt a stubborn rebellious and wilful child and one that is penitent.[2]

This loving side of Fox's character is seen in his

---

[1] At this time the word "admiration" might mean "wonder" (compare Rev. xvii. 6, A.V. and R.V.), but it might equally well have the present-day meaning.

[2] *Epistles*, p. 267, and see *post*, p. 281 ("Let it be your joy"). Concerning Fox's tenderness for children, wrongdoers, and others, see my *Personality of George Fox*, pp. 105 ff., edn. of 1933.

exhortation to diligence in seeking after those who wandered. As a shepherd lad he knew what it was to go after the sheep that had strayed from the unenclosed fields to the swamps and woods and thickets of the waste land which at that time formed so large a part of England. Mindful of those early years, he writes:

> If you should not find that which is lost and driven away at the first, nor second, nor third time of seeking, if you should not find him that is lost, go again, that you may have your joy and rejoice others. . . . And so all be diligent, ye believers in the Light as Christ hath taught you, look up and down in the Light, you will see where the lost sheep are, and such as have been driven away you will spy them out, out of the woods or brambles or pits where there is no water, where they are ready to be famished, where they are tied with thorns and briars; and so with the Light you will see.[1]

Limited though he was in intellectual range, Fox moved in a large space, a leader of men. From early years, his first struggles over, right up to the triumphant end his life resounded with the note of victory. In storms of the English seas and the Atlantic Ocean, in hardships of English and Irish travel and perils of American swamps and forests, in suffering of body from the savagery of the mob and in sickness of heart from the malignancy of false brethren, continually does he make record of the Lord's power going over all. "The top" or "a-top" were among his triumphant expressions: "Keep your feet upon the top of the mountains and sound deep to the witness of God in every man."[2] Characteristic of his whole career

---

[1] *Epistles*, pp. 299–300.

[2] *Ibid.*, p. 152, see *post*, pp. 42, 54, and for other similar references and the subject generally see my *Personality of George Fox*, pp. 79 f., edn. of 1918–19; pp. 155 f. of 1933. Concerning the large part which this conception ("answering the witness of God in every man") played in Fox's life, see *post*, p. 54.

was his experience at Mansfield Woodhouse when he was twenty-five years old. For speaking in church after the priest had done, at that time a recognized custom,[1] he was beaten with fists and books, thrown against the wall of the church, dragged to the stocks and set in them, "and as I sat in the stocks," he says, "they threw stones at me, and my head, arms, breast and shoulders and back and sides were so bruised, mazed and dazzled with the blows." Under the protection of a friendly constable he was set free amid the threats of the mob to take pistols to church and shoot him if he came again; and the story continues:

> When I was passing along the fields Friends met me, and I was so bruised when I was cold that I could not turn me in my bed, and bruised inwardly at my heart, *but after a while the power of the Lord went through me and healed me that I was well, glory to the Lord for ever!*[2]

It is the key to an understanding of Fox's power, a knowledge of his unwavering assurance of victory, assurance rooted, amid outward turmoil, in the quiet of God. "When temptations and troubles appear," he writes, "sink down in that which is pure, and all will be hushed and fly away."[3] Not "other-worldliness," it has been well said, but *over-worldliness* was his native air. To a "Parliament man," who threatened him with a martyr's death at Smithfield, he replied that he "was over their fires." In a time of severe strain he wrote to Friends, "Be of good faith and valiant for the Truth, for the Truth can

---

[1] See Braithwaite, *Beginnings of Quakerism*, p. 133; Barclay, *Inner Life of the Religious Societies of the Commonwealth*, c. xii.; *First Publishers of Truth*, pp. 348–49.

[2] *The Short Journal*, p. 12 (see *ante*, p. 36 note). For other instances of rapid recovery see pp. 11, 26, 27; and in this book, pp. 37–38. For a shocking account of the cruelty to which Fox was on one occasion subjected see *Journal of the Friends Historical Society*, 1934, pp. 8 ff.   [3] *Epistles*, p. 11.

live in the gaols."[1] Writing to his wife in her distress at
the attempt of her son to deprive her of her house, he says,
"as concerning the house, keep over it"; "do not look at,
but keep over all unnaturalness." "Look over all prisons,"
he counselled Friends; "keep over all the bustlings and
wars and strife and the talkers of such things"; "looking
at the good keepeth your minds over the bad"; be "kept
on top of the world."[2]

In the course of his life Fox suffered eight imprisonments, some of them attended with shocking cruelty,
amounting in all to nearly six years. One of the earliest (in
1650–51) was at Derby, where he was sentenced to six
months' confinement on a charge of blasphemy. When this
time was almost ended he was offered the post of captain
in the Commonwealth army over a troop of soldiers who
said that they would have none but him. He declined the
offer, saying that "he lived in the virtue of that life and
power that took away the occasion of all wars," and when
the offer was further pressed upon him, "I told them [he
says] that I was come into the covenant of peace that was
before wars and strifes were." This refusal led to a further
six months' imprisonment, this time in the dungeon
among the rogues and felons, without a bed to lie on.[3]

It was in the year 1650, in the course of his time at
Derby, that Justice Bennett conferred on him the nick-

---

[1] *Epistles*, p. 199.

[2] See my *Personality of George Fox*, pp. 79–81, edn. of 1918–19;
pp. 155–57, edn. of 1933, and Fox, *Epistles*, pp. 11, 198, 202, 205, 213,
225, and the two quotations in the footnote next after this one. "On
top," see *ante*, pp. 7, 40 and *post*, p. 54.

[3] *Journal*, bi-cent, edn., i. 68–69. It is not only here that Fox speaks
of the eternal existence of righteousness before the coming of evil:
"The everlasting power of God that goes over all deceit, which was
before deceit and darkness was" (*Epistles*, p. 142). "Look over that
which maketh to suffer to that which was before it was" (*ibid.* p. 401),
and pp. 38, 58, 76, 111, 168, 184, 185 (thrice), 198, 212, 258, and
others.

name "Quaker" because he bid the Justice tremble at the
word of the Lord. The word was not new, it had already
been applied to a set of religious enthusiasts. Barclay says
that the name was given because of the trembling and
spiritual stress that sometimes was manifest in the
meetings of Friends.[1] The two accounts are not irrecon-
cilable; the name was doubtless given by Bennett, as Fox
and others assert, and it stuck because of its appropriateness. Apart from Fox himself, Friends at first showed no
great dislike to it; Barclay accepts it, "though," as he says,
"it be none of our choosing," and Penn speaks of meeting
in Germany an old man who "for his approaches towards
an inward principle is reproachfully saluted by some with
the honest title of Quaker." " 'Tis much better," continues Penn, "than Papist, Lutheran, or Calvinist, who are
not only ignorant of, but enemies to, quaking and trembling at the word of the Lord as Moses and others did."[2]
"Though our name is new, yet our religion is old," said
Edward Burrough,[3] and Penn wrote a pamphlet entitled
Quakerism a New Nickname for Old Christianity. The
earliest name by which the new community was known
was "Children of the Light," but soon its members

---

[1] *Apology*, xi, 8. In *Truth Prevalent* (1701), p. 16, George Whitehead says that "persecuting adversaries" gave Friends the nickname
"because of their trembling at the word and power of the Lord as
many of His servants and prophets have done." George Keith,
writing from the Tolbooth prison at Edinburgh in 1670, more than
twenty years before he left Friends, says: "These bodily quakings and
tremblings did also seize upon divers, and from this the name
'Quakers' was in scorn cast upon Friends" (*The Benefit Advantage and
Glory of Silent Meetings*, p. 15). John Crook says the same (*Truth's
Progress* (1667), p. 4); and for further information see George
Whitehead, *Christian Progress*, p. 102, John Whitehead, *A Small
Treatise*, etc. (1661), p. 20 (a description of certain Friends' Meetings
in his day), and my *Personality of George Fox*, p. 7, note 4, edn. of
1918–19; p. 22 note, edn. of 1933.
[2] *Travels in Holland and Germany*, under the year 1677.
[3] *Works*, p. 322.

came to call themselves "Friends in Truth," or "Friends." In the later part of the eighteenth century the expressions "Society" and "Religious Society of the people called Quakers" came into common use; the name "Society of Friends" has not so far (1938) been found earlier than 1800.[1]

[1] *Journal of the Friends Historical Society,* xxxii. (1935), p. 83.

Chapter III

THE INNER LIGHT AND SALVATION

IN the preceding chapter mention has been made of the light which dawned on Fox as he sought satisfaction of his spiritual longings and assurance of a principle that would overcome temptation. Indebted as he might be to Church or Book or other outward source for the first communication of truth that otherwise might not have come to him, *his own assurance* of truth inwardly revealed, shining in its own light and not guaranteed by anything more certain than itself, was the *ultimate* ground of his conviction. On this rock he took his stand. He boldly asserted that in all men, even in the heathen who knew not the Scriptures nor Christ in the flesh, there was a principle of God which, as it was heeded, would lead to salvation.[1]

[1] Friends were not the first to assert this; Edwards in *Gangraena* (1646) includes it in his first list of 176 "Errors, Heresies and Blasphemies." The orthodox opinion of the day is expressed by Baxter in his *Quakers' Catechism* (1655), where he puts the question, "Is not he a pagan and no Christian that thinks that the Light which is in all the Indians, Americans and other pagans on earth is sufficient without Scripture?" (Query 13). Nevertheless, in his later life he admits that on this point, as on others which he enumerates, he had changed his opinion, "having some more reason than I knew of before to think that God's dealing with such [the heathen] is much unknown to *us*." (Sylvester, *Reliquiae Baxterianae*, Pt. i. p. 131.) Dryden in *Religio Laici* (1682, more than two years before he professed the Roman Catholic faith) speaks of himself as holding the same opinion, as if it were something strange. Even in the period (to be mentioned later) when most Friends adopted what had come to be called the "Evangelical" way of thought, they never gave up this testimony concerning the salvation of the heathen. For an expression of it in 1798 see *Life of William Savery*, by Francis R. Taylor, p. 425, and see *British Friend*, 1851, p. 238; 1852, p. 254. Joseph John Gurney, the leader of "Evangelical" Quakerism (*post*, p. 232), held the same view (*British Friend*, 1847, p. 133), and see the conclusion of the quotation from the *Yearly Meeting Epistle*, of 1835, *post*, p. 232, also *The Principles of Religion as Professed by . . . Quakers* (Tuke), pp. 36, 37, edn. of 1805.

It was, he says, a divine principle in Nebuchadnezzar, a worshipper of images, that caused him to say, "Blessed be the God of Shadrach, Meshach, and Abed-nego."[1] Writing to certain Friends, captives in Algiers, he exhorts them to stand true to their faith notwithstanding persecution, saying that in the end their captors, the Turks, would be overcome when they saw that this steadfastness was "for conscience' sake towards God, and [proceeded] from the principle of Truth and the Spirit, *in which Spirit and Truth they worship the Most High God.*"[2] Fox and the early Friends identified this principle—the Light, as they called it—with Jesus Christ. Penn said that Friends preferred to speak, not of the "Light within," but of "the Light of Christ within."[3] It was not for them an impersonal abstraction, a substitute for God or Christ; for them it was *Christ*, manifesting Himself in the hearts of men; it was He whom the heathen, obedient to the Light, were obeying; even though they had not heard of His earthly existence, a more eminent manifestation of Himself than any other.[4] This is the Logos doctrine of the Gospel of John. Penington argued that, if, according to

[1] *Gospel Truth Demonstrated (Doctrinals)*, p. 332, and see the whole of the tract in which this passage ocurs, and p. 532, also *post*, p. 303, and Penn, *The Christian Quaker*, cc. 6 ff.; Penington, *Works* (1761), i. 79–80.

[2] *Epistles*, p. 503; see also pp. 455, 477, 493 (twice). At this time a number of Friends were seafaring men, going out from London or Bristol, either as masters of their own ships, or as hired sailors. Some of them were taken captive in the Mediterranean and held to ransom by pirates; Friends all over England were continually getting up subscriptions to ransom them; for further information see other letters of Fox, *Epistles*, pp. 354, 471, 556. In the Minutes of the Meeting for Sufferings (*post*, p. 174) and in the *Yearly Meeting Epistles* of this time, there are many references to the captives and to the efforts made for their release; they are set out in *Account of the Slavery of Friends in the Barbary States* (1848). On p. 13 it is stated that the Friends would not steal from their masters as others did.

[3] *A Reply to a Pretended Anonymous Answer*, etc., 1675.

[4] See Penn, *The Christian Quaker* (1669), cc. 16, 17.

the almost universal belief of his day, all men were involved in the guilt of Adam, even though they had never heard of him, so they might be saved by their faithfulness to the light of Christ in their hearts though they had never heard of His outward appearance.[1] "It is not," he says, "the outward name but the inward life and power which is the Saviour";[2] and again: "It is not the having much knowledge that saves, but the being subject to the measure of the gift which comes from the Lord Jesus Christ, the Saviour."[3] In the following words Fox tells of one of his experiences:

> Now the Lord God opened to me by his invisible power "that every man was enlightened by the divine light of Christ;" and I saw it shine through all.[4]

Concerning the Quaker belief in the "Light" (or the "inner" or "inward Light"), the implications of the belief and the different senses in which the expression has, at one time and another, been used, the attention of readers is directed to a pamphlet, *The Spiritual Message of the Religious Society of Friends*, officially prepared by an international body in view of the Friends World Conference, held in 1937 at Swarthmore, near Philadelphia.

The Quaker pioneers did not undervalue the outward work on earth of Jesus of Nazareth, they took the Gospel story for granted, but, like the Apostle Paul, rejoicing in their new experience, they laid the emphasis on his spirit-

---

[1] *Some Questions and Answers*, the section entitled "Some queries to the strict and zealous professors of this age (such as stick in the letter but are strangers to the life and power) to provoke them to jealousy, lest the heathen and open sinners outstrip them and enter into the kingdom of pure everlasting light before them," *Works* (edn. of 1761), i. 563–64. This is based on 1 Cor. xv. 22.

[2] *Works* (edn. of 1761), ii. 461 and see i. 94.

[3] *Life and Immortality*, § xxi., *Works*, ii. 425 (edn. of 1761).

[4] *Journal*, bi-cent. edn., i. 34.

ual presence in the hearts of all who would follow him. The thought of the time regarded the obedience of Christ, manifested by His sacrifice on Calvary, as the *sole* "meritorious" ground of salvation from hell, inasmuch as God was pleased to accept this act of obedience on man's behalf. To sinful man, having no merit of his own and utterly unable to pay his debt of guilt due to Adam's sin, the merit of Christ was transferred, Christ's righteousness was *imputed* to him or set down to his credit. By this work of "atonement" man was "justified," he stood acquitted at the bar of *justice*, and to this result, *so far*, his own holiness made no contribution, though it was essential to "sanctification" as the "holiness without which no man shall see the Lord." Necessary to salvation was *faith* (as personal trust) in Christ and His righteousness; and no holiness of outward conduct could save a man from hell apart from such "faith" concerning Christ's atoning work as the one "satisfaction" able to cancel the guilt of "original" or birth sin, the objective basis of a sinner's forgiveness and true attitude to the God of grace. Notwithstanding, however, the teaching that the faith which truly saved *would* produce righteousness of life, as a living root produces its proper fruits, and the ready inference that absence of righteousness showed absence of living faith,[1] the practical effect on many minds of this emphasis on "faith" (*including* the right doctrine) was to reduce right conduct to a secondary place. Men came more and more to reckon themselves as effectually saved merely by the work of Christ *outside themselves;* "they presume

---

[1] In *The Pilgrim's Progress* see the discourse of Christian and Hopeful with Ignorance. The original authentic doctrine of Justification by Faith as an experience whereby the root of the matter was quickened in the soul, was essentially a vital idea, the idea of a new *attitude* to God, of trust in His grace for righteousness rather than in self.

upon the sacrifice," said Penn, "*and sin on.*"[1] Baxter in a
vigorous passage speaks of this "false faith" as the chief
hindrance to his ministry, men of evil life claiming to be
saved, not by works, but by faith. "If I tell them," he
says, "of the nature of true faith and the necessity of
obedience, they answer me that they know their own
hearts better than I, and are sure they do really rest on
Christ and trust Him with their souls."[2] Later on he says,
"Deceivers may persuade you that Christ hath done all
and left you nothing to do."[3] The Quaker, like his con-
temporaries, was concerned with "salvation," and with
them he shared the orthodox belief in an everlasting
heaven and hell, but he gave it only a small place, so vivid
was his experience of the Holy Spirit abiding with him
in the place where he was. In Quaker writings there are
no attractive or lurid pictures of a future life, the explicit
references to it being few and short with little stress laid
on it as an inducement or compulsion to righteousness.[4]
The emphasis was placed, not on salvation from the
consequences of sin, but from the power of sin itself. Penn
dwells on the thought of salvation from sin, and *therefore*

[1] *A Key to Distinguish Quakerism from Misrepresentations* (viii.).
Elsewhere Penn speaks of the practical undervaluing of righteousness
(*Innocency with Her Open Face*, iii.; *Address to Protestants*, ii. §§ 4, 6).
In *Primitive Christianity Revived* (c. 8) he says: "They are too apt
to cloak their own active and passive disobedience with the active
and passive obedience of Christ."
[2] *Saints' Rest*, iii. c. 11, § 13. See also the words of Talkative in *The
Pilgrim's Progress.*
[3] *Saints' Rest*, iii. c. 11, § 17.
[4] This reticence is the more noteworthy when compared with the
pictures of hell in (for example) Bunyan's *A Few Sighs from Hell, or
the Groans of a Damned Soul,* and Baxter's *Saints' Rest*, iii. c. 4,
among others. An example of the short Quaker reference to hell is
seen near the beginning of Penn's *No Cross, No Crown.* Even in the
"evangelical" period of Quakerism, to be spoken of later, there was
little, if any, public *teaching* of hell and no mention of it in official
pronouncements.

from wrath.[1] In a moving appeal to Christendom he throws out the challenge,

> Come, what has He saved thee from? Has He saved thee from thy sinful lusts, thy worldly affections and vain conversations? If not, then He is none of thy Saviour.[2]

And Nayler, not having in mind an elaborate formulation of belief, to run the gauntlet of scholastic criticism, but speaking from the deep places of his own living experience, puts the matter simply:

> With the Light we see that he that is in the way of God is in holiness, and he that is not, is in the way of the devil; and that he that's in God is out of self, and there sin is blotted out and forgotten.[3]

Thus the Quaker, in view of a widespread inadequate, and even unethical, presentation of Jesus on the one hand and, on the other, of his own living assurance, *inextricably bound up with personal righteousness*, came to lay emphasis on his new life, "Christ within," as he said, in such a way as tended to withdraw his attention from the man of Galilee and Jerusalem. Friends admitted that inasmuch as facts of the outward life of Christ were generally known, there was less need to preach about them than about the appearance of Christ in the heart which, in mightily enlarged degree, came after His appearance in the flesh— "In minding this and being faithful in this respect we mind our peculiar work," wrote Penington.[4] Thus there

---

[1] See *The Christian Quakers*, cc. 13 and 17; *No Cross, No Crown*, Pt. i., c. 1; *Address to Protestants*, Pt. ii. § 4. There are, however, passages which put forward the idea of paying the debt and of the "substitutionary" conception of Christ's sacrifice (*A Key to Distinguish Quakerism*, § 9, and *Primitive Christianity Revived*, c. 8, §§ 3, 4).

[2] *No Cross, No Crown*, Pt. i., c. 2.

[3] *A Salutation to the Seed of God* (1655), p. 5: in Nayler's *Collected Works*, p. 215.

[4] "A Brief Account of Quakers," *Works*, ii. 261 (edn. of 1761). See also *A Small Treatise*, etc., by John Whitehead (1661), p. 10, and Braithwaite, *Second Period*, p. 486 (Penn on the same subject).

came about a failure to relate the new spiritual experience to the historic life of Christ in such a way as to give each its true value.

> This failure [says Braithwaite] was almost inevitable in the state of thought and knowledge of the age, [but it] does not render invalid the great fact of the indwelling life of Christ out of which Quakerism sprang, and in which it has always been rooted. But it led to much vagueness of thought, and was a chief sterilizing influence in later days. The fuller intellectual outlook of our day is carrying the question to a solution which will enable spiritual Christianity to make a new appeal to the mind of mankind.[1]

It is in no way surprising that those upon whom a great light has risen, to the renewal of their whole life, should be unable to give adequate expression in words to their experience. Although the early Friends protested against the Calvinistic doctrine, widely believed, of the predestination of each individual to heaven or hell, particularly repudiating the idea of a hell for guiltless infants who were not of the elect,[2] they were bound by the spirit of their time more than they themselves knew, and, little as might be the emphasis which they laid on it, they did not set themselves free from the almost universally accepted belief in the total depravity of man, involved as each one was in the sin of Adam. It was, of course, difficult to reconcile this with their discovery of the Light of Christ in all men, and when they came to set forth an ordered formulation of their faith they found themselves impelled to the doctrine that while man was, even in his depravity,

---

[1] *Second Period*, pp. 635–36 and see c. xiv. of the same and p. 495; also a valuable work by Edward Grubb, *The Historic and Inward Christ, A Study in Quaker Thought*, the Swarthmore Lecture of 1914. To this work the attention of readers is directed. Also to *The Spiritual Message of the Religious Society of Friends* (ante, p. 47), p. 11.

[2] Barclay, *Apology*, iv., v., vi., and see my *Personality of George Fox*, pp. 53–54 (edn. of 1918–19); pp. 106 ff. (edn. of 1933).

complete as *man*, to each one was *given*, or "superadded,"
the Divine Seed or Principle which was no part of his
human nature but something distinct and separate from
all the faculties of his soul. This Principle or Light in man
was compared to a candle in a lantern, illuminating it for
a time, *but leaving its essential nature unchanged.*[1] It was
said to be *in* man, but not *of* man,[2] but in view of its
universality Penn was finally driven to the position that
though it (the Light) was *supernatural*, it might, in a
sense, be said to be *natural* inasmuch as to all men it was
given.[3] This in the seventeenth century was the best that
even Barclay and Penn could do *in words*, when they sought
to describe and explain their *living experience* of communion with God. It was not yet open to them to use the
words of a later exponent of Quakerism:

> Man, with all his faults and failures, with all his blunders
> and sins, is a being who lives by ideals which come from
> beyond himself, who organizes all the facts of his experience
> under universal forms of thought that ally him at once with
> a deeper universe of spiritual realities. He is always living
> by values and by visions that raise him out of the category
> of "mere man." Something not of matter nor of space and
> time, something drawn from a realm of Spirit, is woven into
> the very structure of his soul and makes him akin to God,
> whether he chooses to be the conscious child of God or
> not.[4]

[1] Barclay, *Apology*, v., vi. § 16. See *post*, p. 238.
[2] This was a favourite expression of Penn, *Reply to a Pretended
Anonymous Answer to the Key; Rise and Progress of Quakers*, c. 3;
Primitive Christianity Revived, c. 1 (also Penington, *Works*, i. 79, edn.
of 1761). As to the Light being no part of man's constitution, see
c. 4 and *Defence of a Paper Called Gospel Truths* and *The Christian
Quaker*, c. 19.
[3] *Primitive Christianity Revived*, c. 3, and *Reply to a Pretended
Anonymous Answer*, §§ 2, 3.
[4] R. M. Jones, Introduction to Braithwaite's *Second Period*, p. xxxvi,
and see Jones, *Quakers in the American Colonies*, pp. xxiv.–xxvi., and
Grubb, *Authority and the Light Within*, c. ix.

An essential difference between early Quakerism and other organized Christianity of the seventeenth century lay in the fact that, while it did not regard correctness of belief as unimportant, it did not set it in the first place as necessary to salvation.

> The essence of true Christianity it found in a saving experience of the life of God in the soul, transforming the character into the character of Jesus Christ; and it relegated to a secondary place intellectual definitions concerning the nature of His person and of His saving work. Its primary emphasis was inward and ethical. Salvation it regarded as essentially a work to be wrought *in* man, and not merely *for* him; as a transforming experience to be known in the soul here and now, and not merely as a means of escaping penalty in the world to come.[1]

This conception of an "inward" or "divine principle" found expression as *that of God in every man*.[2] Looking out on humanity under this aspect, Fox again and again exhorts Friends so to bear themselves in the world of men as to answer the witness of God in each human soul, by their words and by their whole demeanour calling up all possibilities of good, creating the soil and atmosphere in which good could grow and flourish, all anger and resentment be put away. Of their practical application of this conception in the face of violence done to them, and of its essential bearing on the Quaker testimony against war we shall speak later.[3] From the most horrible of all his prisons, that at Launceston, Fox sounds the triumphant

---

[1] Grubb, beginning of Preface to *The Historic and Inward Christ, A Study in Quaker Thought*. See Braithwaite's *Second Period*, 379.

[2] *Ante*, pp. 43, 45; *post*, pp. 107, 349; see my *Personality of George Fox*, p. 5, note 5 (edn. of 1918–19); p. 16, note 4 (edn. of 1933), concerning *that of God* and *post*, p. 131; also Grubb, *Thoughts on the Divine in Man* (a pamphlet), p. 15.

[3] Pp. 130, 173 note, c. xx.

note which we have already heard; "This," he says, "is the word of the Lord God to you all, and a charge to you all in the presence of the living God":

> Be patterns, be examples in all countries, places, islands, nations wherever you come; that your carriage and life may preach among all sorts of people and to them; then you will come to walk cheerfully over the world, answering that of God in everyone, whereby in them ye may be a blessing and make the witness of God in them to bless you.[1]

Again he calls on Friends to live in love and power,

> . . . having your house established a-top of all the mountains and hills, that ye may answer that of God in every man.[2]

Here we come on one of the dominating thoughts of Fox throughout his life, colouring his message as he saw the outcome of it from every soul which set its course along this way. Most often, as in the two examples already given, does he speak of *answering that of God* in every man; at other times, of answering the witness of God, or the principle of God, or the Light in every man; sometimes in other words does he speak to the same end, and in a footnote are set forth references to eighty places in which this thought finds expression.[3] Apart from a knowledge

---

[1] *Journal*, bi-cent. edn., i. 316.

[2] *Epistles*, p. 116; "A-top," *ante* pp. 7, 40, 42.

[3] *Epistles*, pp. 28, 29, 31 (three times), 53, 73, 77 (twice), 82, 83 (twice), 84, 85, 87, 91, 92, 93 (twice), 95, 106, 107 (three times), 116 (twice), 117, 121, 126, 138, 143, 152 (four times), 153, 156, 158 (thrice), 159 (twice), 160 (four times), 161, 162, 180, 181, 183, 224, 234, 251 (twice), 304 (twice), 321, 322, 329, 415, 424, 431, 455, 462, 471, 477, 493, 504, 540, 542, 543, 553, 554: Fox's *Short Journal*, p. 35 (twice); *Journal*, Camb., edn. i. 317, 319 (twice), (*Journal*, bi-cent. edn., i. 422, 423 twice); ii. 255; *Journal*, bi-cent. edn., i. 317; *The Friend* (Philadelphia), vii. (1834), p. 55. A close study of the nearly eleven hundred folio pages of *Gospel Truth Demonstrated* (*Doctrinals*) would doubtless discover other instances.

of the intensity of this current in the life of Fox there can be no full understanding of himself and of his message. Among a company of people setting their lives by this we can see how keen was their sense of membership one of another (c. viii.).

> Thou must [says Boehe] be a guide into the Kingdom of Heaven, and by thy love and gentleness inspire thy brother that in thee, as in a mirror, he may see a vision of God.

Chapter IV

THE INNER LIGHT AND THE SCRIPTURES: THE EXPRESSION OF THE NEW EXPERIENCE

THE Quaker's sense of inward assurance affected his conception of the Bible. The religious thought of the day insisted on acceptance of it to the letter because it *was* the Bible, inasmuch as on the writers of it there had been conferred a gift or revelation different *in kind* from any that had been bestowed, or ever would again be bestowed, on any other men. "Few in the world have received it from God at the first hand," says Baxter; and he continues: "For though God hath not tied Himself from revelations by the Spirit, yet He hath ceased them."[1] It was this doctrine of finality that gave Nayler occasion for saying that ministers were bound to tell people that "that which is written is all the Word, and what others have seen is all the knowledge that any need ever look for . . . and what others have done, that's all you have to talk on for your righteousness."[2] The Quaker, while disclaiming any power to write a book equal in value to the Bible, nevertheless insisted that an understanding of it was possible only in virtue of the possession of a measure of the same spirit as the writers of it themselves possessed.[3] Barclay asserts that Friends did not claim to have "a revelation of a new Gospel and new doctrines," but "a new revelation

---

[1] *Saints' Rest*, Pt. ii., c. 3, and see quotations from Owen in my *Personality of George Fox*, p. 4 (edn. of 1918–19); p. 15 (edn. of 1933).

[2] *A Salutation to the Seed of God* (1655); in the *Collected Works*, p. 214.

[3] "If you have a revelation from God, I must have a revelation from God too before I can believe you," Benjamin Whichcote (1609–83), taken from *The Learned Knife*, by Lawrence Hyde, p. 92.

of the good old Gospel and doctrines."[1] Nevertheless he
refused to admit that the canon of Scripture was necessarily completed and that no more writings were ever to
be expected to be written by the Holy Spirit.[2] Penington
also refused to shut out the possibility of "the immediate
Word of the Lord" being spoken in his own day by any
man whom the Lord should choose, asserting that any
such word would be "of no less authority, nor more to be
slighted now, than it was in His servants in the days past
by whom the Scriptures were given forth."[3] And, to the
scandal of his day, Fox asserted that "the Everlasting
Gospel [was] being preached again by the same Holy
Ghost as the Apostles were in, and received from heaven
as they received it."[4] Thus, while he continually claimed
for his actions and teaching the warrant of scripture, and
would in no case have gone *contrary* to what he believed
to be Scripture, on one occasion, at least, he claimed
ability to dispense with precedent, if none were forthcoming, for a course which was shown him to be right.
When challenged to justify the position which he was
giving to women in the Church, he went through the
Bible, adducing all manner of texts in support of his
action, and after he had thus met his opponents on their
own ground he continued: *"And if there was no Scripture
for our men and women's meetings, Christ is sufficient."*[5] To

[1] *Apology*, iii. § 9. See also Penington, "A Brief Account of
Quakers," *Works*, ii. 261, edn. of 1761.
[2] *Apology Vindicated, Collected Works* (1692), p. 735.
[3] *Works*, ii. 453, edn. of 1761, and see Phillips, *Vindiciae Veritatis*,
pp. 76–77. Concerning Samuel Fisher's conception of the human and
the Divine co-operation in the writing of Scripture see the passage
quoted in Braithwaite's *Beginnings*, pp. 292–93, noticing the statement that Fisher was in advance of Friends generally.
[4] *Epistles*, p. 7 and see pp. 18, 86, 108, 268 (twice) and *Gospel Truth
Demonstrated (Doctrinals)*, pp. 428, 498, 502, 534, 544.
[5] *Epistles*, p. 388. To seventeenth-century thought this was utter
blasphemy. For other quotations from this particular epistle, and

him and to those who professed with him it seemed that religious people were mechanically using the Bible as an external rule, consulting it as a man consults a book of mathematical tables and taking what he there finds simply on the authority of the book. Burrough, writing in 1655, thus addresses his opponents:

> You say Christ commands it when the letter doth but declare it, and you are not led with the same Light which gave forth the commands . . . to observe them, but [you] say, in such a verse of such a chapter such a command is, not having received the command by the same Spirit (*Works*, p. 105).

Justifiable as this charge probably was in regard to the majority of professing Christians, John Owen and others, in accord with the Westminster Confession of Faith, insisted on the need for the illumination of the Holy Spirit in the understanding of Scripture.[1] They were not, however, prepared to take their ultimate stand on their own inner conviction of truth, and they were careful to draw a sharp distinction between any illumination known by them and the inspiration that was given to the Scripture writers. The thought of the seventeenth century has

for Fox's attitude toward the service of women, see my *Personality of George Fox*, p. 31 (edn. of 1918–19); pp. 64–65 (edn. of 1933). To the references there given add *Epistles*, p. 349.

[1] So far does Owen go in this direction that Penn claims him as supporting the Quaker position (*General Rule of Faith and Practice*), and Goold, in his edition of Owen's works, states that it was a charge brought against him in his own day to inclining toward the doctrine of the inward light (Prefatory Note to vol. iv.). So far as the actual words are concerned, the Westminster Confession might be taken to assert the Quaker position, but certainly it was not so understood. Barclay says that the admission was wrung out of the members of the Assembly ("yet could they not get by this"), but that they were beginning "to be afraid of and guard against the testimony of the Spirit" because of what they saw it would lead to (*Apology*, iii. 1). For some reason the Quakers did not take the opportunity of impaling their opponents on the Westminster Confession as much as might have been expected.

been summed up by a certain writer in speaking of Baxter, whose belief in God, he says,

> . . . based itself primarily, not on his consciousness or intuitions but on the objective evidence of Nature and Scripture—Scripture most of all, and Scripture authenticated by miracle. . . . No doubt there followed the reinforcing witness of the Spirit, but not its witness to any truth independently of the written word. . . . A living, original word of God inspired within him as truly as within prophet or apostle, he thought it a sort of blasphemy to look for; and George Fox's claim to it seemed to him (though not to Cromwell) a dangerous enthusiasm.[1]

The Quakers held that the Scriptures were to be received as a true testimony of what the saints knew in their own experience, but insisted that no one could appropriate their words to himself, unless he also had a measure of that same experience giving him his ultimate assurance of the truth of them.[2] In a discourse between Charles II and Richard Hubberthorne, the King asked the question, "How did you first come to believe the Scriptures were truth?" Hubberthorne answered:

> I have believed the Scriptures from a child to be a declaration of truth when I had but a literal knowledge, natural education and tradition; but now I know the Scriptures to be true by the manifestation and operation of the Spirit of God fulfilling them in me.[3]

This was Fox's great discovery, blasphemous in the eyes of the seventeenth century; but the wonder of the experi-

---

[1] F. J. Powicke, the leading authority (*anno* 1926) on Baxter, *Hibbert Journal*, January 1926, p. 384.

[2] See Penington's *Letters* (1828), pp. 248, 249, and (Penington's use of the Scriptures) pp. 261 f.

[3] *Something that Lately Passed in Discourse between the King and Richard Hubberthorne* (1660), p. 5. For similar declarations by Barclay, Penn and Penington, see *post*, pp. 62–3. Concerning the ease of personal access to the King see *post*, p. 90 note.

ence into which those first Friends entered led them to an
unbalanced presentation of it. Fox himself implies that he
had a direct revelation of truth entirely apart from the
Scriptures, not realizing till afterwards that it was "agreeable to them."[1] Penington asserts that it was for Friends
"a great comfort and sweet refreshment" to find in the
Bible outward testimony concerning things of which they
had inward certainty, *and would have had even if nothing
had ever been written about them.*[2] The quickened insight,
the radiant assurance of the inward teaching of the Spirit,
caused them to minimize, or even forget, their indebtedness to the outward Scripture for the first *suggestion* of the
truths which they now realized as *their own.* This is seen
in an experience of Samuel Bownas. He tells of his first
ministry when he was twenty years old, beginning with
the words, "Fear not them which kill the body but are
not able to kill the soul." Two years later he found, for
the first time he says, that this was a saying of Christ, but
he continues: "*No doubt I had read it, but had taken so
little notice of what I read, it was to me as if it had been
never writ.*"[3]

In all this we see the tiny seed from which later, in a
day of lowered spiritual vitality, there grew up a neglect
of the Scriptures, and sometimes even a depreciation of
them.[4] But there was also among the first Friends another
line of thought due (as we have seen elsewhere) to their
entanglement with the spirit of their time to a greater
extent than they realized. Failing to understand all the
implications of the principle which they had reached, in
their *controversial* use of the Bible they practically

---

[1] *Journal,* bi-cent. edn., i. 36.
[2] *Works,* ii. 59 (edn. of 1761). "Some things relating to Religion."
[3] *Life,* p. 7 (edn. of 1795): this was in 1696. Concerning Bownas
and the Bible see *post,* p. 226 note.
[4] *Post,* p. 222.

accepted the position of their opponents.[1] Their tacit assumption that every part of it was, in equal degree, the work of the same Spirit that spoke in them, and their virtual refusal to give the same position to any other writings, led them to shoot at their opponents isolated proof texts taken from every part, not, however, quoted as decisive from the fact of their being in the Bible, but as being the work of the Spirit to which the Quaker himself bore witness. Barclay asserts that "these Divine, inward revelations which we make absolutely necessary for the building up of true faith" cannot contradict Scripture or right or sound reason,[2] and he speaks of Scripture "as the only fit outward judge of controversies among Christians," "the judge and test" by which Friends are "very willing" that their doctrines and practices should be tried, saying, moreover, that any action, however much it may lay claim to the guidance of the Spirit, if it be contrary to Scripture comes from a delusion of the devil.[3] Nevertheless he contends against the inference that these Divine revelations are to be subjected to the test of either Scripture or reason "as to a more noble or certain rule and touchstone," inasmuch as they are evident and clear of themselves.[4] The Scriptures, he says, are not "to go before the teaching of the Spirit," though he freely concedes to them "the second place,"[5] and, inasmuch as they are "only a declaration of the fountain and not the fountain itself," they are but a secondary rule, "subordinate to the Spirit from which they have all their excellency and certainty."[6] Accordingly, any testing of

[1] Grubb, *Authority and the Light Within*, pp. 39 f., and see the whole of c. iv. On this point see Barclay, *Apology*, ii., iii.
[2] *Apology*, ii. Introduction. [3] *Ibid*. iii. § 6.
[4] *Ibid*. ii. Introduction, and § 15.
[5] *Ibid*, ii. § 5, two passages. See Penington, *Works*, ii. 452 (edn. of 1761). [6] *Ibid*. iii. Introduction.

the inward revelation by them is a condescension to those who cannot do without such evidence.[1]

It is easy to see how Friends lay open to attack, and in later years of traditional acquiescence rather than of personal conviction a certain confusion of thought came to be a source of weakness, but on themselves, at the first, it was powerless for harm so long as it was transcended by their glowing experience of the Light and by their faithful walk in it, their abiding in the place where "formality bows to reality, memory to feeling, letter to spirit and form to power."[2] In a word, "these men and women felt themselves to belong to a new order of life in which all things were seen in changed but far truer values,"[3] and in conformity with this order they set their lives even though they might lack the skill to formulate in adequate words the conclusions which they reached. More important, however, than academic formulation are the living testimonies (like that of Hubberthorne which we have already noted)[4] of those who had entered into the experience, and to some of these we now turn. Barclay, once and for all time, serts forth the essential Quaker position:

> This is the great work of the Scriptures and their service to us, that we may witness them fulfilled *in* us and so discern the stamp of God's Spirit and ways upon them by the inward acquaintance we have with the same Spirit and work in our hearts.[5]

Penn, in his *Summons or Call to Christendom*, challenges the "professors" who opposed him:

> You profess the Holy Scriptures, but what do you witness and experience? What interest have you in them? Can you

[1] *Apology* ii. § 15, and see iii. § 18.
[2] Penn, "Testimony" to John Banks (1711).
[3] Braithwaite, *Beginnings*, p. 131.
[4] Page 59.　　　　　[5] *Apology*, iii. § 5.

set to your seal they are true by the work of the same
Spirit in you that gave them forth in the holy ancients?

By Penington also the Quaker's standing-place is
described:

> We can truly say concerning the Scriptures that now we
> believe, not so much because of the relation of things
> concerning Christ which we have found in them, but
> because we have seen and received the thing which the
> Scriptures speak of.[1]

This note of personal discovery and possession of the
certainty of truth inwardly revealed is a marked characteristic of the message of the early Friends.[2] Under various
figures Fox again and again insists on it: "oil in your own
lamp," "bread in your own house," "water in your own
well," "the pearl in your own field."[3]

In similar strain another wanderer describes his outward seeking and, finally, his inward assurance:

> I thought I would venture on some way where it was
> most likely to find a lost God, and I would pray with them
> that prayed, and fast with them that fasted, and mourn with
> them that mourned, if by any means I might come to rest,
> but found it not until I came to see the candle lighted in my
> own house.[4]

From Penington there comes the same story of outward wandering and seeking and inward finding:

> We had long been looking out abroad, searching very
> diligently the Scriptures and other serious books for great,

---

[1] *Works*, ii. 6 (edn. of 1761), "A Question to the Professors of
Christianity." See also on the Scriptures, *post*, p. 72 (Fox in Ulverston church), and pp. 222–26, also *ante* p. 59 (Hubberthorne).

[2] See Grubb, *What is Quakerism?* c. ii., "The Inward Light."

[3] *Epistles*, pp. 205, 302, 316, 318, the latter of two pp. numbered
331 (following 342) and 334 (following 337), 348, 383, 421, 442, 452,
469 (thrice), 472, 488–89.

[4] John Crook, letter to Isaac Penington, Penington's *Works* (edn.
of 1761), i. 561, and see p. 170 of the same.

full, certain and undoubted wisdom and knowledge; but
now we were directed to turn inwards (even thither where
we thought no good was to be found) to mind the appearance of God there, the Spirit of God testifying to us
(according to the Scriptures of truth) that the Kingdom was
within; and there we were directed to search for the least
of all seeds and to mind the lowest appearance thereof
which was its turning against sin and darkness, and so, by
minding and observing that in us which turned against sin
and darkness, we came by degrees to find we had met with
the pure living, eternal Spirit.[1]

Francis Howgill, addressing the Seekers with whom he
once had fellowship, shows the contrast, in his own mind,
between his earlier experience and the deeper one into
which he had entered:

Them whom you gather it's but into conformity to the
letter and to that which is visible, which all may be done in
the will of man which is fallen from God . . . your justification is all at a distance, grounded upon the report of Christ
dying at Jerusalem and of their report that knew Him, and,
believing this, you call it faith. . . . In love I speak unto
you . . . that you may not build upon a foundation which
will moulder away . . . for this I say to the highest of you,
if you build upon anything or have confidence in anything
which stands in time and is on this side eternity and the
being of beings,[2] your foundation will be swept away, and
night will come upon you, and all your gathered-in things
and taken-on and imitated will all fail you. . . . Why gad
you abroad? Why trim you yourselves with the saints'

[1] *Works*, ii. 528–29 (edn. of 1761), *A Treatise Concerning God's
Teachings*, etc., written in Reading gaol. Concerning the small beginning see *post*, p. 77 note. The conclusion of this passage is in line
with Fox's words, "Mind that which is pure in you to guide you to
God," *ante*, p. 35. Concerning Penington's spiritual pilgrimage, see
Works (1761), ii. 49 ff.
[2] The word "being" does not here, as has been generally supposed,
mean the Divine Being; it means "house" or "dwelling," as shown in
footnote 2 on p. 79. Therefore "the being of beings" means "the
dwelling of dwellings," "the eternal habitation," a meaning that fits
in with the mention of "foundation" and "build."

words when you are ignorant of the life? Return, return to Him that is the first love, and the firstborn of every creature who is the Light of the world. . . . Return home to within; sweep your houses all, the groat is there, the little leaven is there, the grain of mustard-seed you will see, which the Kingdom of God is like . . . and here you will see your Teacher not removed into a corner, but present when you are upon your beds and about your labour, convincing, instructing, leading, correcting, judging and giving peace to all that love and follow Him.[1]

The Quaker insistence on personal conviction as the ultimate ground of assurance was expressed by Stephen Crisp in words that sound strangely modern: "The great thing that I would have ushered into the hearts of men is that they may believe the Truth for Truth's sake."[2] He tells of his early longings "after some other kind of knowledge [of Christ] than that which was to be attained by reading, for I saw that the worst as well as the best could attain to that."[3]

In all this the first Friends were not setting forth something new; on the contrary, they were (apparently without knowing it) in line with groups of men who from the time of the Reformation had been dissatisfied with the work of the Reformers, challenging the system, doctrines and practices which were being set up in the place of those of Rome. Penington writes:

When this nation was rent from Popery (in part I mean, for wholly it was never rent but did still remain in the same spirit, though by the magistrate's sword it was forced from that form and way of worship which the Pope had estab-

[1] Howgill, "A Lamentation for the Scattered Tribes," *Works*, pp. 68–71.
[2] See Braithwaite, *Second Period of Quakerism*, p. 453. Crisp died in 1692.
[3] *Account of Christian Experience* (Crisp's *Journal*), p. 8. For Crisp see *post*, pp. 82, 171, 176.

lished), did it wait on the Lord for the guidance of His Spirit and power thereby to build up a true Church and habitation for God in the Spirit? Or did it take such materials as were ready at hand and frame up a building as well as it could, wherewith the consciences of many (that were tender-hearted towards God) were even then dissatisfied, and felt in the eternal life of God the Reformation not to be right in its beginning?[1]

These groups, standing apart from the Reformation sects, proclaimed the native capacity of the human soul for God, the priority of the inward word and other truths afterwards set forth by Fox:

> The Quakers of the seventeenth century are obviously one of the great historical results of this slowly maturing spiritual movement, and they first gave the unorganized and inarticulate movement a concrete body and organism to express itself through.[2]

Penington insisted that Quakers were "not persons that [had] shot up out of the old root into another appearance as one sect [had] done out of another . . . the ground still remaining the same out of which they all grew."[3] They all demanded some authority as an external infallible guide, presupposing an idea of Divine Grace acting for man's salvation in mechanically irresistible fashion, allowing of no more *personal* relation between God and

[1] *Works*, ("A Question Propounded to the Rulers," etc.), i. 228, edn. of 1761; and see pp. 23, 59, 223–26, 327, 397, of the same. Also Penn on the Reformation. Preface to Fox's *Journal*, bi-cent. edn., i., p. xxiii. "The Reformation, it is maintained, was a mere breach in outward organization which left the old foundation of external authority unassailed in principle, and the body of dogma which rested on it unquestioned in fact" (Oman, *Grace and Personality*, 2nd and 3rd edns., p. 3).

[2] R. M. Jones, *Spiritual Reformers in the Sixteenth and Seventeenth Centuries*, p. 337. Of pp. 336–37 the two preceding paragraphs, except the quotation from Penington, are a summary; and see the same writer, Introduction to Braithwaite's *Second Period of Quakerism*, pp. xxiv–xxvi.

[3] *Works* (edn. of 1761), i. 59.

man than there is between a child in danger of an
oncoming vehicle and the rescuer who snatches it out of
the way. For the Catholic, the sphere of this operation
of omnipotence guided by omniscience was the visible
Church; for the Reformer, it was the body of the elect
made one because each is individually chosen and by
absolute power made regenerate. For each side, reliance
on God meant at some point reliance on overwhelming
force not on recognition of His gift of a heightened
personality which a man now has for *his own*, so that,
through *his own sense of right* and *of his own insight*, he
does the will of God.[1]

The main difference in practice between Fox and
other religious leaders of his time has been summed up
as follows:

> He was prepared to *trust* the direct and personal experi-
> ence of the Spirit's immediate presence and guidance to
> such an extent as to base his whole Church policy upon it
> and therefore to sweep away all the outward safeguards
> which had been built up in the hope of maintaining order
> and unity in the Church: an ordained ministry, with
> sacraments[2] and set forms of worship; traditional creeds,
> and even the letter of Scripture, regarded as an external
> "rule" of belief and practice (Grubb, *What is Quakerism?*
> p. 27, edn. of 1917).

Serious weakness must, indeed, be acknowledged in
the intellectual presentation of Christianity by the early

[1] This paragraph is a summary, in several places as to the exact words,
of the early part of Oman's work. *Grace and Personality*. With
this compare the passage beginning, "You know what I mean:
God's all, man's nought" in Browning's *Christmas Eve*, v.

[2] Concerning the disuse of outward sacraments see Graham, *Faith
of a Quaker*, cc. viii., ix.; Grubb, *The Last Supper, What was Its
Purpose*, and *What is Quakerism?*; R. M. Jones, *The Faith and Practice of the Quakers*, and *The Society of Friends and the Sacraments*;
A. K. Brown, *Sacraments, A Quaker View*; and "Sacraments" in
Index to *Christian Life, Faith and Thought in the Society of Friends*
(*post*, p. 353 note), *post*, p. 354 (sacraments).

Friends. They did not rise far above the ideas of their time in regard to inspiration; they realized insufficiently the limits set by the earthen vessel in which the treasure was contained,[1] and they failed to find adequate terms in which to express the reality they had discovered. Nevertheless it may, without presumption, be said that they had rediscovered the central truth of the Christian religion set forth in the Pauline and Johannine writings, but largely overlooked by the teachers of their day—that Jesus Christ, *the Word of God*, is no mere theological conception and no fading figure of the past, but a living and present reality, continuing and reproducing His own life in the souls of His followers, revealing to them in actual experience at once the character of the God "whom no man hath seen or can see," and the life that God would have them live.[2] Such experience is not invalidated by new discoveries made by science, and by the scientific study of the Bible and religious history; and Friends whose faith has not rested ultimately on outward authority, whether of Church or Book, have found it easier than many other Christians to adjust their minds to the new outlook that these discoveries have made inevitable. In fact, it may be said that much of Christian thought, whatever its denominational label, is approximating more and more to that which Fox and his friends endeavoured to express. While it may not be that all who are thus alive to the inward and practical nature of true Christianity will apply it exactly as Friends have done—as, for instance, to methods of church organization and the conduct of public worship—it is, yet, from this deep source that the special Quaker methods and testimonies proceed. Moreover, it is

[1] On this point see later, p. 133–134, on the exaggeration of James Nayler.
[2] See Grubb, *Thoughts on the Divine in Man*, p. 11, and *The Spiritual Message of the Religious Society of Friends (ante, p. 47)* p. 15.

to a growing consciousness of unity in the one life, amidst differences of administration, that the best hope lies for the reunion of Christendom.

The position has been well stated by a modern historian, who points out that the early Friends, notwithstanding their inadequate expression,

> . . . were the bearers of a religious message which in essence and idea contained much that was permanent and universal. They showed a real genius for feeling out the great elemental truth of Christianity and for avoiding the scholastic formulations which were doomed, sooner or later, to have "mene"[1] written on them. While others were still speculating over the "degrees" and "schemes" of a divine Sovereign, they were living in the joyous consciousness of a divine Father.[2]

A valuable account of the various Declarations of Faith issued in the seventeenth century and of the circumstances which called them forth is given by A. J. Mekeel in his work *Quakerism and a Creed*.

For the first Friends their conception of the "Inner Light" involved no sentimental refusal to recognize the evil in the heart of man. When they likened the great gift of God to the "Seed," they did not think of it as growing up "of itself" as a sound acorn, placed in favourable circumstances, grows into a tree, being unable to do otherwise. They did not make light of the enmity of the carnal mind against God and the call to the holy war, but they set the emphasis, not on the sin, but on the light which showed it; which, if followed, would lead to righteousness.

---

[1] The reference is to Dan. v. 25–26.
[2] Rufus M. Jones, *Quakers in the American Colonies*, pp. 167–68. For a study of the early formulation of the Quaker faith the reader is referred to Braithwaite's *Second Period of Quakerism*, Introduction by Dr. R. M. Jones, pp. xxx f. and c. xiv.

To those who knew their "houses foul and corruptions strong" Fox gave counsel:

> Wait upon God in that which is pure. Though you see little, and know little, and have little, and see your empti-ness, and see your nakedness and barrenness and unfruit-fulness, and see the hardness of your hearts and your own unworthiness, it is the Light that discovers all this, and the love of God to you.[1]

[1] *Epistles*, p. 14, and see Nayler, *Works*, pp. lv. 221. Concerning this Quaker teaching, strange to seventeenth-century thought, namely, that a man could have no knowledge of his sin apart from this posses-sion of a measure of the light which showed it, see my *Personality of George Fox*, (edn. of 1933), pp. 157–58, including note 1 on p. 158.

Chapter V

PUBLISHING THE MESSAGE

At Whitsuntide in 1652 Fox, not yet twenty-eight years old, came into the neighbourhood of Kendal and there met large companies of the "Seekers" of whom mention has been made.[1] In the course of a fortnight, which has been described as "the creative moment in the history of Quakerism," he spoke with prophetic fervour to a few meetings, one of them held on the hillside numbering a thousand people (many "thinking it a strange thing to see a man preach on a hill and not in their church"[2]), and by this means and by close personal intercourse, answering the need of his hearers, he brought them to find that which they sought. The Quaker movement which in Yorkshire had already begun to take definite shape now received a mighty impetus, many of the finders becoming its ardent apostles, some of them within a few years laying down their lives in the service. Of one of these assemblies an account has come down from an eye-witness, Thomas Camm, at the time a schoolboy eleven years old. Writing many years afterwards, he tells how John Audland, having received Fox as his guest, brought him to the meeting held

[1] *Ante*, p. 32; see Penn's Preface to Fox's *Journal*, bi-cent. edn., i., p. xxv and *post*, pp. 110–111.

[2] *Journal*, bi-cent. edn., i. 114. The seventeenth-century wonder at a religious meeting not held in a place of worship appears in the Baptist *Broadmead Records* of Bristol, p. 12 (see *post*, pp. 144–146). A meeting was being held in a house in High Street and the house was attacked "by the rude multitude and seamen" because they thought it strange "for people to meet in a church with a chimney." In 1684 Fox wrote a short work entitled *Concerning Meetings in Houses, Ships, Streets, Mountains and Highways*. It begins: "Here you may see how Christ and His Apostles and John Baptist were not tied to places to preach in," *Gospel Truth Demonstrated* (*Doctrinals*), p. 860, and see also in the same, pp. 225, 797; *Epistles*, p. 524.

monthly at Preston Patrick, and how Fox, declining the invitation to sit by the preacher,

> . . . took a back seat near the door and J. C. [John Camm] sat down by him where he sat silent, waiting upon God about half an hour, in which time of silence F. H. [Francis Howgill] seemed uneasy and pulled out his Bible and opened it and stood up several times, sitting down again and closing his book, a dread and fear being upon him that he durst not begin to preach. After the said silence and waiting G. F. stood up in the mighty power of God, and in the demonstration thereof was his mouth opened to preach Christ Jesus, the Light of life and the way to God and Saviour of all that believe and obey Him, which was delivered in that power and authority that most of the auditory, which were several hundreds, were effectually reached to the heart and convinced of the truth that very day, for it was the day of God's power—a notable day, indeed, never to be forgotten by me (*First Publishers of Truth*, p. 244).

Momentous in another direction for the cause of Quakerism was this visit of Fox to the north-western counties. Shortly after leaving Preston Patrick he came to Ulverston in Lancashire, and one of his friends brought him to Swarthmore Hall, about a mile distant, the hospitable home of Judge Fell and his wife Margaret, open at all times "to entertain ministers and religious people." Here he stayed the night, having discourse with the mistress and her household, the Judge himself being absent on the Welsh circuit. Soon afterwards he attended a service in Ulverston church and by permission he spoke to the congregation. Of his words and of the impression made upon herself, Margaret Fell has left record:

> He said how that Christ was the Light of the world, and lighteth every man that cometh into the world, and that by this Light they might be gathered to God, etc. I stood up in my pew and wondered at his doctrine, for I had never

heard such before. And then he went on and opened the Scriptures and said the Scriptures were the prophets' words and Christ's and the apostle's words, and what, as they spoke, they enjoyed and possessed and had it from the Lord; and said, Then what had any to do with the Scriptures but as they came to the Spirit that gave them forth? You will say, Christ saith this and the apostles say this, but what canst thou say? Art thou a child of Light, and hast thou walked in the Light, and what thou speakest is it inwardly from God, etc.? This opened me so that it cut me to the heart, and then I saw clearly we were all wrong. So I sat down in my pew again and cried bitterly; and I cried in my spirit to the Lord, "We are all thieves, we are all thieves; we have taken the Scriptures in words and know nothing of them in ourselves."[1]

Before long Margaret Fell and most of the Swarthmore household ardently embraced the new teaching. The Judge himself, a man of liberal mind and fine character, never made profession with Friends, but for them, and for Fox in particular, he had high esteem and he often used his influence to protect them from molestation. In 1658 he died, and eleven years later his widow married Fox. Her son was hostile to Friends, but her seven daughters and their husbands joined with her in devoted service for them in many ways. Of great mental capacity and deep spiritual character, the family used the outward means at its disposal to further the cause. With many of the travelling ministers Margaret Fox corresponded, carefully keeping the letters written by them to her. Fox also was concerned to lay up testimony for the future and the result of their care was the preservation at Swarthmore of about 1,400 reliable contemporary documents.[2] To Swarthmore

---

[1] Fox's *Journal*, bi-cent. edn., ii. 512; with this compare quotations from Hubberthorne, Barclay, Penn and Penington, *ante*, pp. 59, 62–63.

[2] These letters, etc., are now in the Friends' Library, Friends House, Euston Road (opposite Euston Station), London, N.W. 1. They are a comparatively small part of the mass of early Quaker

Hall the travelling ministers made their way, so that sometimes it was entertaining visitors from five or six counties
at once. From the time of Margaret Fell's first acquaintance with Fox to her death fifty years later in 1702, her
home was a centre of Quaker life and activity. In the
earliest days in particular, when Friends confined their
labours to the northern counties, it formed a focus or
rallying-point for what might otherwise have been the
scattered or, even, heterogeneous elements of the movement, and Margaret Fell herself was largely responsible
for the early financial organization that was necessary. A
lady of good social standing in the county, she suffered
five years' imprisonment in Lancaster Castle, almost
within sight of her home, rather than betray her faith,
"choosing," as Thomas Camm wrote after her death,
"much rather to join with and suffer affliction and all
manner of reproach for Christ's sake with the people of
God than to enjoy the pleasures, treasures and glory of
this world which she had a share of above many."

> She became [he says] a tender nursing mother unto
> many, condescending in great humility to those of low
> degree . . . not only a great and exemplary sufferer for
> truth, but a visitor and sympathizer with all the faithful in
> their sufferings, zealously labouring and endeavouring with
> such as were in authority for their relief, as being afflicted
> with the afflicted and mourning with those that mourned.
> ("Testimony" at the beginning of M. Fox's *Works*.)

For two years after the great ingathering of the Seekers,
Friends travelled throughout the northern counties
establishing meetings in many places, and in 1654 they
planned an organized mission to the rest of England. In
pursuance of this plan sixty or seventy of them made their
way by twos and threes throughout England and Wales
records. For a detailed account of them see Braithwaite, *Beginnings
of Quakerism*, pp. 134-35 and 538-42.

and before long other workers joined them. Speaking to large companies in crowded rooms, in barns, in the open air; conversing more closely and familiarly with single individuals or with groups, disputing with "priests," facing the fury of the mob, they carried out their mission as triumphant conquerors. At Oxford, John Camm of Westmorland "had great service," and among others he "convinced" Thomas Lee, a tradesman of that city, who, in his turn, drew William Penn into the Quaker fold.[1] Richard Farnsworth writes of the campaign of himself and Thomas Goodaire in the midland counties:

> There is near a hundred that keep constant at one meeting in Warwickshire [Baddesley], and there is many at Leicester and thataways, and towards Lichfield and towards Swannington the river begins to divide into three heads; we had three meetings the last First-day[2] and sweetly carried on.

And, speaking of the opposition that was stirred against them, he continues in the strain of a Hebrew prophet:

> We have pitched our tents, drawn our swords, made ready for the battle; it is begun; and we have wounded the Amorite, and in time we shall have a large inheritance. O sweet labour, pure is our streams, pleasant is the sounding of the trumpets; the day is the Lord's, all our enemies fall before us, praises for ever![0]

The messengers "were for the most part young men in the prime of their ardour and strength, who would follow the movings of life rather than the counsels of prudence."[4] Of their journeyings one of their modern successors has given us this picture:

[1] *Post*, p. 93.   [2] This meant Sunday.
[3] Samuel Watson manuscript collection of letters in the Friends Library, p. 58. For further quotation see Braithwaite, *Beginnings of Quakerism*, p. 176. For the London campaign see *post*, p. 108.
[4] *Ibid.* p. 94.

Through lonely dales where the bracken reddens at autumn and the trout streams tumble to the sea; where the long swell of the moorlands sweeps the horizon; or where the seagulls scream and the spray breaks over the rocks, or the low sandhills melt down the dismal coast; by flat meadow lands with kine and fields of corn; over high, bare hills where the west wind storms with salt and sting of the Atlantic; through the great vale with its far glimpses of cathedral towers; through narrow streets filled with the roar of the shingle on the slipway and the smell of fish and shipping; into broad market squares among the wains and cracking whips and stumbling teams, to city and hamlet, seaport and inland town, fearless and loving, come the Children of the Light (John Wilhelm Rowntree, *Essays and Addresses*, p. 40).

Of these "Publishers of Truth," as they were called, some were of prosperous yeoman stock, others of more lowly position; many of them were possessed of competent Bible knowledge and some had received a fair education.[1] It would, however, seem that in their outward appearance and manner there was, at first, little to commend them. Dr. Gauden, Bishop of Exeter and afterwards of Worcester, in his contempt for them went so far as to assert (with very small warrant) that Quakers "had their beginnings from the very rabble and dregs of people."[2] Isaac Penington, the earnest seeker, several times speaks of his early disappointment at their message and, in fact, of his repulsion from them; to him they seemed "a poor, weak,

[1] Those who wish to know more of the educational equipment of the messengers are referred to Braithwaite, *Beginnings of Quakerism*, pp. 59, 80, 87, 90, 94, 102, 163, 178, 186, 187, 217, 388, 408; also to two essays by Luella M. Wright, namely "Literature and Education in Early Quakerism," University of Iowa Humanistic Studies, vol. v., No. 2; and "Cultural Qualities in Early Quakerism," *Bulletin of Friends Historical Association* (Philadelphia), 1935; for other personal information, e.g. calling and station in life, see an article by Ernest E. Taylor, "The First Publishers of Truth," in *Journal of the Friends Historical Society*, 1922, p. 66.
[2] *A Discourse Containing Public Oaths* (1662).

silly, contemptible generation who had some smatterings of truth in them." Elsewhere he says: "How ridiculous was their manner of coming forth and appearance to the eye of man! About what poor, trivial circumstances, habits, gestures and things did they seem to lay great weight and make great matters of moment. . . . I cannot wonder that any wise man, or sort of professors, did, or do yet, despise them." At last he heard the preaching of Fox opening up "the mystery of iniquity . . . and the mystery of the gospel of peace," and at the call of the uneducated man, several years younger than himself, the scholarly and fastidious gentleman, together with his wife, "gave up himself to the obedience of Truth and took up the Cross." The path which he chose led him to six imprisonments amounting in all to nearly five years.[1] Truly has it been said, "Many a man has been conquered by the winning goodness of his intellectual inferiors."[2] It is not inappropriate to say further of Isaac and Mary Penington that they were among the first persons of considerable worldly standing to join the Quaker community, and in a moving passage, which shows a spirit wholly in accord with what others say of him, Penington describes the hard way set before him:

> What I met with outwardly from my own dear father, from my kindred, from my servants, from the people and powers of the world . . . the Lord my God knoweth before whom my heart and ways are; who preserved me in love

[1] Repeated from my *Personality of George Fox*, p. 37 (edn. of 1918–19); p. 75 (edn. of 1933), based on Penington's *Works* (1761 edn.), i. pp. vi., xxxii., xxxvii., xliii., lvi., 57, 74, 257, 332 (twice), 554, 578, 632; ii. 116, 512. Most of these passages give evidence of Penington's disappointment at the first appearance of what he afterwards saw to be the truth, coming as it did in a lower or meaner guise than he had expected. For his counsel against neglecting humble beginnings see *ibid*. i. 47, 89–90, 100, 553, 558, 559; ii. 117, 529 (quoted *ante*, pp. 63–4), 547.

[2] Gwatkin, *The Knowledge of God*, i. 209.

to them in the midst of all I suffered from them and doth still so preserve me, blessed be His pure and holy Name.[1]

The records left by these "Publishers of Truth" show them to have been men and women who lived in the presence of their Lord, holding themselves at His disposal to go whithersoever He should send them. To a magistrate who asked him why he had come from Yorkshire into Westmorland, James Nayler replied:

> I was at the plough meditating on the things of God, and suddenly I heard a voice saying unto me, "Get thee out from thy kindred and from thy father's house." And I had a promise given in with it. Wherefore I did exceedingly rejoice that I had heard the voice of that God which I had professed from a child, but had never known Him.

He further tells that he was at first unfaithful to the call, so that the wrath of God came on him and none thought he would live, but having at last begun to make some preparation, one day as he was walking with a Friend, "having on an old suit, without any money," he was commanded to go into the West and each day await the command for his work on the next, "which promise," he said, "I find made good every day."[2]

Another Yorkshireman, Marmaduke Stephenson who lived near Market Weighton in the East Riding, tells a similar story of his call to service. He was one of four Friends, three men and a woman, who were hanged at

[1] Penington's *Works* (edn. of 1761), vol. i., p. xxxviii. Isaac Penington was the eldest son of Sir Isaac Penington, a Lord Mayor of London and a representative of the city in the Long Parliament, he was one of the judges of Charles I, but he refused to sign the death warrant. Mary Penington had been the wife of Sir William Springett who died two years after their marriage; their daughter, Gulielma Maria, married William Penn.

[2] Nayler, *Works*, pp. 12–13; also Besse, *Sufferings of the Quakers*, ii. 4. The reader who has heard of Nayler's unhappy conduct at Bristol is asked not to be repelled from him, this being, as will be said later, *post*, p. 135, a sad episode of short duration in a life of great beauty.

Boston under a law of Massachusetts which decreed the penalty of death on any of the "cursed sect" of Quakers who returned to the colony after banishment from it.[1] While awaiting his execution he wrote in prison his record "that all people may know who hear it, that we came not in our own wills but in the will of God."

> In the beginning of the year 1655, I was at the plough in the east parts of Yorkshire in Old England near the place where my outward being[2] was, and as I walked after the plough I was filled with the love and presence of the living God which did ravish my heart when I felt it; for it did increase and abound in me like a living stream, so did the love and life of God run through me like precious ointment, giving a pleasant smell which made me to stand still. And as I stood a little still with my heart and mind stayed upon the Lord, the word of the Lord came to me in a small still voice which I did hear perfectly, saying to me in the secret of my heart and conscience, *I have ordained thee a prophet unto the nations;* and at the hearing of the word of the Lord I was put to a stand, seeing that I was but a child for such a weighty matter.

[1] *Post*, pp. 89-90.

[2] "Being" here means "house," a meaning which *The Oxford English Dictionary* has missed. It is found in Wright's *English Dialect Dictionary*. It occurs a number of times in Quaker writings, sometimes, as here, with the word "outward" before it; Burrough speaks also of "outward residence" (*Epistle to Friends in Truth*) and Alexander Parker of "outward habitations" and "outward abode" (*Letters of Early Friends*, p. 22). Samuel Fisher says that the word of the Lord came to him "at my own outward being at Lydd in Kent" (*Works*, p. 1). Thomas Taylor, telling of a journey, says: "I was got to my outward being in the edge of Yorkshire" (*Truth's Innocency*, p. 3). George Fox says of a certain carrier, "his being is at Bilston, near Wolverhampton," and of another, "whose being is near Bolton in Lancashire" (*Journal of the Friends Historical Society* (1914), xi. 99). A seaman gets leave to go ashore "to my own being" (Besse, *Sufferings of the Quakers*, ii. 119). Roger Hebden records that notwithstanding the persecution that was setting in by reason of the Conventicle Act of 1664, "a hundred Friends of Truth and others" met "at my outward being." *Christian Experiences, Labours*, etc., pp. 134-35. In *David Copperfield* (c. lxiii.) Mr. Peggotty describes his home across the sea, "with the roses a covering our bein' to the roof." In the quotation from Francis Howgill on p. 64, "being" means "house" or "dwelling"; and see *post*, p. 89 note.

Not for three years was his way pointed out to him, and then, having assurance that God "would be as an husband to my wife and as a father to my children, and they should not want in my absence," he obeyed the call to go to Barbados and thence to New England. And of the further and more awful vision that loomed up before him he tells the story:

> So after some time that I had been on the said island [Barbados] in the service of God, I heard that New England had made a law to put the servants of the living God to death if they returned after they were sentenced away, which did come near me at that time; and as I considered the thing and pondered it in my heart immediately came the word of the Lord unto me saying, *Thou knowest not but thou mayest go thither.*[1]

In a time that was ordinarily rough and coarse, among a people demoralized by the Civil War, it was to be expected that the Quaker apostles should go forth as sheep among wolves. Afoot or on horseback, over great stretches of waste land, along the cart tracks that served for roads, from town to town they passed, in street and fair and market challenging the powers of darkness. Their language was not free from the deplorable violence of the seventeenth century; the glowing outpour of their ardour betrayed some of them into conduct that was injudiciously provocative, but between gentle spirit and fiery zealot the savagery of "priest" and layman alike made no discrimination. On Pardshaw Crag in Cumberland Friends met out of doors, and, as a contemporary account relates,

[1] George Bishop, *New England Judged*, i. 131–32. It was Massachusetts, not New England, that made the said law. In Rhode Island there was complete religious toleration under Roger Williams, but even he felt himself strained to the very limit in view of the Quakers. In England about 450 Friends died in prison or directly in consequence of imprisonment, but no one was definitely sentenced to death, although Richard Vickris of Bristol technically came under sentence by a law of Elizabeth's reign. He was finally released.

> . . . abundance of people crowded to the meetings, and great were their sufferings in those parts by scoffing, beating and bloodshed that Friends did undergo from the priests and wicked men. Yet Truth still prevailed and those that kept to it grew stronger and stronger (*First Publishers of Truth*, p. 37).

A little further on in the narrative the note of victory is again sounded:

> Many more profound men and women were raised in this meeting who suffered greatly the spoiling of their goods and imprisonment of their bodies, and were as the stakes of Zion that could not be moved (*ibid.* p. 40).

Typical of scores of adventures that might be related is that of James Lancaster at St. Bees, where he

> . . . bore a public testimony for the Truth. He was sore beat and had his coat torn by the rude people; they drove him upon a bridge and there threw him into the water; and he stood in the water declaring the Truth, they having so wounded him with punching and beating his legs that the blood ran down the water; and afterwards he went to a house where the people out of pity took him in (*ibid.* pp. 36–37).

At Nayland, in Suffolk, on a charge of vagrancy, George Whitehead, twenty years old, was flogged "with a long sharp whip" till many spectators wept and called on the executioner to stop. At Cambridge two women were stripped to the waist and flogged, and shortly afterwards, in the same town, James Parnell was thrown into prison for publishing two papers against the corruption of the magistrates and of the priests. On his release he visited a number of places in Cambridgeshire and Essex, and finally he was arrested at Coggeshall in consequence of a disturbance which arose while he was disputing with a preacher. On a charge of causing a riot he was committed

F

to Colchester gaol and was imprisoned in a hole high in the castle wall. Being refused permission to draw up his food by means of a cord and basket, he used a ladder which stopped short six feet below his hole, and for the intervening space he was compelled to climb up and down a rope. At last, owing to extreme cold, he fell on the stones below and, terribly injured, he was put into a lower hole which had no window. After eight months' imprisonment he died in 1656 at the age of nineteen, being with one exception the first Friend to die in prison. His work lived after him in the life and service of Stephen Crisp of Colchester, a man several years older than himself, a Seeker whom he converted to Quakerism. "These bonds," he wrote from his prison to William Dewsbury, "have been very serviceable to the piercing of the hearts of many."[1] Crisp in later years became one of the wisest leaders of the Quaker movement (pp. 65, 171).

But apart from any process of law, Friends drew upon themselves the attacks of the mob not only in the streets but also in their places of meeting. The sight of men and women pledged to non-resistance of injury, sitting in silence—"mumming and dumming," as in Cornwall people called it—seemed to invite the onslaughts of the rabble, and sometimes, even, of professedly religious people. An account of the Quaker way of worship, with its silence and its lack of arrangement, will be given later; for the moment we turn away from England to tell of the planting of the seed and its growth in Ireland and America.

---

[1] *Letters of Early Friends*, p. 225. With this compare Fox, "The more I was cast into outward prisons, the more people came out of their spiritual and inward prison." *Epistles*, p. 2, and see similar passages on pp. 3, 456 of the same.

Chapter VI

EARLY QUAKERISM IN IRELAND[1] AND AMERICA:
THE WORK OF WILLIAM PENN

AT the time when George Fox and others were sowing the
seed in England, political changes resulted in a large
number of English and Scotsmen occupying in Ireland
the lands of which the owners had been dispossessed. The
links between these colonists and England were very close
and soon some of the Quaker preachers found their way
across the sea. Nevertheless, the real apostle of Quakerism
in that country was one of the settlers themselves, William
Edmundson, a soldier in Cromwell's army at the battle of
Worcester. In 1651 when he was in Derbyshire he heard
various reports, good and bad, of Quakers, "but," he says,
"my heart was drawn towards them for good." Leaving
the army he started business in the north of Ireland, and
shortly afterwards, when, in the course of his trade, he was
travelling in England he sought out James Nayler whose
words so "reached God's witness" in him that on his
return he could not take an oath to clear his goods from
the customs.[2] In 1654 he, with a small group of like-
minded people, began in his house at Lurgan the first
Friends' meeting in Ireland. In the next year he met
George Fox in Leicestershire and for sixty years afterwards he laboured unceasingly for the spread of Truth.
At this interview Fox gave him the following message
to Friends in Ireland, which when they heard the power

---

[1] For these pages of Irish history the author is indebted to Isabel
Grubb.
[2] Concerning the Quaker testimony as to the unlawfulness of oath-
taking see *post*, pp. 128, 153.

of the Lord seized upon them whereby they were mightily shaken and broken into tears and weeping.

> "Friends, in that which convinced you, wait, that you may have that [evil] removed [that] you are convinced of, and all my dear Friends, dwell in the life, and love, and power, and wisdom of God, in unity one with another, and with God; and the peace and wisdom of God fill all your hearts, that nothing may rule in you but the life which stands in the Lord God."[1]

Elizabeth Fletcher and Elizabeth Smith were the first Quaker preachers in Dublin. They were committed to prison by the Lord Mayor, but after their release a meeting was, in 1655, begun near Polegate, in that city. They, together with Edward Burrough and Francis Howgill, "were instrumental to the convincement of many in the province of Munster, and particularly in Cork."[1]

William Edmundson and a number of others gave up shopkeeping and took farms in County Cavan in order to maintain their testimony "against that anti-christian yoke of oppression—the enforcing the payment of tithes in these gospel times." They suffered much persecution and in 1659 they moved to near Mountmellick in Queen's County where, in spite of the opposition of the local clergyman, a large meeting grew up. Meanwhile, Friends travelled all over the country, often in physical danger, and often treated with violence and imprisoned, yet here and there finding seekers who were "convinced" by their messages, so that meetings were settled in various places. On the whole, though the clergy and local officers were inclined to persecute, the higher government officials were lenient with the Quakers because they were English.

In 1666 Thomas Loe, preaching in Cork, was the

---

[1] *Journal of W. Edmundson*, 1715, pp. 16, 17.
[2] *History of Quakers in Ireland*, T. Wight and J. Rutty, 1751, p. 92.

means by which William Penn was induced to throw in
his lot with the Quaker Society and he (Penn) and others
became serviceable to Friends because of their influence
with the government during the persecutions of Charles
II's reign.[1]

In 1669 there were about thirty settled meetings and
George Fox spent three months of hazard and of mar-
vellous deliverances[2] in welding them into an organized
community. The National and Province meetings took the
place of those known in England as Monthly and
Quarterly meetings but by the end of the eighteenth
century the English nomenclature had been adopted in
Ireland. Concerning the Friends themselves, Fox bears
testimony:

> A good weighty people there is, and true and tender and
> sensible of the power of the Lord God and His Truth in
> that nation, worthy to be visited, and very good order they
> have in their meetings and they stand up for righteousness
> and holiness, that dams up the way of wickedness . . .
> There is a gallant spirit in them.[3]

When James II came to the throne in 1685 Friends were
favoured because they had not identified themselves with
the Protestant party. They accepted places on Corpora-
tions and one of them, Anthony Sharp, was Master of the
Weavers' Guild. James's government, however, did not
last for long, and there followed three years of warfare,
1689–92, which were times of great testing for Friends.
Their goods were taken from them, and many lost their
homes also. Nevertheless, in Dublin and other places they
organized a thorough system of relief, they visited and

---

[1] Concerning Penn at Cork see *post*, pp. 93, 108.
[2] See the story as told in the Cambridge edition of his *Journal*,
ii. 137–151: in shorter and less picturesque form, *Jnl.*, bi-cent. edn.,
ii. 107–14.   [3] *Journal*, Camb. edn., ii. 148.

saved the lives of many prisoners, and William Edmundson and others personally attempted to lessen the ani-
mosities between the opposing parties as their troops
wandered over the country. Edmundson himself was taken
prisoner by a band of robbers and barely escaped hanging.
Of the Friends, about five thousand in number, only four
were known to have taken up arms, and only three or
four lost their lives by violence.

After this time of intense trial Irish Friends, like their
brethren in England, settled down into a community
desirous of living to itself, and of maintaining the upright
character which it had acquired. Simplicity in speech,
behaviour and apparel and a Puritan strictness against all
forms of conformity to the "world" marked them throughout the eighteenth century, but in spite of this narrowness
of outlook, the integrity of their lives and their charity
bore witness to the Truth in their day and generation.
They were particularly influential in trade and industry,
for the Catholics were scarcely allowed to trade at all, and
the Protestants were mostly engaged in the government
of the country, so that the Huguenots and the Quakers,
and in the north the Presbyterians, were those who, in
spite of the harsh and unjust economic conditions and
laws, built up such trade as was allowed. Even still in a
country fair in Ireland a refusal to bargain may be met by
the retort, "You are not a Quaker," although there may
not have been a Quaker resident in the district for many
years.[1]

At the end of the eighteenth century, Friends in the
south-east of Ireland had once again to show a constructive testimony for peace, opposing courage and kindliness
to the violence of armed forces. Though in constant

[1] Concerning the Quaker testimony against bargaining see *post*,
p. 137.

danger of their lives from rebels and soldiers they carried on their occupations and meetings, fed the hungry, cared for the destitute and wounded and organized relief on a large scale to help those, in County Wexford especially, who had suffered by the rebellion into which the Catholic peasants had been goaded.

Fifty years later in a time of terrible famine[1] Friends again brought practical relief to the starving peasants of the west and south, and hope and friendship also. On both occasions they were greatly assisted by funds from England and America. Indeed, throughout their history, Friends in Ireland have conveyed their message rather by their lives than through the more intellectual channels of preaching and literary work.[2]

Mention has already been made of the Massachusetts martyrs (p. 78), and we now go back a few years to begin the story, told in short compass, of Quakerism in America.[3] In 1656 two women Friends who had travelled from

[1] The potato famine of 1846–47; see *post*, p. 287.
[2] For books relating to Friends in Ireland see T. Wight and J. Rutty, *History of . . . Quakers in Ireland*, Dublin 1751; Isabel Grubb, *Quakers in Ireland*, London 1927, and the bibliography at the end; the journals of William Edmundson, Joseph Pike, Samuel Neale, and most of the leading English Friends; for the 1798 rebellion, D. W. Goff, *Divine Protection*, London 1857; for sufferings, J. Besse, *Collection of the . . . Sufferings of Quakers*, London 1753; "Ireland," an address by James G. Douglas, *Friends World Conference* (1937) Official Report, p. 61; and see "Ireland" in the Indexes to *The Beginnings of Quakerism* and *The Second Period of Quakerism*, Braithwaite; and *The Later Periods of Quakerism*, Rufus M. Jones.
[3] This part of the chapter is largely taken from *The Quakers in the American Colonies*, by Rufus M. Jones, and *A Quaker Experiment in Government*, by Isaac Sharpless. The Introduction to the former of these two works is warmly commended, even to those who find themselves unable to read more. Braithwaite's *Second Period of Quakerism* has also been drawn upon; see particularly c. xv., "Quaker Colonization," and pp. 55–60 concerning Penn.

England by way of Barbados came on the ship *Swallow*
into Boston harbour. They were Ann Austin of London,
a woman "stricken in years," the mother of five children,
and Mary Fisher, twenty-two years old, who had been a
servant at Selby. She had suffered two imprisonments
at York and a public flogging at Cambridge. So extraordinary had been the reports of Quaker doings in England that (as was said) the colonists were as much alarmed
as if an army had invaded their shores. The boxes of the
two women were searched on shipboard, and a hundred
of their books were seized in order to be burned. They
were taken ashore and put in a dark prison, care being
taken that no one should speak to them. Here they were
subjected to a shocking examination for marks of witchcraft on their bodies, the order for this being given by the
Deputy-Governor, whose own sister-in-law had been
burned as a witch a few months previously. At the end of
five weeks the master of the ship which brought them was
compelled to take them back to Barbados. But two days
after their departure nine more Quakers came—four men
and four women from England and a man from Long
Island. Their boxes also were searched "for erroneous
and hellish pamphlets," and after eleven weeks they too
were sent back. The Colony of Massachusetts now passed
laws providing for the fining of anyone who sheltered a
Quaker and of any ship's captain who had brought him in,
and for the imprisonment, flogging and branding of the
Quakers themselves.[1] But at the very beginning the seed
fell on prepared ground; there were those who accepted
the new teaching, and still more Quakers came, gathering

[1] Unfavourable and not wholly unjust comment is often made on
the treatment of Quakers by those who themselves, no long time
previously, had fled from persecution, but it is to be remembered that,
owing to the tales that had come from England they were in black
terror of Quaker witchcraft working in league with the devil.

converts round them. Terrible is the story of ten years' persecution, fines, imprisonment, appalling flogging of men and women publicly under the Cart and Whip Act (one man was flogged nine times for allowing a meeting to be held in his house), and on Boston Common, in the years 1659–61, one woman and three men were hanged.[1] Never did martyrs go to their death with more triumphant assurance of victory. William Leddra, straitly shut up in a cold, dark room "little larger than a saw pit," chained to a log, thus wrote on his last day of this life:

> The sweet influences of the Morning Star like a flood, distilling into my habitation, have so filled me with the joy of the Lord in the beauty of holiness that my spirit is as if it did not inhabit a tabernacle of clay, but is wholly swallowed up in the beauty of eternity from whence it had its being. . . . As the flowing of the ocean doth fill every creek and branch and then retires again toward its own being and fulness, leaving a savour behind, so doth the life and power of God flow into our hearts, making us partakers of His Divine nature.[2]

At the very moment when sentence was being pronounced on Leddra there came into court Wenlock Christison, who also had been banished. At this challenge to death, face to face, the magistrates were "struck with a great damp." A few days later, when he too was sentenced, he turned on his judges:

> Do not think to weary out the living God by taking away the lives of His servants. What do you gain by it? For the last man you put to death, here are five come in his room. And if you have power to take my life from me, God

---

[1] Concerning Marmaduke Stepenson. See *ante*, p. 78.
[2] Taken from *Quakers in the American Colonies*, by Rufus M. Jones, pp. 88–89. Concerning the ocean retiring to its own being, see notes on this use of the word "being," pp. 64 note, 79 note.

can raise up the same principle of life in ten of His servants and send them among you in my room.[1]

By this time, however, there had grown up among the Colonists an uneasy feeling of having gone too far, drawing on themselves the royal interference in their affairs which they were anxious to avoid. Accordingly, Christison and a number of imprisoned Friends were set free. From the constitutional point of view the most serious part of the matter was the refusal to allow an appeal to England, and it was probably this that carried most weight with Charles II when Edward Burrough told him that a vein of innocent blood was opened in his dominions which would run over all if it were not stopped.[2] Upon this the

[1] Taken from R. M. Jones' *Quakers in the American Colonies*, p. 97. In October 1659 the Government of Massachusetts put out what was intended as a justification of their proceedings. One of their grounds was that the Quakers had only themselves to thank, since their return to the colony after being banished was in disobedience to Christ's injunction, "When they persecute you in one city, flee into the next!" (Penington, *Works*, i. 259, 285; edn. of 1761).

[2] The address to the King is given in Besse's *Sufferings of the Quakers*, vol. i. pp. xxx.–xxxii. In the statement that three persons had been put to death, *three* is a mistake for *four*. The detailed story of New England persecution is told in vol. ii. The ease of access to the King and familiarity of intercourse with him, shown in this story of Burrough and in others of the early Friends, is noted by a French traveller, Sorbière. Writing to the King of France, he says that Charles II in exile had become accustomed to living along with other men as a private citizen, and he goes on to say: "The genuis of the English does require they should be governed after this gentle manner" (*Relation d'un Voyage en Angleterre* (1666), pp. 99–100 Sprat's translation (1709), p. 50). Elizabeth Stirredge tells of writing an address of warning to Charles II and continues: "This testimony I delivered into his hands, with these words in my mouth, 'Hear, O King! and fear the Lord God of heaven and earth.' And I can truly say that the dread of the most high God was so upon me that it made me tremble and great agony was over my spirit, insomuch that paleness came into his face and with a mournful voice he said, ' I thank you, good woman'." *Strength in Weakness Manifest*, by Elizabeth Stirredge, pp. 28–29 (4th edition). Pepys, in his Diary, under date January 11, 1663–64, records that ("this morning") he had been standing by the King, hearing him "arguing with a pretty Quaker woman" who said "thou" to him. For interviews of members of the Fell family with the King, see Crosfield, *Margaret Fox*, pp. 115–17,

King sent to Governor Endicott, who was mainly responsible for the persecution, a mandamus commanding him to put an end to imprisonments, executions and other corporal punishment, and to send prisoners to England to stand their trial there. At Burrough's suggestion, the letter was entrusted to Samuel Shattock, who had been banished from Massachusetts under penalty of death in the event of his return. A Friend's ship was chartered and, fighting through the storms, it reached Boston in six weeks. The story is, perhaps, the most dramatic in Quaker annals. The criminal, with sentence of death upon him, now a royal messenger, came ashore, to the amazement of those who knew him, and went into the Governor's presence wearing his hat in Quaker fashion. Endicott ordered it to be taken off, but when he received the letter, bravely loyal to his King however bitter the pang, he ordered the Quaker's hat to be given back and took off his own. "We shall obey His Majesty's command," he said. The story is told in Whittier's poem, "The King's Missive." It was clearly impracticable to send the prisoners to England, and the imprisonments and executions came to an end, but not for several years did the floggings cease. In fact, it was now that the terrible "Cart and Whip Act" was passed. Dr. Rufus Jones, in his story of the ten years of horror, makes mention of a few individuals goaded into hysterical and fanatical outbursts, but he says that he has found no instance of any Quaker recanting:

> Not only [he says] is the story unsullied by lapses of cowardice, it is further an unbroken record of noble bearing toward the instigators and inflictors of their torment.[1]

173, 182; and with James II, p. 184. See also *The Christian Progress of George Whitehead*, Whitehead's talk, in the Park, Hampton Court, with Charles II, p. 532 ff.; interviews with James II, pp. 570, 575 ff., 616 ff.; with William III, pp. 636 ff.; with George I, pp. 683 ff. Concerning Charles II and Richard Hubberthorne see *ante*, p. 59.

[1] *Quakers in the American Colonies*, p. 110.

Not only in Massachusetts, but in other colonies also, Quakerism was firmly planted before the Restoration, and even before the foundation of Pennsylvania the number of emigrants from England became so great as to weaken the Society at home. A steady stream of English ministering Friends, men and women, visited the country, and from Maine to the Carolinas Quakerism was in many places the dominating religious influence and in some of them the dominating political power. "The extent of the Quaker influence in the political life of the Colonies has not been generally realized."[1]

In 1672 and the following year George Fox and a group of Friends spent thirteen months in the country, the most wonderful part of Fox's life. When he left England he had not recovered from a terrible illness of bodily exhaustion and psychic storm, bringing him to the verge of death, and in Barbados, his first place of landing, his joints swelled in pain, and the bruises left by the beatings which he had undergone were sore, so that it seemed impossible for him to go further. But his great strength of body asserted itself, and, in the Lord's power, as he so often says, he passed through astonishing adventures, of travel, visiting Friends throughout the Colonies, finding many communities standing true in the faith, but others into which evil had come. Of one place he records, "We had a day of washing and sweeping" of those that were defiled. Far and wide the company hold meetings, organize the Quaker community, defend their position before opposers, having intercourse with Friends and people who were friendly, with Roman Catholics and Indians, governors, magistrates and chief men of the country. "The truth sounds abroad every way," says Fox.[2]

[1] R. M. Jones, *Quakers in the American Colonies*, p. xvi.
[2] This passage is repeated from my *Personality of George Fox*, p. 25 (edn. of 1918); p. 52 (edn. of 1933).

More than ten years before this visit, his thoughts
had turned to America as a home of freedom in which
the larger life might be lived. Josiah Coale, a Gloucester-
shire Friend, had been sent over to treat with a tribe of
Indians concerning the purchase of land, but he met with
no success. There was, however, a boy, seventeen years
old in 1661, a student at Oxford, who even then "had an
opening of joy as to these parts" as the place where an ideal
commonwealth might come into being. This was William
Penn, living in a day when the thought of political
Utopias and the framing of constitutions was occupying
men's minds.[1] He had not yet made a profession with
Friends, but he remembered the ministry of Thomas Loe
(of whom mention has been made), heard by him at Cork,
when he was twelve years old. Ten years later, in 1666, he
was again in Ireland, sent there by his father, Admiral
Penn, to the brilliant Court of the Duke of Ormonde in
order to counteract his Quaker turn of mind. The policy
seemed to be successful and the young man adapted himself
to the life of his associates—"the glory of the world over-
took me," he says; he shared their duties in joining with
them in the suppression of a rebellion, and so well pleased
was his father that he put him in charge of his Irish
property. But again Thomas Loe came to Cork, and there
Penn heard him preach from the words *There is a faith that
overcomes the world, and there is a faith that is overcome
by the world.* From this time he cast in his lot with Friends,
to the grievous disappointment of the Admiral, who could
not know that before his son there was opening out a way
of life more glorious than that which he had designed for
him. In the young man's mind there still remained the
dream of America, and before long he was associated with

---

[1] See Braithwaite, *Second Period*, p. 404 note 2, and R. M. Jones,
Quakers in the American Colonies, p. 365. *Penn at Cork*, pp. 85, 108.

John Locke in drawing up a theory of government for Carolina. Soon after this he and others became the owners of New Jersey, first of the western part in 1676 and six years later of the eastern part. For the new Colony, Penn drew up a charter breathing a spirit of religious and political freedom, and up to 1681 more than fourteen hundred Friends had made their way there from England. It has been observed that the part played by him in the settlement of New Jersey has not been adequately recognized.[1]

Nevertheless he had not yet obtained a clear field for his Holy Experiment, as he called it, but his opportunity came when he found that Charles II and his Council were willing to allot him a wide domain in America in order to extinguish a debt of £16,000 which was owing to the estate of Admiral Penn. The province, of course, was to be held under the Crown as part of the English dominion, and to it the King himself gave the name Pennsylvania. The Duke of York, afterwards James II, aided Penn in his schemes, not only putting aside any claim that he himself might have, but also adding what is now the State of Delaware. It was, however, found impossible to carry out this arrangement, and Delaware became a separate province with its own legislature, though having the same Governor as Pennsylvania up to the end of the Colonial period.

It cannot be the purpose of a work like this to tell in more than broad outline the course of events in the new province. In 1682 Penn crossed the Atlantic in the ship *Welcome*, a nine weeks' voyage in the course of which

---

[1] This is taken from the part of R. M. Jones's *Quakers in the American Colonies*, written by Amelia M. Gummere, namely, Book IV, "The Early Quakers in New Jersey." That which follows, concerning Pennsylvania, is taken (sometimes as to the actual words) from Book V, "The Quakers in Pennsylvania," written by Isaac Sharpless, and from that author's work, *A Quaker Experiment in Government*.

thirty out of the hundred on board died of small-pox.
He met the Indians as their friend, but he was not the
first of colonists to buy their land from them. This
had been done by many before him; in fact, in view
of massacres and the extermination of several colonies
in the south, it had come to be recognized as a wise
policy. Baxter, writing in 1673, was able to say of the
New England settlers:

> . . . they take not so much as the native's soil from them
> but by purchase . . . they enslave none of them nor use
> them cruelly, but show them mercy, and are at a great deal
> of care and cost and labour for their salvation (*A Christian
> Directory*).

This last sentence refers to the missionary labours of
John Eliot, who went out in 1631 and thirty-two years
later completed his translation of the Bible into a Massachusetts dialect, one of the first translations of the Scriptures into a language outside the circle of Christendom.
Fox by his will left a copy of it to his wife's son-in-law
Thomas Lower.

But closer and more intimate than even New England
could show (to say nothing of other colonies) were the
personal and political relations between settlers and
natives in Pennsylvania. Provision was made for equit-
able settlement of all disputes between white men and
red, they were guests of one another in wigwam and
home, and under Penn's rule no Indians were made
drunk that they might sign away valuable claims, no
false maps were shown them, no false weights deceived
them in their trading intercourse. In all their transactions they met with the same justice which the white
man demanded for himself, the treatment accorded them
being the necessary outcome of the Quaker's conviction

that to them, as to him, there was given a measure of the Light of God.[1]

Of Penn's share in the framing of the constitutions of Carolina and New Jersey mention has been made. Now for the third time he set his hand to his beloved task, the first time that his hand was free. The constitution of Pennsylvania which he drew up, probably with the aid of his friend Algernon Sidney, was many times changed in form, but it shaped the constitutions of other States and of the Federal Union itself. The province became the most consistently free colony in the country, the most consistently prosperous, the most rapid in its growth in freedom and prosperity. So nearly had the inhabitants everything they could desire that they hesitated to take up the Revolutionary cause in 1775.[2]

This happy outcome of the Holy Experiment was not reached easily. The early settlers showed little gratitude to their benefactor; some of the men on whom he relied to carry out his plan were disloyal to him and at one time his enemies caused the grant of the province to be withdrawn, so that he, having spent a large part of his wealth upon it, was brought into financial straits. It was, however, given back to him;[3] but the early history

---

[1] See *ante*, pp. 46–47, and c. vi., "Friends and the Indians," in *Quakers in the American Colonies*; also the chapters concerning Indians in Taylor's *Life of William Savery*, and Kelsey, *Friends and the Indians, 1665–1917.*

[2] Sharpless, *A Quaker Experiment in Government*, p. 35. Those who can turn to the book will do well to read the long extract there quoted from an address of Andrew Hamilton, the Speaker, given to the Assembly in 1739.

[3] C. S. P. Dom. 1694–95, p. 261: the grant of restoration relates that in consequence of the disorder into which the province had fallen and the inadequacy of provision for its defence it had been put in charge of the Governor of the province of New York. Miss Waterson, in her work, *Mary II, Queen of England*, states that the grant was due to the influence of Mary (p. 80 note). She would doubtless have in mind the close friendship between her father, James II, and Penn.

of Pennsylvania for nearly thirty years furnishes a sad story except for the part played by Penn himself. Through it all the wonderful beauty of his character shines forth as he overcame the rebuffs which would have overwhelmed most men. He was "so ready to forgive enemies that the ungrateful were not excepted."[1]

In the government of the province the Quakers sought for themselves no advantages or positions which were not open to others, though they continued to form a majority of the Assembly even when they were in a minority of the population. But the sons and successors of Penn did not carry out his policy toward the Indians, and these, infuriated by the shameful treatment which they received, became willing tools of the French when the war between England and France was carried into America. They were largely responsible for the defeat of Braddock's army in 1755, a defeat which turned all the waverers definitely against the English. The terrors of Indian warfare to which other colonies had been subjected were now for the first time carried into Pennsylvania, the Governor (not a Quaker) declared war, and the Quakers retired from the Assembly.[2]

Nevertheless their service for their country was not ended. Seeing the root of the mischief they formed "The Friendly Association for gaining and preserving Peace with the Indians by Pacific Measures." They knew that money would be required as compensation for wrongs committed, and though they had objected to paying war taxes, thereby drawing down odium on themselves, they now, in the cause of peace, pledged

---

[1] From the address "To the Reader," beginning of Penn's *Works*, edn. of 1726. He (Penn) "ever loved the Truth in the meanest." Thomas Story, *Journal*, p. 85.
[2] Braithwaite, *Second Period*, pp. 622-23.

themselves to give "a much larger part of our estates than the heaviest taxes of a war can be expected to require." To those who objected to this proceeding as a piece of impertinence, Israel Pemberton answered back that Friends had a standing with the Indians that others had not, and that though their "former kind neighbours" had been turned into "bloody enemies," they were determined that the younger generation of Indians should have cause for holding Friends in as good esteem as their old men cherished for William Penn. For the most outrageous piece of fraud, the "Walking Purchase,"[1] compensation was given and the Indians for a short time settled down in peace until they were again attacked by certain Scots-Irish Presbyterians. These, not having emerged from the stage of morality portrayed in the early part of the Old Testament, felt themselves commissioned to destroy the people of the land, and were incensed against the Quakers for befriending the Indians. But the continuation of this story is beyond the scope of the present work, as is also the dealing of Friends with the Indians toward the close of the eighteenth century.[2]

To those who place overmuch reliance on outward schemes, whether international or social, for the healing of the world's sickness, the tragedy of Pennsylvania should bring home the lesson that no scheme, however skilful its arrangement or pure-minded its inception, will gain success, unless it be worked aright by right-minded

[1] An early arrangement for measuring the land that was to be sold was to reckon the distance that a man could, in normal circumstances, walk in a day and a half. But in 1737 one of Penn's sons arranged that instead of the "walk" two athletes should run over a tract of country from which the undergrowth had been cleared, having horses to carry what they needed and boats to cross streams. The Indians never forgot this.

[2] See *Life of William Savery of Philadelphia*, by Francis R. Taylor, cc. vi., vii. viii., and *Friends and the Indians* 1655–1917, by Kelsey.

workers. Too often is it assumed that the excellence of the scheme is itself a guarantee that these will be forthcoming. Had Penn's method of dealing with the Indians been continued by his successors, his colony would have been saved from the evils which came upon it.

During the eighteenth century a quietism and an excessive deference to tradition, of which the story will be told later, descended upon the Society and in the new world it lasted for a longer time than in the old. There was continual intercourse between the two countries; men and women crossed the sea in each direction, and a large correspondence, official and private, was regularly maintained. The War of Independence made not the smallest breach in the brotherly love between the companies of Friends on opposite sides of the Atlantic. From England and Ireland contributions were sent toward the building of the Philadelphia Yearly Meeting school at Westtown, which was opened in 1799.

The most important matter in the Society's history during this time was the work of John Woolman, Anthony Benezet and others, by means of which Friends in America stood clear of slave-holding before the end of the eighteenth century. Of this, mention will be again made (p. 207) in telling of the work done by Friends in England for the suppression of the slave-trade.

The history of the nineteenth century is largely that of division, and of this the story is too complicated and too lengthy to be told here. There came to be three religious bodies, each calling itself "the Society of Friends," having no official and almost no social intercourse one with another; in fact, looking with hostility on one another. But healing influences are at work: and understanding and fellowship are deepening as Friends of the different "branches" have come together in service not only for their own land but for Europe devastated by the Great War.

To Friends on each side of the Atlantic there is committed a holy world-service. Between the two English-speaking nations it is likely that differences and occasions of strain will arise, and to us it is given to enter into a commonwealth which transcends the bounds of nationality, standing, unpatriotic as the world may count us, in the peaceable mind of Christ. By the acquisition of knowledge and in all ways we may, it is for us to forge links which hold true even if all others be broken. In 1917, a time of war, the Epistle of Indiana Yearly Meeting written to London, after speaking with thankfulness of the hundred years and more of peace between England and America, thus continues:

> We are still more thankful for our fellowship in Christ which makes us citizens of the same spiritual kingdom, and even if the United Kingdom and the United States were at war, Friends would still love Friends, and in our mutual prayers for peace and our works of mercy all men would be included.[1]

[1] *Printed Proceedings of London Yearly Meeting*, 1918. In addition to the works already referred to concerning American Quakerism, reference may be made to *The Later Period of Quakerism*, by R. M. Jones; *A History of Friends in America*, by A. C. and R. H. Thomas; *Separations*, by Grubb; and (a very short account) the article "Friends, Society of," in *Encyc. Brit.*, 11th edn. Concerning the "Hicksite" separation see *post*, p. 230.

Chapter VII

THE QUAKER WORSHIP: MEETINGS IN
EARLY DAYS

THE way of worship already practised by certain groups
of Seekers was adopted by Friends, not as the result of
formal consideration or decision, but as the natural way
from their point of view. In their eyes, an ordered service
and the appointment of one man as minister, to the
exclusion of others, was a limitation of the Holy Spirit;
and to this day they meet for worship, making no arrangement or programme but allowing men and women alike
to speak words of prayer or to give forth such message as
is committed to them. The intervening times of silence
are times of worship equally with those in which words
are spoken; and the union of living silence and living
ministry, each of them helping the other, goes to form
the complete whole.[1] It is among the elements of strength
in Quakerism that no one at any given time, or for any
specified length of time, whatever may then be his state
of mind, is called on to preach or pray; and that the ministry comes from men and women of all ages and of all
stations of life, from farmers, merchants and shopkeepers,
from scholars and others in "professional" life, from
those whose speech may, as Penn said of the speech of
Fox, "sound uncouth and unfashionable to nice ears,"

---

[1] For the benefit of any who seek information it is to be said, by
way of completeness, that in a very few Sunday morning meetings
a passage of Scripture is arranged to be read at the beginning; and
in a few, one or more hymns may be sung, not as part of a programme
but upon the spontaneous request of someone. In a number of evening
meetings arrangement is made for an address intended to be of a
teaching nature; this is sometimes followed by an ordinary "meeting
for worship."

but who, out of the furnace of life, brings a message which cannot be spared.[1] A certain writer thus draws a contrast between the Quaker freedom and the service carried on by one man (or woman) according to an arranged programme:

> There are few forms which secure that all the worshippers shall be equally open to the divine inflowings, equally free from all merely intellectual domination by one or two, and equally able to pass on what may be given to them for others.[2]

It has to be admitted that this liberty lays itself open to ministry which is weak or even unprofitable; sometimes, though rarely, it is deliberately abused; more often are meetings for worship injured by the unfaithfulness of those who refuse to put themselves at the disposal of God as His messengers. As early as 1669, Fox, whilst calling attention to those who outran their Guide in speaking uncalled-for words, laid stress on the harm done by others withholding what they ought to share:

> All Friends everywhere, in the living Spirit and living Power and in the heavenly light dwell; and quench not the motions of it in yourselves nor the movings of it in others; though many have run out and gone beyond their measures, yet many more have quenched the measure of the Spirit of

[1] With regard to the absence of compulsion to speak at any given time, the Friend must be on his guard against allowing freedom to breed slackness; he, on his part, will do well to remember that the fact of a sermon being required causes many a minister to go deep in thought and prayer so as to be spiritually prepared when the set time of service comes. His [the Friend's] own watchfulness, thought, and prayer must be no less than theirs.

[2] Joan M. Fry, *The Communion of Life*, p. 50. Concerning the meeting itself see Brayshaw, *The Things That Are Before Us*, pp. 29–38. *Silence as a Basis for Worship* (a pamphlet), by Jos. S. Rowntree; *Some Practical Thoughts on Worshipping Together* (a leaflet), by Isabel Grubb; *The Naturalness of Religion* (c. vii.), Brown and Harvey; and list of works, *post*, p. 244 note.

God, and after became dead and dull, and questioned through a false fear; and so there hath been hurt both ways.[1]

In 1804 William Forster gave a similar message: "Some are too backward and others too forward, but all proceeds from unsubdued self." (*Memoirs*, i. 42). More than a generation before the rise of Friends, John Smyth, the Baptist, pointed out two ways in which the Spirit was quenched—"by set forms of worship," and by "silence when fit matter is revealed to one that sitteth by and he withholdeth it in time of prophesying."[2] As will be shown later, it is, on the whole, in this direction that Friend's meetings have come short of the ideal, but at various times, including the present, some have suffered from utterance that was shallow and easy, or so continuous as to leave no room for the gathered, living silence which this way of worship demands. Thomas Story tells of a meeting for worship at the Yearly Meeting of 1717; "a crowding time," he describes it, "there not being, for the most part, one minute's time between the end of one testimony and the beginning of another, an indecency I have ever disliked."[3]

But notwithstanding all the risks inseparable from this mode of worship, it is for Friends a necessary expression of their central principle. In the silence wherein there is liberty for men and women to speak and pray (for without this liberty the silence is of an inferior sort) there is known a coming together of spirit with spirit in the pre-

[1] *Epistles*, p. 305 and see pp. 85 (lines 8-9) and 472 of the same, and of this book, p. 244.

[2] *Works of John Smyth*, ed. Whiteley, i. 277. For this quotation I am indebted to Dr. Albert Peel. Concerning Quaker ministry see *post*, p. 227, c. xv., pp. 320-322.

[3] *Journal*, p. 578. Story, who was probably the most able minister present, says that he felt to have something to say but was willing to be restrained. On p. 627 he tells of unsuitable ministry at Bristol.

sence of the Father of all. Then, *out of the silence* (not as an inlay clumsily inserted in it), there is likely to proceed the spoken prayer or message and not seldom does it happen that, before a word is spoken, without any arrangement come to, the thoughts of some of the company are led in the same way, so that the messages of those who are faithful to give them, supplementing and completing one another, speak with strange appropriateness to the condition of waiting hearts. A fine description of the ideal, one that is not seldom realized, has been thus given:

> Any of the worshippers is free to express either in prayer or in communication to his fellow-worshippers the thought to which his mind has been directed in the preceding silence. Communications of this kind have in a powerfully concentrated group of worshippers an effect not so much of breaking *into* the stillness as of breaking *out* of it. Speech here, indeed, may not interrupt the quiet worship; rather it may give spontaneous expression to the silence that precedes direction and substance to the silence that follows. The Quaker practice in which free communication rises out of silence allows in fact of a type of mutual reinforcement that is rarely possible in any other form of worship.[1]

And if ever it should seem that any are mistaken as to their leading (for we are in the body), unprofitably intruding into the silence, often, as all irritation is laid aside, is there known the spirit of healing that allays harm.[2] In the earliest days of Quakerism many in the life of the quiet meetings (the "holy worship in the Holy Spirit and truth" which "never came out of the brain-beaten stuff of man"[3]) found relief from the artificial discourses which had failed to satisfy them, the long sermons set off, as the custom was, with tags of learning and divers quotations

[1] Brown and Harvey, *The Naturalness of Religion*, p. 108 (edn. of 1919).   [2] *Post*, p. 275.   [3] Fox, *Epistles*, p. 326.

in English and other tongues,[1] "conned and gathered stuff," as it is called by Barclay, who thus gives account of his own spiritual finding when he was but eighteen years old;[2]

> Not by strength of arguments, or by a particular disquisition of each doctrine and convincement of my understanding thereby came [I] to receive and bear witness of the Truth, but by being secretly reached by this Life; for when I came into the silent assemblies of God's people I felt a secret power among them which touched my heart; and as I gave way unto it, I found the evil weakening in me and the good raised up.[3]

That this is not to be misunderstood as disparagement of ministry in general is evident from Barclay's completion of his account of a Friends' meeting:

> Many are the blessed experiences which I could relate of this silence and manner of worship, yet I do not so much commend and speak of silence as if we had a law in it to shut out praying or preaching or tied ourselves thereto, not at all, for as our worship consisteth not in words, so neither in silence, as silence, but in an holy dependence of the mind upon God: from which dependence silence necessarily follows in the first place, until words can be brought forth which are from God's spirit. And God is not wanting to move in His children to bring forth words

---

[1] In the later days of Charles II a reaction set in against the old style of sermons with their Greek and Latin quotations, plays upon words, and minute analyses of the text. *Dictionary of National Biography*, i. 403.

[2] "Conned and gathered stuff" is Barclay's own rendering of the Latin in which he wrote his *Apology*—nemo hic Dei Spiritum limitat nec commentos suos et confectos sermones producit. The work was published at Amsterdam in 1676, when Barclay was twenty-eight years old, and his translation appeared two years later. He seems to have been to some extent indebted to George Keith, who in later life became a clergyman and an opponent of Friends (*post*, p. 178). See Braithwaite, *Second Period*, p. 387.

[3] *Apology*, xi. 7. The reader is referred to a valuable pamphlet, *Studies in Quaker Worship*, by D. Elton Trueblood.

of exhortation or prayer when it is needful, so that . . .
there are few meetings that are altogether silent.[1] For when
many are met together in this one Life and Name it doth
most naturally and frequently excite them to pray to and
praise God and stir up one another by mutual exhortation
and instructions (*ibid.* xi. 9).

Barclay goes on to say that this service will not be
entered into hurriedly, but will arise out of a living
silence "during which everyone may be gathered *inward*
to the word and gift of Grace and not to hasten into the
exercise of these things as soon as the bell rings, as other
Christians do."

Further on, the same writer describes the attacks
that were made upon the quiet worshippers:

It would be almost incredible to declare and indeed a
shame that among many men pretending to be Christians
it should be mentioned what things of this kind men's eyes
have seen, and I myself have shared in, with others, of
suffering; there they have often beaten us and cast water
and dirt upon us; there they have danced, leaped, sung and
spoken all manner of profane and ungodly words; offered
violence and shameful behaviour to grave women and
virgins;[2] jeered, mocked and scoffed, asking us "If the
Spirit was not yet come" . . . and all this while we have
been seriously and silently sitting together and waiting
upon the Lord. . . . Sometimes in the midst of this tumult
and opposition God would powerfully move some or other
of us by His Spirit both to testify of that joy which, notwithstanding their malice, we enjoyed and powerfully

[1] George Keith also says this toward the end of his tract, *The
Benefit, Advantage and Glory of Silent Meetings.*
[2] "Grave" is Barclay's translation of *gravidas*, "pregnant." The
original Latin is, violentiam offerentes, impudice erga gravidas
feminas et mulieres se gerentes. Barclay says that "in these beastly
and brutish pranks used to molest us in our spiritual meetings" (in
brutalibus istis et bestialibus perpetrationibus, ad nos in spiritualibus
nostris conventionibus molestandos, excogitatis) the leading part
was taken by university students learning philosophy and divinity,
"the young fry of the clergy" (ab hoc clericorum spermate).

to declare, in the evidence and demonstration of the Spirit, against their folly and wickedness . . . so that sometimes upon such occasions several of our opposers and inter-rupters have hereby been convinced of the Truth, and gathered from being persecutors to be sufferers with us (*ibid.* xi. 13).

This thought of the sufferers so bearing themselves as to make appeal to the inward witness in their perse-cutors was a result of the Quaker outlook on humanity. "Honouring all men is reaching that of God in every man," said Fox,[1] and, setting up as their standard of value not their own safety, but the conversion of their perse-cutors, neither he nor his friends opposed violence with violence, the women did not call on the men to defend them (if there had been a fight there would have been no "reaching that of God" in anyone), they did not flee or discontinue their worship at the appearance of their assailants,[2] but men and women quietly stood their ground in accord with his counsel:

> In the peaceable mind and spirit dwell, for the patient sufferer weareth the crown, and hath the victory at last, and not the hasty, aggravating, revengeful, killing and fighting spirit.[3]

And, referring to the appeal which faithful endurance may make to the persecutors themselves, he writes:

[1] *Epistles*, p. 53.
[2] Concerning certain old meeting houses stories have got about, often repeated by writers of guide books or of newspaper articles, that there was a room in which the women took refuge when the assailants came. There is no evidence for this and there is much that clearly shows the error of this statement. Probably the mistake is due to the fact of there being certain rooms in which the women transacted their part of the congregation's or the Society's business in days before all such meetings were composed of men and women together.
[3] *Epistles*, p. 235, and see *post*, p. 351.

Look not at your sufferings but at the power of God, and that will bring some good out in all your sufferings, and your imprisonemnts will reach to the prisoned that the persecutor prisons in himself.[1]

It was this spirit that was shown by Friends of Cork when William Penn, twenty-three years old, was beginning to attend their meetings before he had reached a full understanding of them. Exasperated by the conduct of a soldier who had come to make a disturbance, the young aristocrat seized him by the collar and would have thrown him downstairs if Friends had not prevented him. The soldier went to the magistrates who sent officers to break up the meeting and Penn along with others was taken to prison. As he went he gave his sword to his man and never wore one afterwards.[2]

The quiet or "retired" meetings, as they were called, of which Barclay speaks, were in many cases composed of earnest-minded people who, having heard the message proclaimed to the multitude, often amid great disturbance, sought out the preachers for intimate discourse. Burrough and Howgill, writing to Margaret Fell from London, in 1655, give account of their method of procedure. They report that on the previous First-day Fox had been in

[1] *Epistles*, p. 80, and see pp. 2, 3 of the same and *Cambridge Journal*, ii. 338 (bi-cent. *Journal*, ii. 251). For love to persecutors, see *Epistles*, pp. 412, 461.

[2] *Journal of the Friends Historical Society*, xxxii. (1935), p. 23. The manuscript in which this is told is dated 1729: at the time of the incident Penn had not yet met Fox and the story conflicts with a later tradition (Janney's *Life of Penn*, p. 50) that Penn asked him whether he should wear his sword and that Fox answered "Wear it as long as thou canst." This anecdote is sometimes misused to imply that Fox did not regard Friends as having any corporate testimony as to the bearing of arms, but left the matter to each individual to do as he would. If this story, and not the earlier one, is true, it is far more likely that Penn's question was a jest and that Fox, so understanding it, meant "Thou won't be wearing it long." For his explicit statement concerning the corporate Quaker testimony against war see *post*, p. 132.

private with Friends, but that they two "were in the general meeting place among the rude world, threshing and ploughing."[1]

> We have thus ordered it since we came; we get Friends on the First-days to meet together in several places out of the rude multitude, etc.; and we two go to the great meeting place which we have which will hold a thousand people, which is always nearly filled, to thresh among the world; and we stay till twelve or one o'clock and then pass away, the one to one place and the other to another place where Friends are met in private; and stay till four or five o'clock (*Letters of Early Friends*, p. 27).

Of one of the great meetings addressed by Burrough, William Crouch gives a lively description:

> He was a man (though but young) of undaunted courage, the Lord set him above the fear of his enemies; and I have beheld him filled with power by the Spirit of the Lord. For instance, at the Bull and Mouth, when the room which was very large hath been filled with people, many of whom have been in uproars, contending one with another, some exclaiming against the Quakers, accusing and charging them with heresy, blasphemy, sedition and whatnot, that they were deceivers and deluded the people, that they denied the Holy Scriptures and the Resurrection; others endeavouring to vindicate them and speaking of them more favourably. In the midst of all which noise and contention this servant of the Lord hath stood upon a bench with his Bible in his hand . . . speaking to the people with great authority . . . and so suitable to the present debate amongst them that the whole multitude were overcome thereby and became exceeding calm and attentive, and departed peaceably and with seeming satisfaction (*Posthuma Christiana*, p. 26).

---

[1] It is probably now necessary to explain that in Quaker language First-day meant Sunday. The meeting place was the Bull and Mouth in Aldersgate, so called from the name of the inn that occupied another part of the building. The old sign is in the Guildhall museum.

To those who remember that Fox's voice and body were powerful beyond those of most men, the exhausting nature of this service is made abundantly clear by a sentence in the letter of Burrough and Howgill already quoted: "George was at the great meeting place two First-days before we came, and his voice and outward man were almost spent among them."

The messengers grasped every opportunity that opened before them for "threshing among the world," or "threshing the heathenish nature" as Fox expressed it. Edward Burrough, on a summer evening walking through the fields of the outskirts of London, came upon a ring of people watching a wrestling match, at that time a popular form of recreation. "A strong and dextrous fellow who had already thrown three others," waiting for a fourth to try his skill, was amazed, together with the spectators, to see Burrough step into the ring where he "began very seriously to speak to the standers-by, and that with such a heart-piercing power, that he was heard by this mixed multitude with no less attention than admiration."[1] Many times, however, as we have seen, the message met with a hostile and, even, savage reception.

But it was not so much among the world at large as among the Seekers that the seed fell on good ground. Mention has been made of the ingathering at Preston Patrick (p. 72), and when John Camm and John Audland, two Westmorland men, in pursuance of the organized mission came to Bristol in 1654, they brought into the Quaker Church hundreds of men and women waiting in expectation of a message of life. At Ross, in Herefordshire, two Friends travelling on foot found a company of people,

---

[1] Sewel, *History of the Quakers*, under the year 1654. "Admiration," see *ante*, p. 39 note.

. . . who had for some time before separated themselves
from the public worship of the world, who did see the
end of the priests' teachings, who did often before meet
together by themselves and would many times sit in silence
and no particular person appointed to speak or preach
amongst them, but each of them did speak by way of
exhortation as had freedom (*First Publishers of Truth*,
p. 124).

Of many places a similar story is told, and it was in
those parts of England where the Seekers had prepared
the way that Quakerism was most readily received.

When they came to know the indwelling life of Christ
for which they had been waiting, their meetings continued
but were now radiant with a new joy.[1]

As a matter of fact, all of the distinguishing tenets and
practices of Friends had been by individuals or by groups,
preached or practised before the appearance of Fox,
though not in conjunction with one another or as the
outcome of any central principle. Of the occurrence of
some of them among the Baptists mention has been made,
and they are to be found scattered up and down in the
list of "Errors, Heresies and Blasphemies" set forth by
the Presbyterian Thomas Edwards in his *Gangraena* which
appeared in 1646.[2] "What was *new*," says Dr. Rufus Jones,
speaking of the Quakers' teaching, "was the fusing of their
ideas into one living truth, which was henceforth to be
done, was to be put into life and made to march."[3]

---

[1] See "Seekers" in the Index to Braithwaite's *Beginnings of
Quakerism*. The passage here quoted is on p. 138.
[2] Those who, in order to gain further information, look this up in
Gangraena should know that each of its three parts must be consulted
separately for the list that it contains.
[3] Introduction to Braithwaite's *Beginnings of Quakerism*, p. xliii.;
and concerning the preparation for Quakerism see the same work
pp. xxviii., xxxiii., 27, 121, 129, 130–31, 138, 139, 163, 165, 188–89,
391, 514, and c. iv., particularly pp. 94–97.

Chapter VIII

MEMBERS ONE OF ANOTHER

THE various groups of Friends for the most part gathered round men and women who exercised a spiritual leadership, not of authority or in virtue of any office or appointment, but a leadership accorded to them by reason of the inspiration shown by their lives. From group to group throughout the country there passed the "Publishers of Truth," not as spiritual superiors claiming the right to exercise discipline, but giving loving counsel and, where necessary, allaying difficulties, as men who followed continually the guidance of their Lord. They were concerned, not primarily to build up a particular religious body, but to set forth the truth as they had received it.[1]

Nevertheless, as the early Christians were driven by force of circumstances to leave the synagogue and meet by themselves, so Friends, in line, as we have seen, with the Seekers, could not find expression for their spiritual experience except in their own way of worship, and this, of course, rendered necessary a certain organization.

> It is a mark of the wisdom and sanity of George Fox that, mystic and idealist as he was, he faced the facts of life, he learned from experience, he came to see that disembodied spiritual movements cannot succeed and do a permanent work in the world; and, when the hour came for it, he took

[1] The following description of the early Church is true of the early Quaker community. "The separate Christian congregations were formally independent of each other. There was no organized unity of the Christian Church as including the little separate communities. [But] while there was no formal dependence of one Christian congregation on another, all these congregations were conscious of a very real and close unity with each other" (Bartlet and Carlyle, *Christianity in History*, p. 375).

the leadership in organizing the Society of Friends for its
abiding expanding mission.[1]

Throughout his life his policy was to provide a right
outlet for all forms of spiritual service. At the age of
twenty-eight he wrote to all those "who have tasted
of the immediate working power of the Lord and do find
an alteration in your minds,"

> Therefore be faithful to God and mind that which is
> committed to you as faithful servants labouring in love,
> some threshing and some ploughing and some to keep the
> sheep (*Epistles*, p. 15).

At first the arrangements were simple; the leaders
or the Friends in general of a district would, at intervals
meet for Christian intercourse at some convenient place,
money was collected for the expense of the travelling
ministers and for the relief of the poor and all who were
brought into want by reason of persecution, arrangement
was made for marriages and for recording of births and
deaths, and the beginning of congregational discipline
is seen in provision for reproof by the Church of dis-
orderly conduct after private admonition had been proved
futile.[2] Not Church discipline, however, but a bond
of fellowship, was the uniting force between people of
widely different social and educational standing, and
between far-separated groups welded into one body by

---

[1] Rufus M. Jones, Introduction to Braithwaite's *Second Period of
Quakerism*, p. xxviii.; concerning organization and discipline see
pp. 328, 401–402, and *Beginnings of Quakerism*, p. 307. See also
quotation from Rufus M. Jones, *ante*, p. 66. "This corporate consciousness [of the early Church] was not due to organization, but was
rather the cause urging the actual Church units to ever more organized
expression of the inherent spirit of unity" (Bartlet and Carlyle,
Christianity in History, p. 296).

[2] See Braithwaite, *Beginnings of Quakerism*, c. xiii.: "Church
Organization." For Fox's more detailed organization later on see
post, pp. 167 f.

the travelling ministers who carried loving greetings together with news of a common experience and of like sufferings for the faith. Apart from a knowledge of this deep fellowship, there is no understanding of early Quakerism nor, in fact, of any effective spiritual movement. The reader will do well to note in the passages quoted in this chapter the frequency of the expression *one another*. Francis Howgill thus tells of early days in Westmorland,

> The Kingdom of Heaven did gather us and catch us all as in a net, and His heavenly power at one time drew many hundreds to land, that we came to know a place to stand in and what to wait in; and the Lord appeared daily to us, to our astonishment, amazement and great admiration, insomuch that we often said one unto another with great joy of heart, "What? Is the Kingdom of God come to be with men? And will He take up His tabernacle among the sons of men, as He did of old? And what? shall we that were reckoned as the outcasts of Israel have this honour of glory communicated amongst us which were but men of small parts and of little abilities in respect of many others as amongst men?" . . . and from that day forward our hearts were knit unto the Lord and unto one another in true and fervent love, not by any external covenant or external form, but we entered into the covenant of life with God, and that was a strong obligation or bond upon all our spirits which united us one unto another . . . and mightily did the word of God grow amongst us ("Testimony" concerning Edward Burrough).

Of this bond of union William Penn also makes mention:

> We were in travail for one another's preservation, not seeking but shunning occasions of any coldness or mis-understanding, treating one another as those that believed and felt God present (Preface to Fox's *Journal*, bi-cent. edn. i., p. li.).

Of the Christian intercourse and fellowship of the Swarthmore household, William Caton tells the story. He was a boy of about sixteen at the time of Fox's first visit in 1652, living with the family as companion to the Judge's only son:

> Oh, the love which in that day abounded among us, especially in that family . . . the nearness and dearness that was amongst us one towards another. . . . And in those days were meetings exceeding precious to us, insomuch that some few of us did commonly every night spend sometimes more, sometimes less time in waiting upon the Lord; yea often after the rest of the family were gone to bed; but oh! the comfort and refreshment which we had together and the benefit which we reaped thereby, how shall I declare it? . . . For I was often overcome, overcome, with the love of my Father which did exceedingly break and ravish my heart, and so I know it was with others of that family; and of the overflowings thereof did we communicate one to another to the comforting and refreshing one of another, and truly willing we were to sympathize, and bear one with another, to be helpful one unto another and in true and tender love to watch one over another (*Life*, edn. of 1689, pp. 6–8).

A year or more after Fox's visit Caton made a journey in the neighbourhood giving forth his message, and after being put in the stocks, stoned and beaten—the boy of seventeen—he tells of his coming back,

> . . . [to] Judge Fell's at Swarthmore in Lancashire. Then was our refreshment very great together in the Lord and with rejoicing did we speak together of His wonderful works (*ibid*. p. 11).

For a moment we turn aside from our story of early Quaker fellowship to follow Caton's career in the twelve years of this life that were left to him. Accompanying

John Stubbs, once a Commonwealth soldier and afterwards a schoolmaster at Lancaster, Caton, not yet twenty
years old, went into Kent. Making their way on foot
and living simply—a Friend tells of his coming on them
at their evening meal and finding them "eating a little
bread and beer without anything to sweeten or relish it"
—the two companions passed from town to town. At
Lydd, Samuel Fisher, an Oxford man, who had been
a Puritan lecturer but was now a Baptist minister, "received them and their testimony to God's glory." He was
one of the most learned of the early Friends, but barely
ten years of service were left to him before he died in a
London prison. It is of interest to note that his two
visitors were able to meet him on his own ground, Stubbs
being, according to the testimony of a strong opponent,
learned in Hebrew and Greek,[1] and Caton, as we shall
see immediately, well versed in Latin. Elsewhere also
the preaching of the two travellers met with good response,
but part of their way was rough. At Dover, in deference
to popular clamour, they were turned out of their inn—
"Baptists, Independents, Brownists and Episcopals all
agreed with one voice that they were deceivers and so cried
them down"—at Folkestone "Caton had hard usage at
their steeplehouse, occasioned chiefly by a rude and
debauched fellow"; at Maidstone they were arrested as
vagrants, their money and other property were taken
from them, and after being kept for three days without
food,

> . . . they were stripped naked, and their necks and arms
> put in the stocks and there cruelly whipped with cords in a
> bloody manner in the sight of many people which forced
> tears from the tender-hearted. . . . And when they had

[1] *Quakers in the American Colonies*, by R. M. Jones, p. 116
note.

thus cruelly proceeded they fastened irons upon them
with great clogs of wood, and put them in amongst trans-
gressors.[1]

By different ways they were sent separately out of the
town and were passed on from one constable to another,
but when they were free they came together and "returned
to Maidstone again and sounded the Gospel in their
streets."

Later on in the same year, 1655, the two companions,
after a short visit to Calais, went to Holland. Caton in
his account of their service, deplores, on one occasion,
the lack of a good interpreter; on another he gave his
message in Latin and through that medium it was translated into Dutch.

Going back to our story of fellowship, we take note,
for our own help to-day, of the love that was known
among those engaged in service together like that of
Stubbs and Caton, and of the keen desire to strengthen
one another. Thomas Thompson, of Holderness, describes
the service of himself and two others in East Yorkshire, one
of them about to go to Beverley, and himself and the other
of them to Malton: 'We sat down and were in prayer and
supplication to the Lord much of the day, William
labouring to strengthen Thomas and encourage him."[2]
William Edmundson, the first apostle of Quakerism in
Ireland, tells of meetings for worship, twice in the week,
"in which our hearts were tender before the Lord, and in

---

[1] *First Publishers of Truth*, p. 139; other details in this story of
Stubbs and Caton are taken from the same source, or from *Love and
Truth in Plainness Manifested* (1704), by Luke Howard, a prosperous
shoemaker at Dover, where he "served the town in offices." He took
Stubbs and Caton into his house when they were turned out of their
inn, and he himself became a Friend.

[2] Testimony concerning John Whitehead, beginning of *Gospel
Labours of John Whitehead.*

His love near and dear one to another." And, after describing the persecution thus brought upon them, he continues:

> In those days the world and the things of it were not near our hearts, but the love of God, His truth and testimony lived in our hearts; we were glad of one another's company though sometimes our outward fare was very mean and our lodging on straw; we did not mind high things, but were glad of one another's welfare in the Lord, and His love dwelt in us (*Journal*, p. 26).

John Burnyeat, also speaking of these days in Ireland, particularly of his fourteen months' travel with Robert Lodge of Yorkshire, bears testimony:

> The Lord gave us sweet concord and peace in all our travels; for I do not remember that we ever were angry or grieved one at the other in all that time (*Works*, p. 28).

Earlier on he had dwelt upon the help flowing from one to another in the meetings for worship:

> . . . the openings of the power that was daily amongst us and wrought sweetly in our hearts, which still united us more and more unto God and knit us together in the perfect bond of love, of fellowship and membership, so that we became a body compact . . . [and] many through the favour of God grew in their gifts and had their mouths opened, and so became instruments in the Lord's hand to bear witness unto the world of the day of the Lord that was broken forth again (*ibid*. pp. 11–12).

Edward Burrough, also, recalls the power of a company, met together, not as isolated individuals, but in unity of spirit which led them to give forth the message,

> . . . waiting upon the Lord in silence as often we did for many hours together, with our minds and hearts toward Him, being stayed in the light of Christ within us from all

thoughts, fleshly motions and desires . . . we received often
the pouring down of the Spirit upon us . . . and our hearts
were made glad, and our tongues loosed, and our mouths
opened . . . and the glory of the Father was revealed . . .
and thus we became followers of the Lamb whithersoever he
goes (Preface to Fox's *Great Mistery*).

In view of the *unbalanced* emphasis on silence in worship, to the disparagement of ministry, which was soon
to settle down on the Society, it is important to note that
the fellowship of those early days valued exceedingly the
word spoken as a means of expression that could not be
left out.[1] In addition to the passages already quoted,
including the testimony of Barclay (p. 105), we may read
an account of the Yearly Meeting of 1679. It occurs in
a letter written to his wife by John Banks of Pardshaw,
in Cumberland, and afterwards of Meare and Street, in
Somerset:

> Now as to our Yearly Meeting. O, how did the Lord's
> power overshadow us, and His pure love and life run as a
> mighty stream amongst us with the pouring forth of His
> Spirit upon us in a plentiful manner; in answer and subjec-
> tion to whose love, power and Holy Spirit we were made
> willing and ready to speak and declare one by one of the
> great work of God for the confirming and establishing one
> another therein.[2]

These Friends, Burnyeat, Burrough, Barclay and Banks
did not claim it as a Quaker merit that they sat long in
silence and dispersed without a word spoken. The point
of this will not be understood by the reader till he has
read c. xv. George Whitehead speaks of the love known
among those who in meetings held largely in silence
were given "a few words livingly to utter . . . to their

[1] See *post*, c. xv.   [2] *Journal of John Banks* (1712), p. 80.

and my own comfort in Him who opened our hearts in great love one to another which then increased and grew among us."[1]

Fox, in his perception of the supreme value of this fellowship (a word not to be used lightly), often commends it: "mind that which is pure in one another which joins you together"; "therefore, all Friends, obey that which is pure within you and know one another in that which brings you to wait on the Lord"; "Friends meet together and know one another in that which is eternal which was before the world was," "feel the power of God in one another," "that all may be as one family, building up one another and helping one another," "know one another in this love that changeth not."[2]

He saw that a necessary bond of fellowship, saving it from disruption, was service shared in common:

> None may stand idle out of the vineyard and out of the service and out of their duty, for such will talk and tattle; and judge with evil thoughts of what they in the vineyard say and do.[3]

[1] *Christian Progress*, p. 10.

[2] *Epistles*, pp. 12, 70, 115, 128, 94, 119 respectively; also see 10, 14, 15, 19, 20, 21, 24, 30, 36, 39, 41, 47, 49, 51, 57, 59, 60, 63, 93 (twice), 100, 138, 139, 143, 171, 354; these are but a few of the passages which speak of "one another." The frequency in the seventeenth century of the words "one another" may be contrasted with their rarity during the eighteenth and most of the nineteenth centuries; see *post*, p. 251. To those who wish to make further study of the fellowship of the early days the following pages of Braithwaite's *Beginnings of Quakerism* are commended (the particular word "fellowship" does not appear on each one of them), xxxiii.–xxxiv., 95, 96, 121, 130, 212, 307, 342, 495, 507, 508, 526, 529. *Second Period*, p. 170.

[3] *Epistles*, p. 235, repeated p. 328. With this passage compare p. 473, where Fox speaks of those "whose candle is gone out, and now cannot endure to hear talk of the light," and see p. 387 (third paragraph). Also Isaac Penington, "There is no such bitter, deadly enemy to Christ and His truth as he who once had some taste of the virtue of it and is now turned from it into the earth." *Works*, i. 344, edn. of 1761; and see p. 571.

One of the most marked differences between these early days and the greater part of the two centuries that followed them is that in this later time the note of joyous fellowship was but little heard.

Conceive, now, of a Church composed of members setting their course of life in this way of *one another*. Nevertheless, they are in the body and there may be some who (perhaps under strain more terrible than anyone knows) will speak or act wrongly, some who are of ill-nature; but in this Church will their fellow members seek to bring healing for their sickness. There will be no evil delight, even on the part of those who have been hurt, at the fall or humiliation of the wrongdoer; no talk or bearing to hinder his recovery, but, far from this, a cleansing wind of love which blows aside, as an evil fog, all resentment and contempt and brooding over affronted dignity or pride. For they, the fellow members, count it their joy to be of the body of Christ, doing, at high cost to themselves it may be, his work of *seeking and saving*. And if the cost be that of forgiveness for hurt done, it will be given, and in no grudging way that leaves in unswept corners some dust of ill-will, for it will be the "Forgiveness [which] does not truly deserve the name, unless it points to such a *renewal of relationships* for which 'reconciliation' seems sometimes too cool and passive a word."[1] And this Church will be a home for many who are seeking, who are lonely, who are hungering for friendship, but who in it will learn to take their part in the work of *answering that of God in one another*.

[1] Brown and Harvey, *The Naturalness of Religion*, p. 152. The whole chapter in which this passage occurs is commended to the reader's notice.

Chapter IX

THE LEADINGS OF THE LIGHT: PLAINNESS, OATHS, WAR, HONESTY: THE EXAGGERATION OF NAYLER

A STRIKING feature of the infant Quaker Church was the uniformity, achieved within a very short time, on various matters of practice, obviously not as the outcome of tradition, but of a common spirit animating all, this being in part due to the influence of Fox and other leaders.[1] Mention has already been made of the way of worship practised by Friends from their earliest days. Not as the result of any ecclesiastical direction, but naturally, throughout the fellowship, there prevailed a simplicity of attire, not the adoption of a specially designed costume, but of the dress of the period shorn of the superfluities with which it was usually decked. A certain Friend, recalling his youthful days, tells of an order which he gave for breeches, doublet and cloak, "all to be hanged with ribbons, as the fashion was"[2] (making people look like fiddlers' boys, as Fox said).[3] Addison, contrasting this foppery with its opposite extreme writes:

> I am much in doubt whether I should give the preference to a Quaker that is trimmed close and almost cut to the quick, or to a beau that is loaden with such a redundancy of excrescences.[4]

[1] Concerning this early achievement of uniformity see Braithwaite *Beginnings of Quakerism*, p. 139.
[2] Luke Howard, *Love and Truth in Plainness Manifested* (1704), pp. 13–14. For Fox's astonishing description of extravagance in attire see my *Personality of George Fox*, pp. 50–51 (edn. of 1918–19); pp. 100–103 (edn. of 1933).
[3] Cambridge *Journal*, i. 176.　　　　[4] *Spectator*, March 19, 1711.

Gilbert Latey, a Cornishman, one of the first converts
to Quakerism in London, was a tailor, doing business

> . . . with persons of considerable rank and quality who
> would have their apparel set off with much cost and
> superfluities of lace and ribbons [but] he came under a
> conscientious concern not to meddle therewith, nor suffer
> his servants to put it on, which made some say he was mad,
> and others, he would be mad.

He lost a large part of his trade and was "despised even
of his own mother's children and, as it were, banished
from his father's house, yet chose to leave all rather than
lose his peace with the Lord."[1] Another Friend, a tailor,
Thomas Wilde of Yorkshire, took the same stand as Latey.[2]

In the matter of "hat-honour," as the Quaker called it,
this uniformity of which we are speaking soon prevailed.
It was not the natural thing for the master in his own
house to take off his hat, though he insisted on his sons
doing so in his presence; the worshipper, and sometimes
even the preacher, wore it in church, taking it off in
time of prayer and the singing of psalms.[3] The Quaker

[1] *Life of Latey*, by Hawkins (1707), pp. 19, 20. On p. 5 it is stated
that he did business with "persons of the first rank and quality then
in the kingdom." This was about 1650. For the abominable imprisonment which he suffered see pp. 27 f. of the same.

[2] *A Collection of Testimonies* concerning Quaker ministers, p. 7.

[3] See my *Personality of George Fox* (edn. of 1918–19), p. 60 note;
(edn. of 1933), p. 119 note. In Pepys' *Diary* under date November 17,
1661, occurs the entry, "To church, and heard a simple fellow upon
the praise of church music and exclaiming against men's wearing their
hats on in the church." Isaac Penington speaks of the custom of men
Friends wearing their hats except in time of vocal prayer, *Works*, ii.
563 (edn. of 1761), and in course of time this, like certain other
"testimonies," degenerated into ritual, see *post*, pp. 192, 296. In 1805
Thomas Shillitoe in Jersey, joining in worship with a non-Quaker
congregation, apologized for keeping on his hat, saying that it was the
"uniform practice" of Friends to do so except in time of prayer. Up
to the late 1870's or even later, men, on entering a meeting for worship always kept their hats on though by that time most would take
them off on reaching their seats or soon after. The present writer
when a boy would keep his on during a good part of the meeting. He

also, to the honour of God, took it off in time of prayer (he did not sing psalms), but he refused to give in to the spirit which led judge or magistrate to demand its removal in his presence and led social "superiors" to demand the payment to them of an honour which they would not pay to their "inferiors." Accordingly he wore his hat on almost all the occasions when others took theirs off. To magistrates and others who were infuriated at the Quaker way Isaac Penington made appeal:

> And for honour to magistrates and superiors, it is not denied, but fleshly honour, corrupt honour . . . cannot but be denied by them which are of God. . . . If ye could search your hearts ye would find that it is not that of God in you which is offended for want of that which ye call honour, but . . . the fleshly pride and loftiness which the Lord will lay low.[1]

can also remember certain Friends, by way of showing their dis-approval of the speaker, refusing in time of prayer either to stand up (as the custom is) or to take off their hats. Some of them if they had already taken them off, would put them on. This was an unhappy legacy from pre-Quaker days, see Edwards, *Gangraena* (1646), Pt. i., p. 65; Pt. iii, p. 96, Ireton's soldiers in church keeping on their hats in prayer and the singing of psalms. See also William Rogers (an apostate Quaker), *The Christian Quaker* (1680), Pt. iii., p. 13.

[1] *Works*, i. 49, edn. of 1761; and see pp. 275 f. Quakers were charged with inconsistency in that they compelled (so it was alleged) their boys to be uncovered in their presence. Daniel Phillips, a doctor, says that it was for the sake of health and not of ceremonious-ness that Quaker boys did not wear their hats indoors. He says that if everyone would get used to doing the same they would not be so liable to have their hair fall off and to "injuries of the air." He con-tinues: "I judge it absolutely necessary for boys to be obliged, on account of their health, to be uncovered when they are within doors, and if girls could be persuaded to go in their hair as boys generally do, it would be advantageous to their health." Phillips points out the inconvenience to schoolmasters in teaching, reading, writing and arithmetic if the boys wore their hats (*Vindiciae Veritatis: A Defence of the Principles of Quakers* (1703), p. 33). On the subject of hat-wearing in the house see Fox's *Journal*, Cambridge edition, ii. 482.

In certain aristocratic London clubs the custom of wearing the hat indoors did not finally die out till some way on in the twentieth century. *Manchester Guardian*, December 10, 1937.

With equal unanimity, refusing to admit the right of some to be addressed as "you" while they themselves said "thou" to those whom they counted beneath them, the Quakers everywhere spoke the "plain language," as they called it, saying "thou" to all men as being the appropriate word for use in the singular number. It is impossible for us now to realize how discourteous this was regarded when addressed by children to parents, servants to masters, or other "inferiors" to "superiors."[1] Fox when confronted with the question whether it was not a shame for a boy to say "thou" to his father and mother replied, with his characteristic use of Scripture, that Jephthah's daughter said "thou" to her father even though he was a judge of Israel.[2] Thus it was that unless the speaker had some obvious right to say "thou," his doing so was taken as impertinence. There was also another ground of dislike to the word. It was said that those who withheld honour from those to whom it was due would go on to question their right to wealth: "Such as now introduce *thou* and *thee* will (if they can) expel *mine* and *thine*."[3]

The suffering which the Quaker's faithfulness in these

[1] See *Lives* of Thomas Ellwood, Richard Davies and other early Friends. Davies says that his mistress hit him on the head with a stick. An anonymous writer challenged Friends as to whether they really said "thou" to their parents, "and if you do, how they look at these wanton chickens that are so fancy with them." *The Querers and Quakers Cause* (1653), p. 21.

[2] *The Great Mystery*, p. 260

[3] Fuller, *Church History* (1655), Introduction to Book viii. The writer thus describes the usage of the time: "*Thou* from superiors to inferiors is proper as a sign of command; from equals to equals is passable as a note of familiarity; but from inferiors to superiors, if proceeding from ignorance, hath a smack of clownishness, if from affectation, a tang of contempt." The writer says of Quakers: "God grant these may be seasonably suppressed before they grow too numerous." At the trial of Raleigh in 1603, Coke thus addressed him: "All that Lord Cobham did was by thy instigation thou viper, for I 'thou' thee, thou traitor."

matters brought upon him was not endured for any unessential or frivolous scruple, but because of his determination to dwell with *the Truth*, standing clear of sham and pretence while repudiating the charge of discourtesy. "True civility stands in truth," said Fox.[1]

> The witness of Friends [says Braithwaite] on points of speech and dress thus touched some of the greatest issues of life, and is not to be treated as an excrescence on their main message. We ought rather to feel that the main message, under the conditions of that age, could not have been uttered in its purity and force if Friends had shrunk from giving it fearless application to these parts of life.[2]

The testimony in favour of simplicity of behaviour is the better understood as we come to have knowledge of the ceremoniousness and insincerity of the time. The customary salutation from one man to another was not the simple greeting that we know; and Ellwood, after he had come to the point of withholding it, thus describes his first meeting with his friends: "When they were come up to me they all saluted me after the usual manner, putting off their hats and bowing, saying, 'Your humble servant, sir,' expecting, no doubt, the same from me." On his failure to make a similar return he tells how "the surgeon (a brisk young man)" clapped him on the shoulder saying, "What, Tom, a Quaker!"[3] Thomas Story tells of the insults that he received when he took the same stand as Ellwood had done. A member of a cultured Anglican family in Cumberland (his brother became Dean of Limerick), he was educated for the Bar and in 1691 in the exercise of his profession he attended the assizes at Carlisle

---

[1] *Gospel Truth Demonstrated* (*Doctrinals*), the former of two pages each numbered 162 (the one that is in its right place). See also *Epistles*, p. 266.

[2] *Beginnings of Quakerism*, p. 495, and see pp. 47, 494.

[3] *Journal*, under the year 1659, Crump's edition, pp. 23–24.

where word had gone round that he had turned Quaker.
He was taunted by his acquaintances, taking off their
hats and offering the customary salutation with mock
elaborateness and then running away laughing loudly or
otherwise showing derision. He thus continues the tale:

> I said very little to any of them but gave them my face
> to their fill of gazing. And some who but a day or two before
> durst not have discovered [bestowed] a disobliging look
> upon me now insulted and triumphed. . . . Yet all these
> things did not provoke or move me, for the grace and
> presence of the Lord was with me and my full strength and
> preservation. My heart was surrounded with a rampart of
> invincible patience and my soul filled with divine love.[1]

Fox speaks of men so much "lifted up in pride" that
no one must come near them without "scraping and
bowing the hat four or five times," and he waxes satirical
over the heart-burnings which these punctilios of etiquette
engendered: "I bowed three times to him and he scarce
bowed once to me and scarce stirred his hat"; "I curtsied
three times, the first almost to the ground, and she scarce
bowed to me, she made but half a curtsey."[2] He describes
the insincerity of "people in the world" who would say,

> . . . "How do you, Sir?" doff the hat, scrape a leg, make
> a curtsey, "I am glad to see you well," "your servant,"
> "your servant, my lord (or sir) or mistress"; and when they
> are past them, with the same tongue wish evil to them,
> speak evil of them . . . and laugh at one another behind
> their backs.[3]

Elsewhere Fox says that this formal salutation "pleaseth

---

[1] *Journal*, p. 39. At this time Story was close upon thirty years of
age.

[2] *Gospel Truth Demonstrated (Doctrinals)*, p. 162, the former of
two pages so numbered; see also p. 31.

[3] *Ibid.* p. 107, and see the former of two pp. each numbered 160
(the one in its right place).

proud flesh, but to say 'thou friend' makes him or her mad."[1] Steele, writing in *The Tatler*, points out that when a Quaker "with an air of good nature and charity calls you 'friend,'" it was unreasonable for him to be ridiculed by those whose extravagant use of terms of honour had emptied them of all meaning.[2]

The story of these Quaker "peculiarities," as they came to be called, has been told, not as an antiquarian chapter of past days, but as giving understanding of subsequent history. The sturdy insistence on them, at the cost of suffering, has been a factor in the formation of an independence of character which inspired respect, and which gave ability to step out along unknown and, sometimes, along unpopular ways. Unfortunately, however, the story will have to be told (c.xvi) of their fading down into a rigid traditional ritualism after the circumstances which in the beginning had called for them no longer existed.

This same passion for *truth* led the Quaker to refuse to confirm his word by an oath in courts of law. Before his time there had been those who had known a similar scruple, relying on the Scriptural injunction "Swear not at all." Like them, Friends quoted in defence of their position Matt. v. 33–37 and James v. 12, but they also took their stand on their fundamental principle. Penington contends that the taking of oaths did not come into the world till man fell from the state of innocency in which he was at the first created, a state "wherein man could not lie or deceive" and that while a Jew or a heathen may take an oath because he knows no better way of confirming his word, the Christian must show forth the principle of Christ, *the Truth*, into which he has come, being more firmly

---

[1] *Gospel Truth Demonstrated* (*Doctrinals*), pp. 160–61, the former of the pages so numbered.   [2] *The Tatler*, No. 240, June 29, 1710.

bound thereby than any Jew or heathen can be. Thus for *him* it is a lowering to take an oath, "a way of confirmation of things which is short of his own." (*The Great Question Concerning . . . Swearing*). In view of the double standard which an oath sets up, Penn points out that if truth-speaking ever is to become the rule of the world so that oaths are unnecessary, there must be those who will lead the way, themselves showing forth the principle which they have reached. In two epigrams he sums up his case: "We dare not swear, because we dare not lie"; and again: "People swear to the end they may speak truth; Christ would have them speak truth to the end they might not swear"[1] By one who is not a Friend the position has been well stated:

> Oaths are condemned [by Jesus] as likely to take from the severe demands of truthful speech. The yea must be yea, the nay, nay. An oath lowers the value of normal speech.[2]

In the stand which they took on this matter Friends were confirmed by repeated evidence of the futility of

[1] *A Treatise of Oaths*, ii. and ix. This pamphlet was presented to the King and Parliament in 1675; it is signed by Penn and twelve other Friends to some of whom at any rate the credit of producing is almost certainly due. It is written with great learning and is interesting by reason of its references to and quotations from a very large number of writers ancient and modern.

[2] Hastings' *Dictionary of Christ and the Gospels* (1908), Article "Sincerity," by Rev. Edw. Shillito. In his comment on Matt. v. 33–37, T. W. Manson writes in his work, *The Teaching of Jesus*, "This is far more than a mere demand for the abolition of oaths in the law courts or elsewhere. What Jesus envisages here is a state of affairs in which oaths, cross-examinations and punishments for perjury are alike unnecessary, because a man's word is enough; because, in other words, he can be trusted to tell the truth. And he can be so trusted because he has been changed in himself, with the result that truthfulness has become more precious in his eyes than any seeming advantage that might be gained by falsehood" (p. 298, edn. of 1931). In Arnold Bennett's story, *The City of Pleasure*, one of the characters challenges another to confirm "on his honour" a statement that he had made. "No," he replied proudly, "not on my honour. When I talk to a

1

oaths. Penn's description of the adaptability of both clergy and laity to each new change imposed on them in the days of the Tudors has already been quoted.[1] And in their own day they saw some who had subscribed to the Solemn League and Covenant of 1643, making formal declaration that the oath which they had taken counted for nothing.[2] A sermon preached in York Minster before the judges of assize in the year 1650 contains a lament on the frequent perjury of witnesses, the preacher expressing a wish that, instead of an oath being administered, a fine might be inflicted for falsehood, "so might the land be much freed from the burden of oaths under which it groans."[3] The suffering brought upon Friends by faithful adherence to their conviction of the unlawfulness of oath-taking will be spoken of later (p. 153), it is enough to say here that many of them endured years of imprisonment for this one cause alone.

On similarly broad grounds Barclay took his stand in dealing with the unlawfulness of war for a Quaker. As to the Jews certain ceremonies continued to be permitted "because that spirit was not yet raised up in them whereby they could be delivered from such rudiments," in like manner it might be said that to the European States of his

person as I am talking to you, if I say a thing is so, it is so. I decline to back my assertions with my honour."

[1] *Ante*, p. 20.

[2] A number of these declarations appear in the records of the proceedings of the municipal council of Bristol. Butler, in *Hudibras* (1663–64), satirizes the easy evasion or breaking of oaths, Pt. ii. cant. 2. In "An Heroical Epistle," standing at the end of the poem he again takes up the subject:

> Besides, oaths are not bound to bear
> The literal sense the words infer.
>
> .   .   .   .   .
>
> For no man takes or keeps a vow
> But just as he sees others do.

[3] The preacher was John Shaw of Hull (*Publications of the Surtees Society*, vol. lxv. (1875), p. 405). See also an article, "Kissing the Book," written by myself, in *The Friend* of 1909.

day war was permitted because they were still in that spirit which would not refrain from defending itself by means of carnal weapons. But for such as Christ has brought into His own Spirit "it is not lawful to defend themselves by arms, but they ought over all to trust to the Lord" (*Apology*, xv. 15).

It is to be noted, however, that the Quaker testimony concerning war does not set up as its standard of value the attainment of individual or national safety, neither is it based primarily on the iniquity of taking human life, profoundly important as that aspect of the question is. It is based ultimately on the conception of "that of God in every man" to which the Christian in the presence of evil is called on to make appeal, following out a line of thought and conduct which, involving suffering as it may do is, in the long run, *the most likely* to reach to the inward witness and so change the evil mind into the right mind. This result is not achieved by war. "Pacifism is not the expression of a sentimental and exaggerated regard for the human body, but the acknowledgment of a religious reverence for the human spirit."[1]

The positive ground thus stated of the early Quaker testimony is that on which, at the present day, stress is laid, although full weight is given to the obvious humanitarian considerations. To the middle period of Quakerism (no less resolute in its testimony than other periods) humanitarian considerations made the greater appeal, and at all times Friends have tested their position by the mind of Christ as shown forth in His teaching and life.[2]

The Quaker Church calls on its members, even if they cannot yet claim to have attained this spirit, to

---

[1] "Max Plowman," *The Faith Called Pacifism*, p. 48 (edn. of 1936).
[2] For Friends' testimony concerning war see also *ante*, pp. 42, 108 note (Penn's sword), and *post*, pp. 173 note, 214–5, c. xx.

be earnestly concerned so to set their lives in this direction as to refrain from war. Mention has been made of the answer of Fox to those who would take him for a soldier, and of the suffering which his faithfulness brought upon him (*ante*, p. 42). It was not for a few years that unanimity was reached, inasmuch as the matter was not widely and continually pressed on individuals so as to require decision in one way or another, as the command to take an oath was pressed on them. A number of Friends in the army had scruples about saluting their officers before they saw the necessity of leaving the service altogether,[1] but the implication of their fundamental position soon became manifest, and the Quaker discovered that he could not remain a soldier. In 1660, Fox, in reply to a question whether it was desirable that a certain Friend "who had partly engaged to be a captain" should carry out his intention, answered that such a proceeding "was contrary to our principles, for our weapons are spiritual and not carnal."[2] To a Justice of the Peace who charged Friends with disturbance and insurrection, alleging their participation in the Civil War, Oliver Sansom made reply that some who had fought "came afterwards to own the Truth and leave the wars." He further asserted that none of these "after they came to own and abide in the Truth did ever take up arms or use a carnal weapon."[3] Edward Burrough,

---

[1] Firth, *Cromwell's Army*, pp. 344–45.

[2] Braithwaite, *Beginnings of Quakerism*, p. 462, and see pp. 230, 414, 519.

[3] *Life*, p. 203. This was at Windsor in 1674. See also George Whitehead, *Truth Prevalent* (1701), p. 146. About a hundred and fifty Parliamentary soldiers joined Friends and a few Royalists. One of these latter, Christopher Bacon, came to be a leading Friend in Somerset. For attendance at a meeting at Glastonbury he was brought before the Bishop of Wells, who called him a rebel. Friends showed astonishing patience under the insults heaped on them, but a man who had fought for his king found the word "rebel" beyond endurance, and he answered: "Dost thou call me a rebel? I would

writing in 1660 an Address to the King, admits that some of those who had joined Friends, had previously fought in the Parliamentary army, but he says that they did not fight to compass the King's destruction or, as some had done, to get honours and riches for themselves, but to oppose oppression and seek after reformation. "We are now," he continues, "better informed than once we were for though we do more than ever oppose oppression and seek after reformation, yet we do it not in that way of outward wars and fightings."[1]

In those days of confusion it was but natural that the new spiritual movement should attract to it a number of men and women of unbalanced enthusiasm which betrayed them into actions injudicious or, in fact, evil. There were those who railed on magistrates and ministers and by indecorous conduct hurt the cause which they professed. It is, however, to be remembered that in these first years there was no formal or definite membership, and it was open to anyone, by attending Quaker meetings and thereby gaining the reputation of being a Quaker, to bring reproach upon the whole body. But the most serious harm was done by those who, in ill-proportioned measure, held the essential doctrine of the Divine Light or Seed dwelling in the hearts of all men. Failing to realize that the "Christ within" did not speak through men as through mechanical instruments unconscious of service, they overlooked the fact that in the expression of the divine message the conscious human instrument contributed something of his imperfect self. Unversed in psychology, they claimed infallibility for the message spoken through them, repudiating all claim to it as *their own* and asserting

have thee to know I have jeoparded my life for the King in the high places of the field when such as thou lay behind hedges." The bishop let him go (Whiting, *Persecution Exposed*, p. 14, edn. of 1715).

[1] *Works*, (edn. of 1672), p. 671.

that it came from the infallible Spirit of God. On un-balanced minds the effect of this belief was disastrous, and the tragedy of James Nayler made manifest the danger into which Quakerism might have drifted. One of the most persuasive preachers in the early campaign in London, he passed in the year 1656 to the West of England, and, physically and mentally overstrained, he became ensnared by flatterers who led him riding into Bristol as they strewed garments in the way, singing, "Holy, holy, holy, Lord God of Israel." For some time before this Fox and others had seen the cloud that was coming over him, but to their grave warnings he gave no heed. He was examined at the bar of the House of Commons, where he strenuously asserted, probably in all sincerity, that it was not to him that he had allowed worship to be paid, but "to the appearance of God in him, as to a sign of Christ's second coming and being revealed in His saints." By a narrow majority he escaped the penalty of death, but uncon-stitutionally and against the will of Cromwell an atrocious sentence was passed upon him. He suffered terrible flogging through the streets, he was set in the pillory for two hours, his forehead was branded with a B (blas-phemer), and his tongue was bored through with a hot iron. After this he was imprisoned. At this time he was forty years old.[1] The story of this went over England and,

[1] Concerning Nayler's action as illustrating early Quaker thought see Braithwaite, *Beginnings of Quakerism*, c. xi., "Nayler's Fall," and additional particulars given in *Second Period*, p. 250, note 2. A Life of Nayler has been written by Mabel R. Brailsford, it is entitled *A Quaker from Cromwell's Army* (1927); and *James Nayler the Rebel Saint* (1931) by Emilia Fogelklou, translated from the Swedish. Each authoress has brought to light much valuable information but each, having less understanding of Fox, has not made fair allowance for him concerning his part in the matter. See articles by Gerald K. Hibbert, supplement to the *Friend*, October 9, 1931, p. iv., and by Dr. Rufus M. Jones, *The Friend*, December 25, 1931, p. ii. 83. Also articles by Elisabeth Brockbank, *Journal Friends Historical Society*, xxvi. (1929), xxvii. (1929), p. 11, and by Professor Henry J. Cadbury, *ibid.* xxvii. (1930), p. 33, and xxviii. p. 67.

in fact, over western Europe and brought terrible scandal
on the infant Quaker Church.

But notwithstanding this sad episode of short duration,
Nayler was one of the finest minds among the early
Friends, and it is an unhappy thing that his "fall" is
the only part of his life that is generally known. After
his release, in the brief space of life that was left to him,
he showed a spirit of wonderful beauty in his utter forgiveness of those who had done evil to him and in his
remorse for the evil brought by him upon his brethren.
"Concerning you, the tender plants of my Father," he
wrote, "who have suffered through me or with me in what
the Lord hath suffered to be done with me in this time
of great trial and temptation . . . the Lord knows it was
never in my heart to cause you to mourn, whose sufferings
is my greatest sorrow that ever yet came upon me, for you
are innocent herein."[1] Large numbers again flocked to his
preaching in London, but before long he set out on foot
to his home near Wakefield. He was found dying in a field
near Huntingdon. Shortly before his end he uttered
the testimony which showed part of his Christian service
and which in large measure guided other Quaker pioneers,
enabling them to rise above suffering and, many times,
to reach the witness of God in their persecutors:

> There is a spirit which I feel that delights to do no evil
> nor to revenge any wrong, but delights to endure all things
> in hope to enjoy its own in the end. Its hope is to outlive
> all wrath and contention and to weary out all exaltation and
> cruelty or whatever is of a nature contrary to itself. It sees
> to the end of all temptations. As it bears no evil in itself, so
> it conceives none in thoughts to any other. If it be betrayed,
> it bears it, for its ground and spring is the mercies and

[1] *Works* (edn. of 1716), p. xxx. The passage is part of an address,
To All the Dearly Beloved People of God, Mercy and Peace: the whole
of it is beautiful reading.

forgiveness of God. Its crown is meekness, its life, is ever-lasting love unfeigned; and takes its kingdom with entreaty and not with contention, and keeps it by lowliness of mind. In God alone it can rejoice, though none else regard it, or can own its life (*Works*, p. 696).

The emphasis laid on this spirit, and on the every-day righteousness that was necessarily the outcome of it, saved Quakerism from going the way of the Ranters who, in ill-balanced measure, also made profession of knowing the indwelling Spirit of God. With them, however, this profession degenerated "into a vague pantheism which blurred the distinction between good and evil," and the doctrine (Antinomianism, as it is called) that the fact of an individual being "in grace" placed him "above the law" led to indulgence of carnal desires. John Owen, the Independent writer, speaks of "too many professors" pretending "to such a deliverance from the law that they would consult its guidance and direction no more" and says that this principle "having taken possession . . . hath turned the will and affections loose to all manner of abominations."[1] This line of thought was a serious danger to England, and to it a strong counteracting influence was exercised by the Quakers, who, starting from the same point as the Ranters, differed from them by their insis-tence on the fact that obedience to the Light could not result in immoral conduct. Baxter, the saintly opponent of the Quakers, says that they "were but the Ranters turned from horrid profaneness and blasphemy to a life of extreme austerity on the other side."[2] This testimony

[1] *Mortification of Sin in Believers*, c. xi. See also Penn, *Address to Protestants*, Pt. 2 §§ 3, 4 and Preface to Fox's *Journal*, bi-cent. edition i., p. xxv.

[2] *Reliquiae Baxterianae* (Sylvester), i. 77. Bunyan also insisted on the identity of the Ranters' and the Quakers' doctrines, "Only," he says, "the Ranters had made them threadbare at an ale-house and the Quakers have set a new gloss on them again by an outward legal

to their right living, however, was not intended as commendation, but as the basis of a charge of self-righteousness.[1] Their position is thus set forth by Nayler:

> If you will take heed to this Light to obey and love it, then it will show that to you what no outward declaration of man can show you. It will let you see all your sins done in secret, and whom you have wronged and how you have spent your time, and it will bring you to repentance and to tenderness of heart towards all people, and will bring you to exercise a pure conscience in the fear of God towards God and man in uprightness, and so will lead up to justification and peace.[2]

This walking in the Light led the Quaker shopkeepers, with that unanimity throughout the Society which we have already noticed, to break away from the general practice of asking higher prices than they intended to

holiness or righteousness," *A Vindication of Gospel Truths*. This righteousness, according to the religious thought of the time, being merely the works of the law and not the righteousness of Christ imputed to the sinner, contributed nothing to his salvation from hell, see *ante*, p. 48. John Edwards, in *A Discourse Concerning Truth and Error* (1701), bears the highest testimony to the Quakers' writings and way of life (their "chastity, gravity, humility and other moral accomplishments"), but he says "these are a mask for their errors, and falsehoods (I mean they are so intended by the evil spirit who actuates them)," pp. 128–131. For Ranters see *Encyc. Brit.* and Index to Beginnings of Quakerism (Braithwaite), and to *Studies in Mystical Religion* (R. M. Jones); also by R. M. Jones, *Spiritual Reformers in the Sixteenth and Seventeenth Centuries*, pp. 210, 320. For other references see my *Personality of George Fox*, p. 30 note 3, (edn. of 1918-19); p. 62 n. (edn. of 1933), and Fox's *Journal* (Cambridge edition), ii. 498 and Index.

[1] Penn complained that the uprightness of the Quakers' lives was continually misrepresented as hypocrisy or self-seeking: *Maxims*, Pt. ii. 89; *Address to Protestants*, Pt. ii. §4; *The Christian Quaker*, Preface; *Wisdom Justified*, c. 10; *Defence of . . . Gospel Truths*.

[2] *The Power and Glory of the Lord*, etc. This particular passage was singled out for reprobation by Thomas Weld and four other ministers of Newcastle in a pamphlet, *The Perfect Pharisee Under Monkish Holiness* (1654), pp. 10–11. Their contention was that men are justified by faith in the blood of Christ, whereas (they said) Quakers believed men to be justified by the righteousness which Christ within enabled them to perform.

take, asserting that such conduct did not accord with truth. Fox speaks in condemnation of those who, seeing their customers finally refusing their terms and walking away, "have your boys and lasses to fetch them back again." By reason of this faithfulness to their conviction, Friends suffered unpopularity and severe loss, but when the public came to see the advantage of the fixed price and the honesty of Friends throughout, they returned to them and gave them more custom than before. Fox says that people expected from Friends a higher standard than they did from others.[1] Nevertheless as late as the beginning of the eighteenth century the abuse had not died down. In the following passage the references to pride, to the few words, the sour looks,[2] and particularly the foxes, show that Quakers were being aimed at. The writer, after speaking of the dishonesty of tradesmen, continues:

> Some old standers, indeed, that pretend to more honesty (or what is more likely, have more pride) than their neighbours are used to make but few words with their customers, and refuse to sell at a lower price than what they asked at first. But these are commonly cunning foxes that are above the world and know that those who have money get often more by being surly than others by being obliging. The vulgar imagine they can find more sincerity in the sour looks of a grave old fellow than there appears in the submissive air and inviting complacency of a young beginner.[3]

But the Quaker way prevailed and the stand for truthfulness was a valuable contribution to the national life, inaugurating as it did a better method of trading under

---

[1] *Epistles*, pp. 102, 251, 424.

[2] These three points in particular were continually charged against Friends. Concerning Quaker shopkeepers see Fox, *Jnl.* (bi-cent.), i. 185–86, and *Gospel Truth Demonstrated* (*Doctrinals*), p. 826.

[3] Mandeville, *The Fable of the Bees, or Private Vices Public Benefits*, edn. of 1714, p. 56, Remark (D).

which the fixed price replaced the custom of bargaining for each purchase.[1]

In his concern for everyday righteousness Fox was particularly insistent on honesty in business, and of the business life he took a large view:

> Wrong no man [he writes], overreach no man (if it may be never so much to your advantage) but be plain, righteous and holy; in this are ye serviceable to your own nation and others by your change and exchanging of things and merchandise; and to the Lord God ye come to be a blessing in the creation and generation (*Epistles*, p. 157).

From the same epistle two other quotations may be taken, typical of Fox's repeated counsel:

> A man that would be great and goes beyond his estate, lifts himself up, runs into debt and lives highly of other men's means . . . he is not serviceable to the creation, but a destroyer of the creation and creatures, and cumbereth himself and troubleth others, and is lifted up, who would appear to be somebody (p. 159).

And further on we find:

> It is a bad thing to be lifted up and to make a noise and a show for a time with other people's goods (p. 161)[2]

---

[1] See Braithwaite, *Beginnings of Quakerism*, pp. 152, 211, 523; *Second Period*, pp. 556, 560–61, and c. xviii., "The Quaker Way of Life."

[2] The beginning of the long title of this epistle is "The Line of Righteousness and Justice stretched forth over all Merchants, etc., and an Exhortation unto all Friends and People whatsoever who are Merchants, Tradesmen, Husbandmen or Seamen." It was written in 1661, and reprinted in 1674 and again, in part, in 1710, this time officially by the Yearly Meeting, which advised that it be read once a year in Quarterly and Monthly Meetings. See also *Epistles*, pp. 104, 251, 527; *Journal*, bi-cent. edn., i. 186; *Gospel Truth Demonstrated*, pp. 128, 826; also Burrough, *Works*, p. 220, and my *Personality of George Fox*, pp. 40, 58, 61–62 (edn. of 1918); pp. 121–25 (edn. of 1933). Concerning the whole subject see two interesting and valuable works, *Quakerism and Industry before 1800*, by Isabel Grubb, and *Quaker Ways*, by A. Ruth Fry, c. xiii.

Chapter X

THE RESTORATION: PERSECUTION

IN 1660, on the return from exile of Charles II, the Presbyterian and Independent rule came to an end, and the restored Anglican Church demanded the suppression of Dissent. For this they could count on the aid of the Government which, not without justification, was apprehensive of plots formed against it. Thus a new period of persecution set in, Friends and other Nonconformists being now punishable by law for carrying on worship in their own way.[1] Among other measures that were passed were the Quaker Act of 1662 and the more comprehensive Conventicle Act of 1664 which applied to all Dissenters, making it illegal for more than four persons to meet for worship otherwise than in accordance with the practice of the Anglican Church. In 1670 this was renewed in more deadly form, giving to informers an interest in detecting and reporting Nonconformist meetings. They were to have one-third of the fine that was imposed and magistrates and judges were directed to construe the law strictly against the accused.[2]

Under these Acts enormous fines were levied and hundreds of Friends were imprisoned. Croese, a Dutch historian, describes the pillaging of Quaker shops and houses, his testimony being chosen from many others because he was by no means well disposed to Friends. The informers and others, he says,

[1] Concerning persecution before and after the Restoration see an essay, "The Penal Laws Affecting Early Friends in England," by Braithwaite, *First Publishers of Truth*, p. 343.
[2] Concerning the shameful doings of these men see Braithwaite, *Second Period of Quakerism*, Index, "Informers."

. . . took away what they could find, oxen and cattle from their lands and instruments for husbandry from their houses, merchandise, household stuff, feather beds, blankets, vessels and raiment, yea, their very meat they spared not of what value so ever. Some carried home wagons loaded with their goods, leaving nothing that was either portable or movable. These goods were often put up to public sale, but some were so honest that they loved not to buy what had been lost with grief and could only be purchased with shame. Some of their goods were taken secretly away by night (*History of the Quakers*, English ed., translated from the original Latin, 1696, Pt. ii. p. 69).

And an account of the breaking up of a meeting by process of law may be given, not the most atrocious that can be found, but chosen for its description of the Quaker bearing in the face of violence, marking Friends off, in the eyes of the world, as a strange people. Josiah Coale of Winterbourne, near Bristol, writing in 1664 from Newgate prison to George Fox, tells how a week previously the Sheriff and nearly fifty officers had rushed violently into the Bull and Mouth meeting in London and had begun hitting Friends with swords and staves. Coale spoke to them "of the unmanliness of their proceedings" towards "an innocent, peaceable people that would not resist them," and thus his narrative continues:

. . . they were ashamed and commanded the swords to be put up. So afterwards they fetched out the rest of the meeting more quietly; and two or three of the officers took me and led me alone to the Guildhall; and afterwards brought Friends, two, three, four and six at a time, to me till they had brought near two hundred. And I drew them together about the judgment seat, and had there a very precious meeting, for the power and presence of the Lord was plentifully manifested amongst us.[1]

[1] *Letters of Early Friends*, pp. 135–36. Coale says that the persecutors next turned their attention to the Baptists and Independents, and at the end of his letter describes another attack on the Bull and Mouth meeting worse than the one described above.

More than 250 years later, again in the Guildhall, this scene was repeated. In 1918, a time of national fury stirred up by the Great War, three Friends were convicted under the Defence of the Realm Act on a charge of issuing a leaflet, *A Challenge to Militarism,* without first submitting it to the censor. Each of them was imprisoned. When the magistrate retired to consider his decision the Friends in court united in silent worship in the course of which words of prayer were spoken. The *Manchester Guardian* described the scene as being "like a throw-back to the seventeenth century."[1]

Most Noncomformists tried the expedient of meeting secretly, but they were so often trapped or betrayed that in many places they ceased to meet at all. Friends (with rare exceptions) refused to take this course, and, though a number of them were frightened off, nevertheless, all over England, meetings were held by worshippers assembling in their accustomed way and braving the consequences.[2]

At Bristol and at Reading for a time, when the men and women were in prison, the meetings were attended by

---

[1] The trial took place on May 23 and 24, 1918; there is an account of it in the *Friend,* and in the *Friends' Fellowship Papers,* July 1918. Two men, one of whom was about to be chosen as the next Lord Mayor of Birmingham, underwent six months' imprisonment, and a woman, in default of payment of a heavy fine, three months.

[2] There was a weakness at Preston Patrick, some Friends meeting "in gills, holes and woods, and unaccustomed places." This led to a secession from the Society, headed by John Story and John Wilkinson, but the rest signed their names to a paper publicly condemning their action of going "from our ancient meeting houses to meet out of doors in a kind of a private, slavish manner, to the dishonour of that noble profession of truth that we had taken upon us, the evil example of [to] others and the great dishonour of our meetings." Taken from the Kendal records (3) in the Westmorland portfolio of the Braithwaite manuscripts in the Friends' Library. This was in 1678: a number of those who signed the paper suffered persecution afterwards. For Story and Wilkinson see *post,* p. 171 note.

children, some of whom were put in the stocks or beaten and otherwise ill-used.

William Sewel, a Dutch historian, records that other Nonconformists, afraid to meet openly, would in their nocturnal meetings pray God to keep the Quakers steadfast.[1] George Whitehead says that at first many of the Baptists suffered imprisonment, but the blow chiefly "fell upon us, the poor Quakers," and that he had heard of "other Dissenters who durst not meet publicly" thanking God "that He had enabled the Quakers to stand in the gap and bear the brunt and keep the blow off them."[2] Thomas Ellwood, speaking of South Buckinghamshire, has a similar story. Others, he says, particularly the Baptists, would call Friends "the bulwark that kept off the force of the stroke from them, praying that we might be preserved and enabled to break the strength of the enemy."[3]

Robert Barclay, addressing the King in 1676, throws down a challenge that could easily have been taken up, had it not been justified in fact:

> In the hottest times of persecution and the most violent prosecution of those laws made against meetings (being clothed with innocency) they [the Quakers] have boldly stood by their testimony for God without creeping into holes and corners, or once hiding themselves as all other Dissenters have done, but daily met according to their custom in the public places appointed for that end, so that none of thy officers can say of them that they have surprised them in a corner, overtaken them in a private conventicle, or catched them lurking in their secret chambers; nor needed they to send out spies to get them whom they were

---

[1] *History of the Quakers* (edn. of 1811), ii. 394, under 1683. Sewel was a Friend.   [2] *Christian Progress*, pp. 370–71.
[3] Ellwood, *Life*, under the year 1673 (Crump's edn., p. 187; Graveson's, p. 257). There were, however, others who vilified Quakers to prevent those who were thus well disposed to them joining them.

sure daily to find in their open assemblies testifying for
God and His truth (Preface to the *Apology*).

Conscious of standing on firm ground, James Jackson,
addressing his "loving friends, kindred and acquaintance" among the Independents of Nottinghamshire with
whom he had formerly professed, puts his question:

> When did they [the Quakers] shrink in the least or turn
> back from their duty when loss of estate, liberty, yea
> danger of banishment, attended it? . . . When did they
> meet at night for fear of being seen, or creep in at back
> doors into cellars, holes and secret places to hide
> themselves?[1]

This often-repeated testimony of Friends themselves
receives confirmation from other quarters, notably from
their opponents, Richard Baxter and Bishop Burnet.
The former says that "the fanatics called Quakers" so
monopolized the attention of the persecutors "that they
had the less leisure to look after the meetings of soberer

---

[1] *The Strong Man Armed*, "By James Jackson, formerly a parish
priest, and a teacher among the Independents"—p. 15 (1674). See
the appeal of Samuel Duncon of Norwich to his fellow townsmen
to resume public worship: "take heed," he says, "of fathering your
weakness on Christ, calling it Christian prudence," Eddington, *History
of Norwich Friends*, p. 80. For the conduct and sufferings by fine and
imprisonment of the Baptists in Bristol see *The Broadmead Records*,
edited for the Hanserd Knollys Society by Underhill, 1847. In one
of their meetings the preacher was hidden by a curtain so that he
could not be identified, and they "filled up the stairs with women and
maids that sat in it, that the informers could not quickly run up"
(p. 226, and see p. 223). In another place the preacher, hidden by a
screen, could get into the next house (p. 227). There was also a trap-
door by which he could escape (pp. 227, 280). Nevertheless, there is
a brave confession of shortcoming under the date 1686, July 25. It
is stated that the Church was able to come together again after
three years and five months' interruption, "partly occasioned by our
violent persecutors and partly by our own fears and backwardness."
Elsewhere the device was tried of having four people in one house and
four in another hearing the preacher through the open windows or
through the wall, but this was decided to be illegal (*Reliquiae Baxterianae* (Sylvester), Bk. i. 436).

men, which was much to their present ease." The Quakers, he says,

> . . . assembled openly . . . and were dragged away daily to the common gaol; and yet desisted not, but the rest came the next day nevertheless, so that the gaol at Newgate was filled with them. Abundance of them died in prison and yet they continued their assemblies still. And the poor deluded souls would sometimes meet only to sit still in silence. . . . Many turned Quakers because the Quakers kept their meetings openly and went to prison for it cheerfully.[1]

Fox relates that "about 1671" the King asked the Governor of Dover Castle whether he had dispersed all the sectaries' meetings. The Governor replied that he had, but he went on to say:

> . . . the Quakers the devil himself could not. For if that he did imprison them or break them up, they would meet again; and if he should beat them, and knock them down or kill some of them, all was one; they would meet, and not resist, again (*Epistles*, p. 5).

Even before the Conventicle Acts we read the same story. A minister (not a Friend) who had been one of Cromwell's chaplains wrote to another minister in America an account of the persecution suffered by Nonconformists under the Act of Uniformity of 1662. He states that the Baptists continued in the holding of their meetings longer

---

[1] *Reliquiae Baxterianae* (Sylvester, pp. 436–37 and for the firmness of Friends see Braithwaite, *Second Period of Quakerism*, pp. 41–42, 50–51, 55 (Burnet's testimony), 102, 108–109, 111, 225. See also *More Sad and Lamentable News from Bristol*, anonymous, but clearly non-Quaker; and a curious story in Fox's *Journal*, bi-cent. edn., ii. 85–86. *The Broadmead Records*, under the year 1682 (N.S.), states that in Bristol the Quakers were meeting in the street, their meeting house being nailed up (thus confirming Quaker statements), and that they were the only Dissenters not meeting privately. This was in January.

than most, and, he adds, "the Quakers held their ground to the last and have smarted more than any."[1]

In this way there grew more pronounced between Friends and all others the separation which from the first had existed and which, as we shall see, lasted long after the days of persecution.[2] Penn advised Friends to keep apart from others to avoid the infection of their terror; "Yet," he continues, "we must make their case as our own and travail alike in spirit for them as for ourselves."[3]

In 1672 Charles II exercised his pretended dispensing power in matters ecclesiastical by issuing a Declaration of Indulgence suspending the execution of the penal laws against Roman Catholics and other dissenters from the established Church. So strong was the opposition of Parliament to this proceeding that he was compelled to cancel it within a year, but in the meantime many dissenters got relief from suffering and gained ground which they could not wholly lose. The instrument affecting Friends contained 491 names including, by permission, those of a few non-Friends among whom was John Bunyan. Before this time he had strongly attacked Friends but he did not again do so. The story of the carrying of the enormous document—eleven skins of vellum with the Great Seal attached—from prison to prison where Friends were confined and of the overcoming of many difficulties in the way of their release is told by George Whitehead.[4]

---

[1] *Extracts from State Papers* (Friends Historical Society), p. 169. For another piece of testimony to the same effect see Congregational Historical Society, "Transactions," September 1937 (vol. xiii. p. 34.)

[2] In *The Broadmead Records (ante,* pp. 71, 144) is an account of the funeral of a Baptist minister who died in prison in 1675. It was attended by "professors" of all sorts except Quakers, p. 225. For this separateness see *post,* c. xii., pp. 220–221, 300 note.

[3] *To the Children of Light in this Generation* (1678).

[4] *Christian Progress,* pp. 347 ff. See Braithwaite, *Second Period,* pp. 81 ff.

The document itself is preserved in the Friends' Library in London.

We shall the more deeply value the courage of those whose steadfastness had smoothed our way, as we set ourselves to picture the young man or maiden in whom the current of life ran strong, or the father and mother with home and children dependent on them, or the man and woman of advancing years with small store of strength, coming to the parting of the ways and facing the alternatives. This we may the more easily do as we read the pathetic story of those who found the hard way too hard. From the Nottingham Quarterly Meeting records of 1671 are taken the following reasons for non-attendance of meeting[1]—a man says that "his wife is discontented, and he hath a great family, so that he cannot give up to suffer." A man and his wife "said it was the truth, but fear of persecution was the cause why they came not." Further on it is reported that a certain man would like to continue coming to meeting, "but the times are so at present that if he should come, his wife and he is like to part." It is with nothing but tenderness that we think of them, along with all our gratitude to those who stood firm.

In all parts of the country Friends were kept out of their meeting houses, and they held their meetings in

[1] This word "meeting" has always been used by Friends, who have never adopted "church" or "chapel." Their places of assembly they still call "meetinghouses," the term apparently used first by Protestants separatists from the Anglican Church. The places of worship set up by the nonconforming clergy ejected from the Church in 1662 were called chapels, but it was not till the nineteenth century that "chapel" finally replaced "meetinghouse" for everyone except Friends. (A few nonconformist places of worship still retain the old term "meetinghouse.") Now "church" has mostly superseded "chapel" (*Oxford English Dictionary*, under "Chapel").

the street, being persuaded that God required this service of them. Naturally, a crowd gathered round and the ministers, standing on a bench or chair, took the opportunity of preaching to the people. Sometimes three or four of them, standing some distance apart, were thus engaged simultaneously; and when the men had been marched off to prison their places were taken by women and by youths not much more than boys.[1] Through all seasons and in all weathers Friends held their course, even, says George Whitehead,

> . . . in the great severe and long frost and snow in the year 1683, for about three months together, when the River Thames was so frozen up that horses, coaches and carts could pass to and fro upon it, and a street also be erected and stand over it.[2]

It was at one of these meetings held in Gracechurch Street, London, in 1670, that William Penn and William Meade were arrested. They were indicted for a riot, but, to the indignation of the Recorder who tried them, the jury returned a verdict "Guilty of speaking in Gracechurch Street." This was no crime, and on the jury being bullied by both Recorder and Lord Mayor they returned a further verdict, "Not Guilty." For this they were fined, being imprisoned till the money should be paid, but when the matter was brought to trial it was, once and for all, settled as a principle of English law that no jury could be punished

---

[1] Sewel, *History of the Quakers* (edn. of 1811), ii. 4–5, under 1662.

[2] *Christian Progress*, pp. 543–44. According to the Old Style reckoning up to 1752, the new year came in March 25th, so where Whitehead says 1683 we should say 1683–84. The severity of this winter, 1683–84, and of the following one caused the death of many Friends in prison, and much other suffering. See *post*, p. 159. There is an account of atrocious cruelty at this time given by Besse, *Sufferings*, i. 460, but it is curious how little in Quaker writings mention is made of the intense cold. It lay over Western Europe down into Spain; the Thames was frozen over nearly as far as Southend. See Evelyn's *Diary*.

for its verdict. The case is known as "Bushell's case," one of the landmarks of our constitutional freedom.

In pursuance of the policy of repression, at least two of the London meeting houses, Horsleydown (Southwark) and Ratcliffe, were wholly or in part destroyed, the demolition of the former being, by order of the King in Council, committed to "Christopher Wren, Esq., Surveyor General of His Majesty's works." Friends cleared away the rubbish "that they might meet on the ground where their own house stood," but several times they were removed by soldiers, a large number of men and women being shamefully used.[1] It was on incidents like these and on a passage of Barclay's *Apology* pointing out the advantage of the Friends' way of worship in times of persecution, that Professor Masson of Edinburgh founded his description of the success of the Quaker method. It has been pointed out that in his picture he has massed the high lights which were not all found together in any one instance.[2]

> No denomination so amazed and perplexed the authorities by their obstinacy as the Quakers. It was their boast that their worship, from its very nature could not be stopped "by men or devils." . . . In a meeting of Lutherans or Episcopalians, or in a meeting of Presbyterians or Independents or Baptists or Socinians there is always some implement or set of implements on which all depends, be it the liturgy, the gown or surplice, the Bible or the hourglass; remove these and make noise enough, and there can be no service. Not so with a Quaker meeting. There, men and women worship with their hearts, without implements, in silence as well as by speech. You may break in upon them,

---

[1] *Christian Progress of George Whitehead*, pp. 341 f. For the attacks on Friends and their meeting house at Ratcliffe, see *Memoirs of Benjamin Bangs*, pp. 8–10, edn. of 1798, often bound up with *A Journal of John Banks*; also Besse's *Sufferings*, i. 416, 428–29.

[2] Braithwaite, *Second Period*, p. 21.

hoot at them, roar at them, drag them about; the meeting, if it is of any size, essentially still goes on till all the component individuals are murdered. Throw them out at the doors in twos and threes, and they but re-enter at the window and quietly resume their places. Pull their meeting house down, and they reassemble next day most punctually amid the broken walls and rafters. Shovel sand or earth down upon them, and there they sit, a sight to see, musing immovably among the rubbish. This is no description from fancy; it was the actual practice of the Quakers all over the country. They held their meetings, regularly, perseveringly, and without the least concealment, keeping the doors of their meeting houses purposely open that all might enter, informers, constables, or soldiers, and do whatever they chose. In fact, the Quakers behaved magnificently. By their peculiar method of open violation of the law and passive resistance only, they rendered a service to the common cause of all the Nonconformist sects which has never been sufficiently acknowledged.[1]

It is of importance to note that the more instructed Friends, at any rate, had a wide outlook. Besides obedience to their own sense of duty and loyalty to their religious Society, they were conscious of standing in an evil time for the liberties of Englishmen. A prisoner with Fox at Launceston, Edward Pyott, once a captain in the Parliamentary army, addressed the Chief Justice of England who had presided at their trial, pointing out, both on legal and on moral grounds, the harm which was likely to result

[1] Masson, *Life of Milton in Connexion with his Times*, vi. 587–88. The passage is based on Barclay, *Apology*, Prop. xiv. § vi., quoted by Braithwaite, *Second Period*, p. 88. The *Church Times*, the organ of the Anglo-Catholic party of the Anglican Church, bears generous testimony to the same effect. In the course of a book review referring to the treatment of Dissenters in the seventeenth century occurs the following passage, "The unfortunate Quakers deserve much sympathy, for their gentle persistence in face of all trials had a great deal to do with bringing into being religious liberty as we know it to-day." March 29, 1931, p. 366. The book under review was *Studies in English Puritanism*, by Whiting (S.P.C.K.).

from action such as he had taken.[1] The writings of Penn
continually show his concern for his country, which he saw
was being hurt by the persecution. And looking out on the
wickedness of the land in the Restoration period, thus
he pleads:

> O England, my native country! come to judgment!
> Bring thy deeds to the true Light; see whether they are
> wrought in God or no![2]

Elsewhere he calls upon Friends "in troubles not to be
dejected and in jeopardies not to be concerned to make
to ourselves defences," but to be a holy company whom
God could use "as saviours to the people."

> Next, Friends, this know, we are the people above all
> others that must stand in the gap and pray for the putting
> away of the wrath so that this land be not made an utter
> desolation, and God expects it at our hands. . . . Let none
> gaze or look out, I beseech you; that is the enemy's work to
> weaken you within; but be ye retired, be ye centred in the
> Eternal One, and meditate upon the Lord and His living
> law, that ye may be wise in heart and travail in spirit for this
> poor land, and that for enemies as well as friends (*To the
> Children of Light in this Generation*, 1678).

In the day of persecution it was with determination,
and sometimes even with joy, that Friends went through
the storm.

> Oh! those that flee before informers [wrote Penn] and
> run at the sight of persecutors, (yea, though an army of
> them), either never had or have parted from this noble

---

[1] Fox's *Journal*, bi-cent. edn., i. 287; and see p. 318, Pyott's
letter to Major-General Desborough; and John Crook, *The Cry of
the Innocent* (1662).

[2] *Address to Protestants*, 1679. Braithwaite speaks of this as "one
of Penn's best writings" (*Second Period*, p. 96). In 1662 Caton, in
a protest against persecution, wrote: "Hear, O England! and consider
the things which the Lord hath done in thee, thou choicest of the
nations!" (*Testimony of a Cloud of Witnesses*, p. 48).

faith which is pure confidence in God and entire resignation to His divine will, come what will come! Christ will not have one coward in His spiritual army (*Saul Smitten to the Ground*, 1675).

Those who were in prison steadily refused to accept release on any compromising conditions.[1] "Do nothing to make it easy for your persecutors," was the counsel of Penn. William Dewsbury (who at one time had been "a trumpeter in Oliver's army")[2] "perhaps the sweetest and wisest of the early Friends," recalling long years of imprisonment at Warwick, bore his testimony as he came near his end:

> For this I can say I never since played the coward, but joyfully entered prisons as palaces, telling mine enemies to hold me there as long as they could; and in the prison house I sung praises to my God and esteemed the bolts and locks put upon me as jewels; and in the name of the eternal God I alway got the victory, for they could keep me no longer than the determined time of my God (*Works*, unnumbered page near beginning).

In like manner Isaac Penington makes record of his prison days:

> I have had experience myself of the Lord's goodness and preservation of me in my suffering . . . for the testimony of His truth, who made my bonds pleasant to me, and my noisome prison (enough to have destroyed my weakly and tender-educated nature)[3] place of pleasure and delight, where I was comforted by my God night and day and filled with prayers for His people, as also with love to, and

---

[1] See my *Personality of George Fox* (edn. of 1918–19) p. 28, and footnote 4 on the same; edn. of 1933, pp. 58–59.

[2] *A True and Faithful Relation of Five Hundred False Prophecies*, etc., by Pickworth (1776), p. 81.

[3] The reader is recommended to turn back to pp. 77–78 note which tell of Penington's position in life.

prayers for, those who had been the means of outwardly afflicting me and others upon the Lord's account.[1]

One who was several times in prison with him out of his own experience confirms Penington's words. After speaking of his "great patience, cheerfulness, contentedness and true nobility of spirit," the writer continues:

> I do not remember that ever I saw him cast down or dejected in his spirit in the time of his close confinement, nor speak hardly of those that persecuted him. . . . Indeed, I may say in the prison he was a help to the weak, being made instrumental in the hand of the Lord for that end. . . . O, the remembrance of the glory that did often overshadow us in the place of confinement, so that, indeed, the prison was made by the Lord unto us (who was powerfully with us) as a pleasant palace! I was often, with many more, by those streamings of life that did many times run through his vessel, greatly overcome with the pure presence and overcoming Love of God.[2]

Apart from the operation of the Conventicle Acts which applied to all Nonconformists, Friends were exposed to suffering by their refusal to take the oath for reasons which have been already explained (p.128). The Government, nervous as to its security of tenure, encouraged magistrates and judges to tender widely the Oath of Allegiance; and when the Quaker could not be convicted of any offence he was commanded to *swear* to his loyalty, in order that his refusal might furnish a pretext for imprisoning him. He would give his word to be true to the King and to the government, he would insist that Friends never had been concerned in plots and that it was against their principles to be so, but this was of no avail. By reason of his steadfastness Francis Howgill lay for five years in Appleby gaol,

---

[1] *Works*, i. 578 (edn. of 1761). *Three Queries Propounded to the King and Parliament.*
[2] "Testimony" of Robert Jones at the beginning of Penington's *Collected Works.*

being released by death near his fiftieth birthday; Margaret Fell suffered four years imprisonment, and later on, after her marriage with Fox, a fifth at Lancaster; and Fox himself was almost brought to his end by an imprisonment of nearly three years at Lancaster and Scarborough. At Reading a certain Friend, "a poor smith," refused in court to prove *on oath* that three cows which had been stolen from him were his, whereupon the judge said that if one of his neighbours would swear to the fact, they should be restored to him. Accordingly, one of his neighbours, who had no scruple in the matter, did so, and the judge then insisted that before the Friend got his property back he should take the Oath of Allegiance. For his refusal to do so he was sent to prison.[1] It was this immovable loyalty to principle, repeated hundreds of times, that, as early as 1661, gave Penington good reason for feeling sure of his ground when, in view of the slight regard paid to oaths which we have already noted (p. 130), he took the risk of throwing out the challenge:

> Who of those who have observed and known our conversation and upright speaking and behaviour for these many years . . . would not prefer our *Yea* and *Nay* before the oaths of others?[2]

But the right to make this challenge was won at terrible cost. It seems that, on this account and for one reason or another, at least 21,000 Friends suffered fines or imprisonment, many of them more than once, and at least 450 died either during imprisonment or soon afterwards as the result of it (Braithwaite, *Second Period*, pp. 114–15). This, of course, takes no account of acts of cruelty times without number committed by the lawless mob.

[1] Besse, *Sufferings*, i. 13.
[2] *Works* (edn. of 1761), i. 438: *The Great Question Concerning . . . Swearing*.

In order to enter into sympathy with the men and women of those days we do well to picture the separation of families incidental to all missionary enterprise, and the anxiety concerning loved ones of whose imprisonment or death tidings at any moment might come. First we recall the humorous complaint of Miles Halhead's wife before she herself became a Friend, concerning her husband's frequent service in the ministry: "Would God I had married a drunkard, then I might have found him at the alehouse, but now I can't tell where to find my husband."[1] Graver are the words of William Dewsbury to a wife dreading the imprisonment of her husband:

> Woman, thy sorrow is great: I sorrow with thee. Now the time is come that those who marry must be as though they married not, and those who have husbands as though they had none, for the Lord calls for all to be offered up.[2]

Of their twenty-one years of married life Fox and his wife passed little more than five in one another's company. United though they were in deepest love, their work lay apart; and twice only after his marriage did Fox visit Swarthmore Hall, spending there in the aggregate three years and a quarter. When he was not in prison or in America, he stayed for the most part near the headquarters of Friends in London, while his wife had the care of her family and estate more than two hundred miles away in North Lancashire.

> Though the Lord had provided an outward habitation for him [she wrote after his death] . . . we were very willing both of us to live apart for some years on God's account and His truth's service, and to deny ourselves of that comfort which we might have had in being together for the sake and service of the Lord and His truth.[3]

[1] Sewel, *History of the Quakers* (edn. of 1722), p. 71, under 1653.
[2] *Some Memoirs of the Life of John Roberts*, p. 10 (edn. of 1746).
[3] Fox's *Journal*, bi-cent. edn., ii. 519.

Nor was Margaret Fox the only wife who joyfully up-held her husband in his distant travel. From her Westmorland home Ann Audland, in 1654, wrote triumphantly to her husband, John Audland, twenty-four years old, as he laboured in the first Quaker mission to the South of England:

> . . . I received thy letters and all my soul desireth is to hear from thee in the life. Dear heart, in life dwell, there I am with thee out of all time, out of all words, in the pure power of the Lord; there is my joy and strength. Oh, how I am refreshed to hear from thee, to hear of thy faithfulness and boldness in the work of the Lord. . . . O, dear heart, go on conquering and to conquer, knowing this that thy crown is sure. So, dear heart, now is the time of the Lord's work and few are willing to go forth into it . . . but blessed be the Lord for ever who hath called us from doing our own work into His great work. . . . Oh, it is past my utterance to express the joy I have for thee, I am full, I am full of love towards thee, never such love as this; the mighty power of the Lord go along with thee . . . a joyful word it was to me that thou wast moved to go for Bristol. O, my own heart, my own life, in that which now stands act and obey, that thou mayst stand upon thy alone guard, so, dear heart, let thy prayers be for me that I may be kept pure, out of all temptations, singly to dwell in the life. So farewell (*Memory of the Righteous Revived*, pp. 22–24).

Ten years later Audland died, his body worn out in the service.

Many are the prison stories that have come down to us, no inconsiderable number of them containing loathsome details and accounts of special cruelty. In order, however, to have a picture which, being free from these, may be taken as typical rather than extreme, we may read George Whitehead's narrative of his imprisonment in Norwich Castle from January to May 1661, when he was about twenty-four years old. He was one of more than 4,200 Friends whom the Government, in its nervousness (the King having returned only a short time previously), put into prison on the outbreak of the trivial Fifth Monarchy Riot in January of the said year. "The sudden storm swept many counties bare of men Friends."[1] With Whitehead were three of his friends, two of whom he describes as "having been men of note and captains in the Commonwealth's day," and all of them as being "well accommodated at their own houses in all respects." Of an imprisonment in the same place, six years earlier, he had said of himself that it pressed the more hardly on him, in that he had been "tenderly brought up" by his parents. Of this later time he says:

> We were so crowded in the Castle that we had not convenient room for lodging, about thirty or above being then crowded in that old nasty gaol.

Having taken up their quarters "in a poor narrow hole,"

> . . . we got up [he continues] two little beds and lodged two in each, John Lawrence and his brother Joseph in one bed and William Barber and I in the other. . . . The rain came so much in upon us that we could not well keep it off our beds, though we set dishes or basins to keep off what we could. In the cold of winter we burned a little charcoal in evenings, which we found somewhat injurious and suffocating, having no chimney . . . and in the day time we endeavoured often to keep ourselves warm by walking upon the Castle Hill . . . though 'twas but a bleak cold place in winter, yet we were glad that we had that benefit of the air.

Whitehead goes on to say that in March he almost died

[1] Braithwaite, *Second Period*, p. 9; and see *Beginnings*, p. 512. Thirty-five (some say fifty) persons, led by Thomas Venner, threw London into a four days' panic.

of ague and fever, and in his illness was nearly suffocated one night by the charcoal fumes.[1]

John Whiting, of Nailsea and Wrington in Somerset, after a horrifying description of the persecution in Bristol, tells of his visit to the gaol in that city shortly before three women and two men died there, "being suffocated for want of air and room." To his comment on the crowded state of the place a woman answered in words that came natural to a seaport dweller, "Aye, we are full freight, ready to set sail the first fair wind." "This," says Whiting, "she and some others did into the ocean of Eternity not long after."[2]

In the years immediately following 1680 the last and, perhaps, the heaviest storm swept down. Baxter, writing in 1683, says that the gaols were filled with Nonconformists, nine ministers being in Newgate and many more elsewhere, while those not in prison were "fain to fly or abscond."[3] In the same year mention was made of Fox's attendance at a Meeting for Sufferings "where there was many grievous sufferings read that came out of many parts of the nation"[4]; and two years later he wrote to Friends in Pennsylvania, "We are under great sufferings and spoiling of goods and imprisonments and they have of late increased in spoiling of our goods."[5] Throughout

---

[1] *Christian Progress of George Whitehead* (1636–1732), pp. 245–46 and 35. Whitehead tells how one morning as they lay in bed "Joseph Lawrence (after his pleasant manner) said to his brother John 'O Captain Lawrence, I have seen the day that thou wouldst not have lain here.' "

[2] *Persecution Exposed*, 1715 edn., p. 79.

[3] Taken from *Documents Relating to the Settlement of the Church of England*, ed. Bayne, p. 135.

[4] *The Short Journal and Itinerary Journals of George Fox*, p. 83. See *Epistles*, p. 490; the assertion that between 1,300 and 1,400 were in prison, besides fines and spoiling of goods.

[5] *Epistles*, p. 540; and see p. 542. Meeting for Sufferings, see *post*, pp. 163, 174.

this time Friends showed themselves no less resolute than they had been from the first, and the terrible winters round about the beginning and end of 1684 added largely to their suffering.[1] Elizabeth Stirredge tells of an attack made, at the instance of the priest of the parish, on a meeting that was being held at Chew Magna in 1683, and of the imprisonment of herself and other Friends at Ilchester in Somerset. They were put in the common gaol with three condemned felons and not allowed any straw to lie on "though we would have paid for it."

> Truly [she continues] that was a most dismal place where we had neither stock nor stone to sit upon, nor any resting place to lean against but the black stone wall covered over with soot, and the damp cold ground to lie upon. But before we lay down, three of our Friends that were prisoners in the room adjoining to that we were in put through the grates in unto us four dust, or chaff, pillows and a little straw whereon we lay down like a flock of sheep in a pen, in that very cold winter that we had never had the like since I had a remembrance, where most of us took our rest very sweetly. But when I lay down in that dismal place it came into my heart a consideration of these things, saying in my heart, "Lord, thou knowest for what we are exposed to this hardship, it is because we cannot betray our testimony nor wrong our conscience" . . . Then the Lord was pleased . . . to fill [my heart] with His living mercy and comfortable presence . . . that I could have sung aloud of the goodness of the Lord . . . But I, looking over my fellow prisoners and seeing them so sound asleep, I did forbear to open my mouth.[2]

The imprisonment, which lasted on into the time of intense cold, began on the eighth of September.

[1] *Ante*, p. 148.
[2] *Life of Elizabeth Stirredge*, pp. 97, 98, edn. of 1795. The depth of horror of certain imprisonments is seen in accounts of Friends being kept for days together in a single room from which they were not allowed to go out *for any purpose whatever*.

In 1684 Friends in the south of Ireland sent a sum of over £260 for the relief of sufferers in England.[1]

To the Royalist and Anglican mind this treatment of Dissenters was justified on two main grounds. It had come to be held that the very act of separation from the "Church" constituted the sin of schism: in 1610 Joseph Hall (afterwards Bishop of Exeter and of Norwich) wrote, "The Church of England justly matches separatists with the vilest persons . . . wise generals punish mutinous persons more than robbers or adulterers." He adduces examples of certain kings of Judah compelling the people to serve God (2 Chron. xv. 13; xxxiii, 16; xxxiv. 32–33) and he asks, "Whether Queen Elizabeth or King James have done more or what other?"[2] Moreover, it was said that Dissenters' conventicles were places of hatching plots and that, even apart from this, their separation from the national worship was a breach of national unity. An eminent Church dignitary of the time asserts that men "often miscall that by the odious name of persecution which is nothing but the execution of just and, sometimes, of necesary and wholesome laws."[3] Penn had ample justification for his saying, "Truth has never been persecuted under its own name."[4] The preamble to each of the two Conventicle Acts attempts to justify such legislation as

[1] *Minute of Limerick Six Weeks Meeting*, 16. vi., 1684. In connection with this matter Isabel Grubb has drawn my attention to the continual interchange of relief between England, Ireland and America as need arose. In 1666 Friends of Moate (Ireland) sent £100 for Quaker sufferers from the fire of London. In 1691 Friends of Tortola (West Indies) sent relief for sufferers from the war in Ireland.

[2] *A Common Apology Against Brownists.*

[3] Dr. George Hickes, *The True Nature of Persecution Stated*, 1682. Hickes, a few years later, himself suffered for his principles as a non-juror, and he may have changed his opinion.

[4] *Wisdom Justified*, c. i. "Persecution is so hateful (and hath such a blackness of spirit in it) that it cannot endure to appear in its own colour". Penington, "Concerning Persecution," *Works*, i. 468, edn. of 1761.

being necessary in consequence of the "dangerous practices of seditious sectaries and other disloyal persons, who, under pretence of tender consciences, do at their meetings contrive insurrections as late experience hath shown."[1] This fear is seen in the Toleration Act of 1689, which gave relief to Dissenters' meetings provided they were not held in rooms of which the doors were fastened. Although, as we have seen (pp. 142, 150), Friends by their refusal to hold secret meetings, differed from other Dissenters; they were, nevertheless, exposed to suspicion by reason of their frequent coming together from different places to their Monthly, Quarterly, and Yearly Meetings;[2] and also by reason of the activity of their travelling ministers, the fact of a number from different parts of the country meeting together being taken as clear evidence of a plot.[3] The extensive correspondence, continually maintained, added to the suspicion. There is, however, no reason to believe that any Friend was concerned in any plot.

The conception of national unity as broken by Dissenters' meetings is seen in the following passages, revealing, as they do, a line of thought which at one time held sway:

> All Christian princes have seen a necessity to preserve, as much as they could, the unity of religion as one of the foundations of their subjects' peace; and, when divisions

[1] Edward Pyott, writing in 1667, pointed out that there was far more danger of treason to be feared from private meetings of four persons as allowed by the Conventicle Act than from the public assemblies of Friends held with the doors open (*The Quakers Vindicated*, p. 9). Richard Hubberthorne had used a similar argument when speaking at the bar of the House of Commons against the Quaker Act of 1662 (Braithwaite, *Second Period*, p. 23).

[2] See *post*, p. 167, concerning these meetings.

[3] See *Life of Thomas Ellwood*, account of an arrest at Isaac Penington's house in 1661, Crump's ed., pp. 77–80; Graveson's, pp. 106–10. Also, *A True Testimony of Faithful Witnesses Recorded* (1657); by Robert Wastfeild, p. 27, and pp. 29 ff.

L

have happened within their territories, by consulting such persons as might be presumed the fittest judges in the case, they have searched for the truth (which being once found) they have maintained it by a restraint on all contradiction to it.[1]

Dr. John Gauden, Bishop of Exeter and afterwards of Worcester, writing shortly after the Restoration, states his opinion,

> . . . that some little pecuniary mulct [fine], as one or two shillings to the poor, for every Lord's day's absence from the public church or assembly may be justly laid (as a mark of public dislike) upon Dissenters and Separaters from the established religion, not for private difference in judgment (which possibly is not their fault) but for their public deformity in practice to the scandal of the established religion and to the endangering of the public welfare whose strength and solidity consist in unity, and this in uniformity to the settled rule and in conformity to outward practice.

Later on he gives expression to his fear of danger to the State:

> For Dissenters to have multitudinous conventicles, as it were musterings of the forces, when, where and as many as they please, cannot be safe, for thereby they not only affront the established religion but confirm each other in their opinions.[2]

It was on the ground of reasonableness that the Lord Mayor of London made a personal appeal to Fox on the first Sunday after the Conventicle Act of 1670 came into force. Fox, having gone to Gracechurch Street meeting, where he "expected the storm was most likely to begin," was brought before the Lord Mayor, who, however,

---

[1] *Indulgence not Justified* (p. 2), 1668, by Perrinchief. It was written in reply to *A Peace Offering . . . A Plea for Indulgence and Liberty of Conscience,* by John Owen, 1667.
[2] *A Discourse Concerning Public Oaths* (1662).

was "very civil" and let him go, after pressing on him the argument that, inasmuch as Christ had promised to be with the two or three gathered in His name, Friends might be satisfied to meet in companies of four as allowed by the Act and thus retain their position as law-abiding citizens. Fox replied that the Act would have prevented Christ meeting with the twelve apostles.[1]

Another line of attack on Dissenters was the penalizing of schoolmasters who taught without licence from the bishop. The prohibition was contained in a series of Acts, directed in the first instance against Roman Catholics, beginning in the reign of Elizabeth and prosecutions against Friends were continued even after the Toleration Act of 1689.[2] At least a score of Friends were fined, imprisoned or excommunicated, the first of them, so far as at present known, being Thurston Read who in 1664 "was imprisoned in the Moothall by William Moore, Mayor of Colchester, for teaching school without licence, and continued there till he died."[3]

In order to cope with the distress caused by the persecution, a committee, known as the Meeting for Sufferings, was set up in 1675. It still meets monthly, its name remaining unchanged, and it is the executive body of the Society of Friends in Great Britain. A fuller account of its activities is given on page 174.

At last relief came. In dread of the Romanizing policy of James II, the Anglicans, Independents and Presbyterians drew nearer together, and when, in 1688, the King

---

[1] *Journal*, ii. 123 ff. (bi-cent. edn.). This particular argument Fox had previously used, *Gospel Truth Demonstrated*, pp. 259, 306.

[2] Braithwaite, *Second Period*, p. 532, and also pp. 216 n, 526 n.

[3] Besse, *Sufferings*, i. 202. I am indebted to Miss Dorothy G. B. Hubbard for pointing this out. The result of her research into the whole subject is likely to be published shortly (1938). Further mention of this persecution for school-keeping is made on p. 213.

was deposed in favour of William and Mary, the Anglican Church could no longer withhold the ease which the Nonconformists sought. Accordingly, in 1689, the Toleration Act was passed, a grudging measure which did not remove the persecuting laws from the statute book but enacted that there should be no penalty for breaking them. It did not relieve Roman Catholics and Unitarians, but in practice they were no longer disturbed in their worship.[1]

The spirit which bore up Friends for more than a generation of storm is nowhere more manifest than in the challenge sent by Isaac Penington to the King and Parliament in 1665. It was the year after the passing of the Conventicle Act, and he wrote:

> I could say in the joy of my heart and in the sense of the good will of my God to us who suffereth these things to come to pass, *Go on; try it out with the Spirit of the Lord; come forth with your laws and prisons and spoiling of our goods and banishment and death (if the Lord please), and see if ye can carry it.* For we come not forth against you in our own wills, or in any enmity against your persons or government, or in any stubbornness or refractoriness of spirit, but with the Lamb-like nature which the Lord our God hath begotten in us which is taught and enabled by Him both to do His will and to suffer for His name's sake. And if we cannot thus overcome you (even in patience of spirit and

---

[1] Seaton, *The Theory of Toleration Under the Later Stuarts*, pp. 278, 288. In 1789 a strained construction of the Toleration Act removed Methodists from the benefit of it and some of them were fined under the Conventicle Act against which they were now rendered defenceless. In 1811, Lord Sidmouth unsuccessfully tried to pass a Bill excluding from the benefit of the Toleration Act people who in his judgment ought not to be ministers of religion, such as blacksmiths, cobblers, chimney sweeps and others. This stirred up such a strong protest that in 1812 (after another prosecution) the Quaker, the Conventicle and the Five Mile Acts were definitely repealed. See Atmore's edition (1813) of Chandler's *History of Persecution*, pp. 420 f.; also a *New History of Methodism*, Townsend, Workman and Eayrs, i. 566–67, *History of English Congregationalism*, Dale, pp. 575–76 (edn. of 1907) and Sydney Smith's "Essay on Toleration," *Edinburgh Review*, 1811.

in love to you), and if the Lord our God please not to appear for us, we are content to be overcome by you.[1]

In 1668 Thomas Salthouse wrote from Somerset to Margaret Fell telling her that a few days previously there had been read from the High Cross (he does not name the town) a proclamation against Papists and Nonconformists and he continues,

> we are preparing our minds for prisons in these parts . . . though the Papists are named, yet we are like to bear the greatest part of the suffering, if it do any execution. We are resolved to meet, preach and pray, in public and private, in season and out of season, in city town or country, as if it had never been; well knowing that the same power by which we have been preserved and delivered out of the den, is with us, and will be with us to the end if we abide faithful.[2]

[1] *Works*, i. 579, edn. of 1761.
[2] *Letters of Early Friends*, pp. 245–46.

NOTE.—The attention of readers is called to two works telling of the part played by Penn and other Friends in their advocacy of religious toleration: *The Theory of Religious Toleration Under the Later Stuarts*, by A. A. Seaton: by P. S. Belasco, *Authority in Church and State*, Part I. "The Political Ideas of the Quakers of the Seventeenth Century," c. i. "Quakerism"; c. ii. "Liberty of Conscience."

Chapter XI

THE QUAKER MEETING FOR CHURCH BUSINESS: THE CORPORATE WITNESS

THE problem of the shattered state of the Society owing to the death and imprisonment of its leaders confronted Fox when he came out from his imprisonment at Scarborough in the late summer of 1666. Although no more than forty-two years old, he was so benumbed and swollen by reason of his confinement in rooms that let in wind and rain that he could hardly get on his horse, or bend his knees, or endure fire and warm meat, so long had he been kept from them. Nevertheless, his powerful constitution asserted itself; and immediately he set out on a four years' travel through all parts of England, establishing the Church organization which has lasted to the present day.

Before describing this, however, we may note that at this time, when the Quaker Church seemed at its lowest, it received two of its most eminent converts, William Penn and Robert Barclay. In the ardour of early youth, aged respectively twenty-three and eighteen, they resembled one another in other ways also. Of aristocratic standing, of singular charm and beauty of character, possessed of academic learning and knowing a deep spiritual life, they came to exercise on the Church of their allegiance a profound and lasting influence. Up to this point the Quaker literature, of which there had already been a large output, had, with some exception, been formless and even uncouth,[1] but

---

[1] See Braithwaite, *Beginnings of Quakerism*, c. xii., "Controversy," and p. 506. The exception referred to consists mainly of the writings of Penington and Ellwood.

before long the scholarly presentation of Penn and Barclay made its way into quarters which had been closed to others. Each of them suffered imprisonment for his faith.[1]

We now turn to a brief description of the Quaker organization set up, as already stated, by Fox. Naturally the experience of two and a half centuries has led to certain modifications, but the essential features and many of the details remain unchanged. The scheme is that each congregation shall form a "Preparative Meeting" for the management of its own affairs, that a group of "Preparative Meetings" shall form a "Monthly Meeting," the executive body of Friends in a particular district, that several "Monthly Meetings" shall form a "Quarterly Meeting" mainly for the purpose of Christian intercourse and conference, and that a number of "Quarterly Meetings" shall be organized as a "Yearly Meeting," the legislative body of the whole. Great Britain forms a group known as London Yearly Meeting;[2] Ireland a group known as Dublin Yearly Meeting; and on the American Continent and

---

[1] For an estimate of the characters of Penn and Barclay respectively the reader is particularly referred to Braithwaite, *Second Period*, pp. 210–11 and 445–47.

[2] In London Yearly Meeting are included a number of Friends in Australia, New Zealand and South Africa, the total membership in Great Britain being at the end of 1936 about 19,300, inclusive of children and of a large number who for many years have not attended worship or shown any interest in the Society (see *post*, p. 209 concerning birthright membership). In addition to actual members there are probably near 5,000 who regularly attend Friends' Meetings but are not yet members; these are technically called "Attenders." The number in Ireland at the same time was 2,053. For a history of the assembly itself see *London Yearly Meeting During 250 Years, 1668–1918*, by several writers. Concerning the work committed to each of above-mentioned meetings see *Church Government*, officially put forth by the Society of Friends in Great Britain (1931, with slight revision 1934), being Part iii of *Christian Discipline; Church Government in the Society of Friends*, Edith J. Wilson; *The Quaker Method of Church Government*, J. S. Rowntree.

elsewhere there are a number of others. Each of these is independent of the rest.[1]

All Friends, men and women, are entitled to attend any of these meetings and, in any of which they are members, to take part. A man or woman (along with an "assistant clerk") acts as "clerk" (i.e. as combined chairman and secretary) and records the decision to which he considers the meeting has come. There is no voting or applause or noise of dissent. *Almost never* is the clerk's decision challenged, although there may be some discussion as to the wording of the minute which he draws up, but there is no attempt to fight a rearguard action in the hope of snatching a victory after all. The ideal of that early day, an ideal which, not seldom, is still realized, has been thus set forth:

> Every business meeting was concerned with knowing the mind of the Lord, and sought to guide its action by the weight of spiritual judgment rather than by the mechanical counting of heads, or the rhetorical and argumentative skill of the speakers. "Friends," wrote Fox, "are not to meet like a company of people about town or parish business, neither in their men's nor women's meetings, but to wait upon the Lord"[2] (Braithwaite, *Second Period of Quakerism*, p. 278, and see pp. 341–42).

This willingness to *wait* and *persuade* until a large measure of spiritual unity is reached is one of the most cherished possessions of Friends, saving them as it does from smart scoring of debating points or impatience in pressing for a decision. It has to be admitted that often, in

---

[1] Representatives of most of the "orthodox" Yearly Meetings on the American Continent meet once in five years and to this assembly London and Dublin send "fraternal delegates." They meet for Christian intercourse and consideration of matters affecting the welfare of all, but leaving a large measure of autonomy to each constituent meeting. There are one or two official ties between London and Dublin Yearly Meetings.   [2] *Epistles*, p. 349.

deference to timid individuals, a desirable forward step is
over-long delayed, but, once taken, it meets with general
acquiescence free from the bitterness which might at an
earlier stage have arisen had one side carried its point by
force of majority. Not infrequently it happens that those
who have been against the proposed step will, when once
it has been decided on, help to carry it out. Edward
Burrough, in 1662, exhorts Friends:

> . . . being orderly come together, not to spend time
> with needless, unnecessary and fruitless discourses; but to
> proceed in the wisdom of God . . . not in the way of the
> world as a worldly assembly of men, by hot contests, by
> seeking to outspeak and overreach one another in discourse,
> as if it were . . . two sides violently striving for dominion
> in the way of carrying on some worldly interests for self-
> advantage; not deciding affairs by the greater vote or the
> number of men, as the world who have not the wisdom and
> power of God . . . but in the wisdom, love and fellowship
> of God, in gravity, patience, meekness, in unity and con-
> cord, submitting one to another in lowliness of heart . . .
> hearing and determining every matter coming before you
> in love, coolness, gentleness and dear unity (*Letters of
> Early Friends*, p. 305).

This method of conducting the business meetings of
the Church is no accidental growth, nor is it something
that can on occasion be laid aside. It is an outcome and
an illustration of a certain way of thought on which
Friends have always laid stress. At this point the reader
will do well to turn to the passage hereafter quoted on
page 352. In the official statement of Quaker practice
the ideal is thus set forth:

> As it is our hope that in our Meetings for Discipline the
> will of God shall prevail rather than the desires of men, we
> do not set great store by rhetoric or clever argument. The
> mere gaining of debating points is found to be unhelpful

and alien to the spirit of worship which should govern the rightly ordered Meeting. Instead of rising hastily to reply to another, it is better to give time for what has been said to make its own appeal, and to take its right place in the mind of the Meeting. . . . We cherish, therefore, the tradition that excludes voting from our meetings, and trust that clerks and Friends generally will observe the spirit of it, not permitting themselves to be influenced in their judgment either by mere numbers or by persistence. The clerks should be content to wait upon God with the Meeting as long as may be necessary for the emergence of a decision which clearly commends itself to the heart and mind of the Meeting as the right one.[1]

By a modern writer this fine conception of the right conduct of a business meeting of the Church has been set forth with equal power:

It is not the mere absence of voting that makes a Quaker business meeting. It should be conducted in such a spirit that the sense of the Divine presence is not far removed from our thoughts, so that it is natural to wait for a while in silence and to find through the windows of prayer an opening leading our thoughts out above the controversies which separate us, letting in the spirit that may unite us and lead us forward together.[2]

The importance of this matter justifies the setting forth of one more message of wise counsel that has come down from early days. This method of conducting business, demanding as it does a high standard of courtesy and of consideration not only for the opinions but also for the feelings of others, is capable of having a fine educational effect on the community at large, but it lies peculiarly open to the devastation caused by obscurantism or

[1] *Christian Practice* (the second part of *Christian Discipline*), 1925, pp. 32–33.
[2] T. E. Harvey, *Authority and Freedom in the Experience of the Quakers*, p. 45.

obstinacy, self-assertiveness or party-spirit, should these evil things make their appearance. Stephen Crisp, already mentioned as a convert of the boy martyr, Parnell, writing in 1690, points out that among those who "have a single eye to the Lord to do the Lord's business in the leadings of His Spirit," difference of opinion in itself "makes no breach of unity nor hinders the brotherly kindness," and that when each one, in this atmosphere, has liberty to express his mind freely, a right way is opened up,

> . . . for [he continues] the danger in society doth not lie so much in that some few may have a differing apprehension in some things from the general sense, as it doth in this, namely, when such that so differ do suffer themselves to be led out of the bond of charity and shall labour to impose their private sense upon the rest of their brethren, and to be offended and angry, if it be not received, this is the seed of sedition and strife that hath grown up in too many to their own hurt.[1]

The establishment of an organized arrangement for the conduct of Church affairs and discipline was not carried through without strain. There were some who saw in it an infringement of the liberty of each individual to obey what he conceived to be his own divine guidance, and, but for the wisdom of Fox and other leaders, an anarchy destructive of all corporate life might have ensued.[2] Friends have never stood for a bare individualistic principle of the "Inner Light" *apart from certain practices and a general way of life into which, as they believe, a faithful following of the Light would lead them.* It is important to

---

[1] *An Epistle of Tender Love*, p. 8: it is given in Sewel's *History of Friends*, under the year 1690. Concerning Stephen Crisp see *ante*, pp. 65, 82.
[2] The controversy to which this gave rise is known as the Wilkinson-Story Controversy: see John Stephenson Rowntree, *Micah's Mother*; Braithwaite, *Second Period*, Index; *ante*, p. 142 note.

bear this in mind inasmuch as at various times the claim
has been set up that the mere fact of anyone asserting
that he was following his Light (*wherever* it led him)[1]
entitled him to be counted as a "Friend." It was in reply
to this claim that Barclay, in 1674, wrote *The Anarchy of
the Ranters* in which he says:

> We [are] a people gathered together by the power of
> God . . . into the belief of certain principles and doctrines
> and also certain practices and performances by which we
> come to be separated and distinguished from others, so as
> to meet apart and to suffer deeply for our joint testimony
> (p. 34).

"The new truth," as a modern writer has stated, "manifested a wonderful constructive energy, quickly finding
expression in a consistent body of principles. . . . Seldom
has a great spiritual truth been followed along its untried
consequences with surer and more resolute steps."[2]
The Light

> . . . had led the first Friends out from the world into a
> definite body of testimonies which had been the natural
> expression in life of the great indwelling experience which
> they enjoyed, and from the first years fellowship had meant
> this common witness to a common body of truth.[3]

In other words, the Society of Friends is not merely
a religious club, having as its basis of membership nothing
more than profession of belief in the "Inner Light";
it exists to bear *corporate* witness to the principles *and
practices* for which it stands, calling for the loyalty of those

---

[1] The reader's attention is specially directed to p. 173 note 1.
[2] Braithwaite, *Beginnings of Quakerism*, p. 137.
[3] Braithwaite, *Second Period of Quakerism*, p. 249; and see *George
Fox* (p. 114), by H. G. Wood; *The Universal Light, a Statement of
Quaker Faith* (p. 12), by A. Barratt Brown; and my *Friends and the
Inner Light.*

who voluntarily remain its members.[1] At some periods of its history this has not been clearly perceived, and a sympathetic observer viewing Friends with knowledge at the time from an outside standpoint, has thus drawn attention to a weakness which has, at times, overtaken them:

> The doctrine of the Inner Light sometimes issues in an amiably hospitable frame of mind which presumes some measure of truth in any view sincerely held, and which is content to give an equal welcome to incompatible ideas. Friends are occasionally inclined to delight in theological haziness or religious novelties, and sometimes this suggests lack of intellectual thoroughness rather than breadth of mind (H. G. Wood, *Quakerism and the Future of the Church*, p. 72).

In the stand for its principles taken by the Society of Friends, or by any other religious society, *as a united body which any of its members may injure*, it will in practice be found that there need be no strain between corporate authority and individual freedom among those whose first concern is to maintain a deep *spiritual* fellowship, not primarily for itself but for the building of the City of God.[2]

[1] Concerning one particular application of this, the Quaker testimony to the incompatibility of *all* war with the mind of Christ, it has been said: "That testimony is not an accident, it is no mere excrescence like the wearing of the hat or the use of 'thee' and 'thou.' It is a vital application of the principle on which it was founded. To forgo it would be to strike a fatal blow at the very existence of the Society of Friends. To retain our witness to the Inward Light without holding fast to so vital an application of the principle would be of small value" (William Littleboy, *Friends and Peace*—a pamphlet). For this testimony see *ante*, pp. 42, 130 ff. and *post*, c. xx.

[2] See Braithwaite, *Second Period of Quakerism*, pp. 342, 346, 350, 499, and *Authority and Freedom in the Experience of the Quakers*, by T. Edmund Harvey. The Christian Church as portrayed in the early chapters of Acts "shows, like parallel cases of a religious movement in its fresh prime, a vital blend of corporate and individual experience, each helping to intensify the other" (Bartlet and Carlyle, *Christianity in History*, p. 44, and see pp. 289, 336, of the same).

Before passing from the account of Quaker organization further mention must be made of the Meeting for Sufferings of which the name has been already explained (p. 163). It meets monthly and is composed of representatives, men and women, from the different Quarterly Meetings and of *ex-officio* members, namely, the elders appointed by the Monthly Meetings to have care of the ministry,[1] and the surviving recorded ministers.[2] Not only does it act as the executive committee of the Yearly Meeting, it takes note of Peace movements in England and elsewhere and of others in which the Society has special interest; it pays attention to legislative and other proposals and emergencies which have particular bearing on the cause of righteousness, whether they directly affect the Society of Friends or not; to it Friends bring their "concerns" for service in different parts of the world. The "concern" may be for travel in the ministry in foreign parts, for the relief of suffering due to war, famine and other cause, or for such other service as the Friend may feel to be "laid upon" him or her. An instance of such "concern" is given later (p. 331).[3] It is impossible to set forth the whole range of the Meeting's activities, but it is true to say that they are not limited by either continent or race.[4]

---

[1] *Post*, p. 275.   [2] *Post*, p. 266 note.   [3] See also pp. 330, 346, 347.
[4] Attention is particularly directed to "London Meeting for Sufferings in the Nineteenth Century," c. xx. of R. M. Jones's *Later Periods of Quakerism*.

Chapter XII

THE EIGHTEENTH CENTURY:
QUIETISM AND SECLUSION:
FAITHFULNESS TO CONVICTION:
THE "CIRCULAR MEETINGS":
TRADITION

THE passing of the Toleration Act in 1689 opened a
new chapter in the history of Friends. We are not surprised to find that many who would have endured further
persecution, had it come in their way, now that they were
freed from it lay back, as it were, gasping for breath
and disinclined for new adventure. This was partly due
to their advance in outward prosperity, their honesty in
trade having brought increase of riches; and even in
early days, Fox had been concerned to warn them against
saying "My business, my business," when spiritual service
was set before them.[1] Shortly after this he wrote to those
"who are of the royal seed of God": "I warn and charge
you from the Lord not to make any of the world's jewels
your God" (*Epistles*, pp. 127–28).

Other causes of weakness were internal controversy,[2]
the emigration of thousands of Friends to America, and
the loss by untimely death of leaders who would have
exercised an ever-deepening influence, and raised up
successors to themselves. Aldam, Parnell, John Camm
and Nayler did not live beyond 1660, and in the next
six years there died (some of them in prison) Farnsworth,
Fisher, Burrough, Hubberthorne, Humphrey Smith,

[1] *Epistles*, p. 102; see also p. 228 and Fox's *Journal* (bi-cent. edn).,
ii. 523.
[2] See *ante*, pp. 142 note, 171 note, Braithwaite, *Second Period*,
c. vii.

Ames, Caton, Joseph Coale and Audland. Fisher, ten years a Friend, lived on to sixty-one, and of neither Farnsworth nor of Ames is the year of birth known, but the average age at death of the remaining ten was thirty-six. In 1669 Howgill died in prison at the age of fifty. Of those who survived into later years, at such times as they were not themselves in prison, a large part of the energy which would have otherwise been spent in setting forth the spiritual message of Friends had been used up in care for the families of imprisoned members and in endeavours to gain relief from suffering. "For thirty years the energies of Friends were occupied with the defence of their right to live."[1] They were not broken by the persecution, but they were bent and weakened. The Quaker society had, however, been saved from utter destruction "by the quiet meetings resolutely maintained up and down the land [which had] remained centres of power, and [had] offered an almost invincible resistance to the persecutors."[2]

But now, just as Friends were entering into their liberty, they suffered further loss. In the early days of 1691 Fox died at the age of sixty-six, triumphant to the last, saying, as he felt the cold strike to his heart on coming out of meeting two days before his end, "Now I am clear, I am fully clear." Two years earlier Dewsbury was taken, and less than two years later, Stephen Crisp, and within this period others of the early leaders passed from sight. Very

---

[1] Braithwaite, *Second Period of Quakerism*, p. 351, and for the weakening effect of the persecution see pp. 217–19, 223–25, 250, 366, 401, 544. The writer speaks (p. 225) of the persecution stopping the itinerating work so that the Quaker communities came to be isolated as by the winter snow. In 1670 Fox wrote to Bristol, "Few travel now the countries, it may be well to visit them lest any should faint." *Epistles*, p. 317.

[2] Quoted from Braithwaite's *Second Period*, p. 225 (quoted *post*, p. 198), and see pp. 228, 540, 637 of the same.

few survived into the next century. Of each of them the day's work was well done when the evening found him, but there was yet one from whom more might have been hoped. Wealthy in this world's goods, of aristocratic standing and personal charm, learned and of a deep spiritual life, Barclay was marked out as a leader of men. Of a long-lived, powerful race (his father, Whittier's "Barclay of Ury," had had the reputation of being the strongest man in Scotland and no other could use his sword), he might have looked forward to a further generation of life, but at the age of forty-one he was stricken of a fever and died a few weeks before Fox. His death is the tragedy of the Society; had his personal influence shaped its course in its early days of freedom, its later history might have been different. Penn, the equal of Barclay, was yet to do good work by his writings, but, as we have seen, he was pressed down by the care of Pennsylvania; and there were others, some of whom had suffered for their faith, who for years to come were to exercise a kindly and high-minded influence; but the great note of *inspiration* was no more heard. "There was no proper cultivation of a soil for the growing of leaders, and it followed that the human harvest was poor."[1]

Moreover, the prospect of a return of persecution was not remote, and the fear of it was deepened by the storm of ridicule and abuse which burst upon Dissenters early in the new century. Penn, writing in 1703, says that ever since the Toleration Act "some busy and forward priests" had done all they could to set magistrates and other people against Friends[2] but he goes on to say that there was growing up a better understanding of them. Nevertheless Friends in particular had cause for alarm inasmuch as

---

[1] Braithwaite, *Second Period*, p. 538. The whole chapter (xix.) ought to be read in order to gain understanding of the change that was setting in.

[2] Preface to *Vindiciae Veritatis*, by Daniel Phillips.

M

the Toleration Act applied only to "orthodox" Dissenters and at this time their orthodoxy was being seriously challenged. Their most formidable opponents were two clergymen of the Church of England—Charles Leslie, author of *The Snake in the Grass*, and George Keith, who had once been a leading Friend.[1] Besides this, they sought indulgence beyond that accorded to other Nonconformists, in that they required relief from the necessity of taking the oath in courts of law and in other affairs of life where it was regularly demanded to a greater extent than it is in our time. Thus it was that Friends were confirmed in their instinct of seclusion from the world by their anxiety to avoid drawing hostile attention to themselves (beyond that which their peculiar attire, speech, and manners inevitably attracted), and in this way there grew up a suspicion of activity that might carry them into the company of others. This, as we shall see later, led on to a conventional repressiveness, a suppression of any deviation from the established uniformity, and this, in many lives, to an inertia indistinguishable from indolence. There was considerable uneasiness at the work of Elizabeth Fry by reason of her association with people of importance outside the Society.[2] This instinct of separateness and the long memory of persecution are seen in a letter

---

[1] *Ante*, pp. 105 note, 106 note. For these attacks on Friends see Braithwaite, *Second Period*, c. xvii. Leslie was a Non-juror.

[2] The (Philadelphia) *Friend* in 1848, near the conclusion of a series of articles on the recently published *Life of Elizabeth Fry*, says that her "whirl of philanthropic business . . . inducing premature old age," was "highly unfavourable" to spiritual growth, and adds, "her self-complacency was evidently gratified and fed by the notice and applause which her labours attracted" (p. 414). The *British Friend* drew attention to these articles (1848, p. 219, and 1853, p. 128) which it published as a supplement to its issue of Second Month (February) 1849. Nevertheless that periodical afterwards spoke of her with affection, though holding her to have been mistaken (1853, p. 128). See also *post*, pp. 188 note, 220 note, 300 note.

written eighty years after the Toleration Act by a Friend to his wife in America. He says that in the political world there is much cause for uneasiness, but he continues:

> I cannot by any means think our people [i.e. Friends] the proper instrument for setting things right which may appear out of order; as we were the other day but a poor handful, despised and persecuted for our religious dissent, and glad our forefathers were, by all their labour and solicitude, to obtain the liberty we have of late enjoyed. I hope, therefore, that the members of our Society will be very cautious how they intermeddle in politics or government.[1]

In their Yearly Meeting Epistle and elsewhere, Friends not infrequently expressed thankfulness for the security they were enjoying and for their good standing in the eyes of the Government.[2] Not for themselves only, but also for their country had their fathers braved the storm for religious freedom, but now gone was the day of mighty daring when men and women, not counting their lives dear, went forth with the power of God behind them in challenge of the existing order, esteeming it a matter of small or of no concern whether they enjoyed good standing in the eyes of the Government or not.

The effect of this quietism was a binding together of Friends in a rigid uniformity, emphasizing the separation that from the first had existed between them and the world. From other Dissenters they were, as we have seen, separated as much as they were from the Anglican Church, and now their secluded life found few interests beyond the management of their business and homes, the organization of their religious body and the calls of philanthropy.

[1] *Isaac and Rachel Wilson, Quakers of Kendal, 1714–85,* by Somervell, p. 97. This letter was written in 1769.
[2] For instances of this see the Epistles of 1701, 1720, 1730. For an example of timidity, ludicrous or pathetic according as it is viewed, see *First Publishers of Truth,* p. 11.

But although, for this reason, the story of the eighteenth century is of less obvious interest than that of the first years of storm and heroism, a knowledge of it is essential to an understanding of present-day Quakerism. In this century a character was formed and a reputation acquired, and from it certain currents have flowed down to our day, their force being not yet spent.

In the first generation, as has been stated, obedience to the Light had led men and women to a plainness of dress, not the wearing of a special costume, but the discarding of the fantastic ornamentation of the period. But even before the end of the seventeenth century "plainness" had come to have a conventional meaning, and by the imposition of stringent rules attempts were made to secure a uniformity of what had come to be old-fashioned attire. Margaret Fox in her old age saw the impending danger of (as she says),

> this narrowness and strictness entering in, that many cannot tell what to do or not do. . . . We are coming into Jewism, into that which Christ cried woe against, minding altogether outward things, neglecting the inward work of Almighty God in our hearts . . . insomuch that poor Friends is mangled in their minds, that they know not what to do.

She points out that contrary to the teaching of Christ, who bade us take no thought for raiment, considering the lilies,

> we must [she writes] not look at colours nor make anything that is changeable colours as the hills are, nor sell them nor wear them, but we must all be in one dress and one colour. This is a silly, poor gospel. . . . I have stood against it several years.

This was written in 1700, and has obvious reference to a minute of Margaret Fox's own Quarterly Meeting of

Lancashire held in 1693, which counselled Friends to "stand clear" of "making, selling or wearing striped cloth, stuff or striped silk or any sort of flowered or figured thing of different colours." In 1703, the year after Margaret Fox's death, this was repeated.

It was not the first time that the mother in Israel had warned Friends against the lowered vitality that was setting in. In 1698, a year after a similar minute had been sent from London throughout England, she wrote:

> It's a dangerous thing to lead young Friends much into the observation of outward things, which may be easily done; for they can soon get into an outward garb to be all alike outwardly, but this will not make them true Christians. It's the Spirit that gives life.[1]

Pathetic is the sight of the wise old woman of eighty-six years, with her memories of prison walls, pleading in vain with a younger generation who, in an easier time, were exalting ecclesiastical discipline over living conviction. Her warning was not heeded, and for more than a century

---

[1] These three quotations from Margaret Fox are taken from Braithwaite, *Second Period*, pp. 518–19; and for the absurdly minute rules laid down see pp. 509–14. The London minute above referred to was sent from the Quarterly Meeting held 5th of Fifth month, 1697. It was entitled "An Epistle to women Friends, but more especially to a young generation with children, of believing parents." It expresses the wish "that if it be possible there might be a stop put to the vanity that into many of our sex is entered," and warns against "ruffled and fantastical and high dresses, gaudy attire, flowered and striped silks of divers colours," etc. Margaret Fox must have known of this, the piquancy of the situation being that of the thirty-four women who signed the Epistle, four were her own daughters, the eldest of them being close on sixty-five years of age. I have come on a copy of this in a Lincolnshire Quarterly Meeting book; "A Record wherein are several writings containing wholesome advice to the Quarterly and Monthly Meetings," etc. The original has not, so far, been found, but there is another copy in the Swarthmore MSS. (at Friends House), vol. v., No. 90. For further information on this matter see Barclay, *Inner Life of the Religious Societies of the Commonwealth* (1879), pp. 490–93; John Wilhelm Rowntree, *Essays and Addresses* (1905), p. 60; and *The Burtts, a Lincolnshire Family*, p. 89

and a half no one could be admitted to the Quaker fellowship who was not prepared to be marked off from other
men by his antique dress and speech. Nevertheless, to
the rules that were laid down many who were born into
the Society refused to conform, following the dress and
manners of "the world's people," but though they were
not expelled it was clearly understood that they were not
to be allowed any part in the service of the Church.[1]
William Savery, an American, records his impression of
Norwich meeting which he visited in 1798:

> There might be two hundred under our name [i.e.
> Friends], but very few of the middle-aged and young
> that had a consistent appearance in their dress. Indeed,
> I thought it the gayest Friends' meeting I ever sat in and
> was grieved to see it.[2]

Nevertheless the larger number of Friends continued
through all changes of fashion to wear the costume and
maintain the manners and speech of early days, and, being
visibly marked out as a separate people, they acquired
for the Society a reputation which, in the main, was that of
respect but which, on another side, was reflected in
caricature and lampoon.[3] At the beginning of the

---

[1] The story of the painful dissolving away in the middle of the
nineteenth century of certain observances that had come to be empty
ritual is told in c. xvi.

[2] Taken from *Life of William Savery of Philadelphia*, by Francis R.
Taylor, p. 429. It was in this meeting that Elizabeth Fry, then
Elizabeth Gurney, seventeen years old, through the ministry of
William Savery, knew the spiritual uprising which shaped her life
(see *post*, p. 190).

[3] Speaking of the reign of James II (1685–88) Bishop Burnet
(1643–1715) says: "The Quakers had set up such a visible distinction
in the matter of the hat and saying *thou* and *thee*, that they had all
as it were a badge fixed on them: so they were easily known" (*History
of My Own Time*, iii. 152, edn. of 1823). Elsewhere, speaking of the
same time, he says that the Church of England formed the main
body of the nation, that the Presbyterians and Independents were
more than two-thirds of the rest and owing to their "depressed
estate" were looked on as one body; and that the Baptists and

eighteenth century a scurrilous attack on the Low Church
and the Nonconformists bodies, in its description of
Friends making their way to Yearly Meeting, says of them:

> Their coats were of so old a fashion,
> As if derived from the Creation.[1]

A more kindly effusion coming from the same time
refers to their manner of speech:

> We next will ramble to the Bull and Mouth,
> To hear the Yea and Nay man holding forth.[2]

But although the writer goes on to bear witness that

> . . . some are so refined,
> They scarce do quake in body, dress, or mind,

it was, as already stated, the external signs, insisted on
by the majority, which stamped the whole Society. In
accordance with the old Puritan testimony against Popish
or superstitious observance of customs, times and seasons,

Quakers "were not very numerous but they were more united; the
former [were] men of great virtue and of a universal charity; and the
latter had so many little distinctions in their whole deportment that
they were everywhere known: they lived in great simplicity and
equality among themselves and were all as one man" (*Supplement
to Burnet's History of My Own Time*, ed. Foxcroft, 1902, p. 218).
Braithwaite estimates the number of Friends in 1660 as from 30,000
to 40,000 in a population of about five millions (*Beginnings*, p. 512),
and in the years 1670–79 at about 40,000 or, at most, 50,000 out
of a population of 5½ million (*Second Period*, p. 459). John Bellers,
writing in 1724, says: "We are but a handful of people to the nation,
like the gleanings after the harvest" (*An Abstract of George Fox's
Advice and Warning . . . with some Observations Thereon*, p. 7).
   [1] Edward Ward, *Hudibras Redivivus*, which appeared in parts from
1705 to 1707. See *post*, p. 187 note 2, for another quotation. There
is much that is more abusive than either of these. *The Quaker, a
Study in Costume*, by Amelia M. Gummere, is a curious antiquarian
chapter of Quaker history.
   [2] From *The Pulpit Fool, a Satyr*, anonymous, 1707. For the
Bull and Mouth see *ante*, p. 109 note. The man referred to as a "pulpit
fool" is William Penn, of whom the writer speaks disparagingly, but
otherwise his description of Friends is, along with some criticism,
cordial and even affectionate (*Journal F.H.S.*, xvii. 130).

the Quaker wife wore no wedding ring, and a school which had winter holidays carefully timed them to begin *after* Christmas.[1] On Christmas Day and Good Friday the Quaker shop was open (and was sometimes stormed by zealots resenting such profanation of the holy season[2]) but on one morning of each week of the year the locked door of the same shop and the shuttered windows told the neighbours that the Friend was attending his mid-week meeting for worship.[3] To single individuals, his customers and others, he said "thee" and "thou," and the days of the week and months of the year he called not by their "heathen" names but by their numbers.[4]

[1] This was as late as 1849, and in 1857 the scruple was dropped. The school was Bootham, York. The headmaster, an advanced educationist for his time, said that rather than have the holiday called "Christmas" he would have none at all. Shortly after 1860 Ackworth School for the first time in its history had a half-holiday on Christmas Day, the headmaster explaining that it was granted at the request of a Friend and not because the day happened to be Christmas. The following is taken from the minutes of Strickland (Westmorland) Monthly Meeting of 2. xii. 1708, "It is the advice of the Quarterly Meeting that no Friends who have cattle for slaughter do sell or dispose of them against the time called by the word 'Christmas' nor any other commodities for provision, nor anything else that may allude to the spreading of the observation of that time." The original Puritan objection to recognition of the day had been directed against the Popish idea of "mass" (*Christ's Mass*). As to the use of the ring in marriage, this was, in the sixteenth century, one of the chief battlegrounds between the Puritans and their opponents, the former objectto it as a Popish practice (see *post*, p. 291).

[2] See, for example, *The First Fifty Years of Quakerism in Norwich*, by Arthur J. Eddington, pp. 94–95.

[3] I knew a Friend who came to the point of closing his shop on Good Friday and Christmas Day, but, wishing to avoid any appearance of superstitious observance of them, he put a notice on his shutters, "Closed for recreation." In 1873 a conservative Friend wrote to his son entreating him to keep his warehouse open on Christmas Day, "as Friends have been wont to do, as a testimony of their allegiance to the King of kings and Lord of lords" (*Diary of John G. Sargent*, p. 211). See *post*, p. 292.

[4] Friends, on the strength of Exod. xxiii. 13, refused to speak the names of heathen deities. To this day *Bradshaw's Railway Guide*, begun by George Bradshaw, a ministering Friend of Manchester, bears on the outside cover of some issues the number as well as the name of the month.

The prefixes "Mr.," "Mrs.," and "Miss" his soul abhorred as being "flattering titles."[1] Deservedly he enjoyed a reputation for a rigid standard of honesty and truth speaking; but in this latter respect his caution not infrequently led to such guarded or involved expression as to arouse a suspicion of slyness and evasiveness. Charles Lamb, while professing his own inability to join the Quakers, combats this charge that was brought against them, saying that they, more than other people, took careful heed to their words.[2] They certainly acquired a habit of understatement and circumlocution understood among themselves but puzzling to others. Elizabeth Fry expressed her disapproval "of that mysterious, ambiguous mode of expression in which Friends at times clothe their observations and their ministry." "I like," she says, "the truth in simplicity, it needs no mysterious garment."[3] The

---

[1] This scruple was based on Job xxxii. 22: "I know not to give flattering titles, else would my Maker soon take me away." In parts of America this conservatism lasted longer than it did in England; in 1899 I heard a Friend say in Philadelphia Yearly Meeting: "The custom of saying *Mr.* and *Mrs.* is striking at the very root of our spiritual life." See the *British Friend*, 1860, p. 9.

[2] Essay, "Imperfect Sympathies," and Clarkson's *Portraiture*, ii. c. 16 (*post*, p. 216).

[3] *Memoir*, ii. 5. It is part of an account given by Elizabeth Fry of the Yearly Meeting of 1826, *Pen Pictures of London Yearly Meeting*, p. 180. A typical saying was that of a Friend on his death-bed to whom someone expressed the hope that he felt beneath him the Everlasting Arms. The dying man replied, "Measurably so, I trust." A certain Monthly Meeting, refusing to admit to membership an individual who made application, thus framed its minute (after some other verbiage): "We apprehend it may not be improper to defer the application," etc. A Friend setting out under a "concern" to pay a round of ministerial visits has nothing to say beyond the expression of a hope that he may be preserved from doing harm. A woman Friend, after accompanying her intended husband, as the rule then was, to give official notice to the Monthly Meeting of their engagement, recorded in her diary the day's proceedings, and added that she had been "permitted not to cast away a confiding hope" that the contemplated step was in right ordering. On this subject see *Quaker Language*, by T. Edmund Harvey: he tells of a Friend who to an

"consistent" Friend, courteous in manner and in mind as he might be, refused to raise his hat in salutation. For his most dearly beloved dead he wore no sign of mourning, and over their graves he placed no memorial stone, such a practice being "a vain and empty custom" and, as an ancient minute says, "of no service to the deceased."[1] In his home music found no place[2] and pictures on the

enquiry concerning the health of his wife replied, "Thank thee, I think I may safely say that she is much as she sometimes is." Concerning Elizabeth Fry's attitude to traditional observance, see *post*, p. 285. For an instance of understatement, see *post*, p. 206.

[1] The minute is as follows: "Whereas there have been a more perticular Case of Difference about a Tomb-stone which have Long Laine on the Grave of (Elinour Jones first husband) Josiah Thoms It being a practice generally disliked by Friends through this Nation and of no service to the Deceased. Wherefore it is our judgment that the stone be removed out of sight by order of Joseph Jones or his wife." At the next meeting report was made that this had been done: Minutes of Dorset Q.M., 27, iv., and 3, viii., 1705. In certain meetings there was trouble with those who insisted on putting stones on the graves of their relatives (see minutes of Strickland (Westmorland) M.M. 1717–18; Pontefract M.M. 1765, 1767, and Norwich M.M. 1757 and 1765, and finally, by minutes of the Y.M. of 1850, 1861 and 1885, the practice was allowed, subject to the conditions that the stones were to state no more than the name and age of the deceased and dates of birth and death, that "such a uniformity may be preserved as may effectually guard against any distinction being made in that place between the rich and the poor" (see *post*, p. 291, and Braithwaite, *Second Period*, p. 471).

[2] In 1804 a Friend was disowned (i.e. separated from membership) on the ground that she "encourages and approves of her children being taught the practice of music." Three years earlier her husband had been disowned for "paying tithes and encouraging diversions in his house" (*My Ancestors*, by Norman Penney, p. 47). More than a hundred years after this a survivor of the old school, quoting Tennyson's line, "May make one music as before," for the dreaded word "music" substituted "harmony." A pathetic story, which must go back to near the beginning of the nineteenth century, has been told me by an ex-clerk of London Yearly Meeting concerning a relative of his who, from a "gay" Friend, became a "plain" Friend. This involved giving up music, but once a year he went to the top of the Monument in London and there, where his action could do no harm to anyone, he played his flute. About the same time there joined Friends a man who had played the 'cello in a Methodist choir. He now felt it wrong either to keep, give away or sell his instrument, he could not bear to break it up or burn it and so he buried it. Bernard Thistlethwaite, *The Bax Family*, p. 308.

walls raised suspicion of laxity, although public opinion tolerated a certain three (rarely all seen at once) namely, Penn's treaty with the Indians, the interior of a slave ship and a plan of Ackworth School.[1] By reason of its strangeness and separateness, the Society came to be looked on almost as a monastic order. Other Dissenters used the church for their marriages and not infrequently the churchyard for their burials; the Quaker, resolute in refusal to recognize the paid minister, in his meetinghouse married in his own way and in his own graveyard he buried his dead. Marriages in the Quaker way were not recognized as lawful unless both man and woman were Friends, and "disownment," i.e. expulsion from membership, was the fate of any who, in order to marry one of another Church, resorted to a "priest."[2]

[1] Clarkson, *Portraiture of Quakerism*, i. 292–94. For Clarkson (not a Friend) see *post*, p. 216. This was about the beginning of the nineteenth century. William Howitt, writing later, says that at that time the three Quaker pictures were a portrait of Clarkson, Penn's treaty, and the West family (*Tait's Edinburgh Magazine*, October 1837). Benjamin West, a Friend, painted the well-known picture of Penn's treaty with the Indians.

[2] Concerning the abandonment of this practice see *post*, p. 293. By Lord Hardwick's Act of 1753, directed against clandestine marriages, all marriages were to be solemnized at church, except those of Jews and Quakers, the two bodies of people whose determined adherence to their own way gained this and other concessions. The Act was repealed in 1836. *Hudibras Redivivus* (*ante*, p. 183 note 1) says of Quakers:

> Because this nonconforming sect
> Ne'er marry as our laws direct—

but it says falsely that they would marry properly "when lands are in the case," to save their children from the illegitimacy which might have prevented them inheriting. This point came up at Nottingham Assizes in 1661, and the judge ruled that a Quaker marriage was valid (Fox's *Journal*, bi-cent. edn., i. 520). A similar decision was given at Carlisle in 1681: for this information I am indebted to Arthur J. Eddington, who has come on it in a letter of George Whitehead at Norwich. As to burials, it was not till 1880 that they might be conducted in a churchyard with a service other than that of the Church of England. For a long time other Dissenters had,

A Friend who attended such a marriage was, if not actually disowned, visited with severe censure. A member who fell into poverty was relieved by the Society and not by the parish. For his children the Friend sought out teachers and employers of his own persuasion, and, in accord with official advice, in the bestowal of his custom he dealt with other Friends as far as he might. In fact, he himself came to regard separation and outward difference from others as his normal way of life, an attitude of mind which might lead to spiritual pride. John Woolman records that when, in his striving after simplicity, he began to wear a hat of undyed fur, his fellow-members were distressed at its coincidence with the fashion of the day. Nevertheless he continued to wear it.[1] It is hardly an exaggeration to say that a Friend was likely to feel uncomfortable at catching himself doing the same as other people. Many times does this instinct of seclusion find expression, a typical example being the caution of Samuel Scott in 1780 against Friends taking part in elections except to record each his own vote. He con-

in some parts, acquired their own graveyards, but at the beginning this was a Quaker peculiarity. In *A Modern Account of Scotland*, published anonymously but written by Thomas Kirke in 1679, it is stated that in that country people are buried "in the kirk garths or in a burying place on purpose, called the *hoof*, at the further end of the town (like our Quakers) enclosed with a wall." See also *Journal of the Friends' Historical Society*, xvii. (1920), p. 120. Fox advised Friends to see that their graveyards were "decently and well fenced" (*Epistles*, p. 291).

[1] This was in America, but it was typical of English Quaker thought. I myself can remember the instinctive dislike of Friends to even a sensible and useful fashion, simply because it was the fashion. In the eighteenth century, when umbrellas came into use, Friends generally had a "testimony" against them. An anecdote, trivial in itself, may show to future generations this instinct of separateness. In the years shortly after 1890 each Friends' school, following the custom of others, adopted a uniform cap or hat for its boys and girls, and a boy of ancient Quaker family said to me that it did not seem very Friendly.

tinues: "Israel is to dwell alone, and not to be mixed with the people."[1]

The Quaker adherence to his scruples, advertising the aloofness of his Society from the world, and (thanks to generations of sturdy faithfulness) the deference paid to these scruples, can find no more typical illustration than is afforded by the action of Joseph Pease, the first Friend to sit in the House of Commons.[2] He was, in 1833, returned to the first Reformed Parliament as member for South Durham, but he refused to take the oath required of all members, and a Committee appointed to consider the matter reported in favour of his taking the Quaker affirmation. This, however, was not the only scruple that demanded satisfaction. As a member, he

[1] *Diary*, p. 12. The quotation marks are in the diary, but the passage is not in the Bible; it recalls Num. xxiii. 9, Neh. xiii. 3, and Hos. vii. 8. For many years it was a favourite expression of Friends; Margaret Woods, writing in 1779, expresses her disapproval of it: *Journal*, p. 97. In 1768 John Roper of Norwich wrote "An Epistle to Parents, etc. . . . Respecting Dress and Address" in which he says, "Although to the eye of natural wisdom the cock of the hat, the cut of a coat, the form of a cap, or most of the preceding may appear insignificant . . . yet the spiritual eye can see they are all mercifully designed by infinite Wisdom to build a separation, to form, though by such despicable briars and thorns, a hedge that pricks on both sides to prevent an improper, unsafe communication, association and intermarrying with those among whom we dwell." Reynolds MSS. This seclusion and clannishness give point to an essay by Swift, *A True and Faithful Narrative of what Passed in London*. The writer represents his Quaker neighbour as refusing adherence to a widespread belief in the immediate end of the world on the ground that if there were any truth in it, some Friend or other would have had it revealed to him. "This, indeed," says Swift, "(as in all other spiritual cases with this set of people) was his only reason against believing me." He adds that the Quaker advised him not to sell his stock at the low price of the moment, inasmuch as it would rise again when the scare was over.

[2] John Archdale, a Buckinghamshire Quaker squire, was elected for Chipping Wycombe in 1698, but his refusal to take the oath prevented him taking his seat (Braithwaite, *Second Period*, pp. 412–14). For the same reason John Gurney, great-uncle of Joseph John Gurney, was, in the eighteenth century, obliged to refuse the offer of a safe seat made to him by Sir Robert Walpole.

acquired the privilege of "franking" letters for himself and his friends; that is, of sending them through the post free of charge, a privilege which was withdrawn in 1840 on the introduction of the penny post. It was necessary that he should write the date on each exercise of this privilege, and his insistence on writing the number of the month, instead of its name, caused the Post Office officials to consult the Law Officers of the Crown as to the legality of this proceeding. They returned a written opinion to the effect that while the designation of a month by its number would be illegal in an indictment, "yet considering the indulgences granted to Quakers in matters of conscience, under which head their peculiar mode of dating must be classed," they were of opinion that Mr. Pease might frank letters in his own way.[1]

Within the Society itself, public opinion confined the ministry and other services of the Church to those who adopted the Quaker attire and other conventions; and if one of the "gay" Friends entered on a more serious way of life the change was marked by the adoption of the "plain" dress and manner. "The step was not seldom attended by a profound religious experience, like that which has often marked the entrance upon life in a monastery, or an instantaneous conversion."[2] The large Gurney household into which Elizabeth Fry was born in 1780 ranked among the county families of Norfolk, and, religious and philanthropic as was its atmosphere, it conformed with most of the manners and recreations of its social equals. But when Elizabeth's spiritual longings were ministered to by William Savery in the meeting already mentioned, it dawned upon her that she was to be

[1] *The Yorkshireman*, i. 287. On separateness see *ante*, p. 178; *post*, pp. 220, 221, 300 note.
[2] R. M. Jones, *Later Periods*, pp. 177–78.

a "plain Friend"; and the early part of her diary is a record of one difficult step after another taken in this direction before she was twenty years old.[1] On her brother, Joseph John Gurney, when he was "rather more than twenty-one," a "light from above" beamed, pointing out to him "in a very explicit manner the duty of submitting to decided Quakerism, more particularly to the humbling sacrifice of [so ran the Quaker phrase] plainness of speech, behaviour and apparel."[2] After a time he found himself able to record that he "was now plainer in dress and using Friends' language in part" (Life, i. 77).[3] Then he is doubtful whether it was not his duty when paying a certain visit to enter the room with his hat on, and at last, before he reached the age of twenty-five, he made the sacrifice. He was engaged, he said, "to a dinner party at the house of one of our first county gentlemen"; and for three weeks before it he was in great agitation as the time for taking his stand came near. Dressed as a Quaker, with his hat on his head, he entered the drawing-room, shook hands with his hostess and then deposited his hat in the hall. This he did shortly afterwards when visiting the Bishop of Norwich. It was well understood that the courteous gentleman, as he was throughout his life, had, in his loyalty to conviction,

---

[1] About the same time her cousin, Elizabeth Chapman Gurney (afterwards Backhouse), underwent a similar struggle at the age of twenty-one (Journal, c. ii.). For further details about the Gurney family see an article entitled "On Turning Plain," Journal of the Friends' Historical Society, xxii. (1925), p. 25, and R. M. Jones, Later Periods, pp. 350 f. The attitude of conservative Friends is seen in An Address to the Youth of Norwich, written by Joseph Phipps, of that city, in 1776.   [2] Post, p. 296.

[3] This progress in the way of "plainness" is seen in other lives. Joseph Bevan Braithwaite, who from a boy had worn the distinctive Quaker garb, in 1843, at the age of twenty-five, adopted the stiff white cravat as a further mark of the desire to appear as a "consistent Friend" (Life, p. 94). For an insight into the agony of the struggle and the joy of victory see the stories told in the (Philadelphia) Friend (xxi.) First Month 29, 1848, p. 150, reprinted in the British Friend 1848, p. 71. See Letters of John Barclay (1841), pp. 56–57.

intended no discourtesy; but the fact that he had definitely taken his stand as a Quaker cut him off from further invitations to dinner. As we exercise our imagination to sympathize with the motive of the young man, cultured and fine minded and appreciative of good society, we shall think less of the eccentricity and more of our indebtedness to him and many others who, by their faithful travel in a hard way, won for their religious society a character which it has not worn out. Nevertheless the particular form in which this faithfulness was manifest, the emphasis on rules of outward conduct, often degenerated into a worship of externals. The Society of Friends, on a small scale, repeated the history of the Church at large in the ritualistic clinging to relics of its past, when they had come to hinder its present service. We have already noted the warning uttered by Margaret Fox as early as 1700 (p. 180). In early days the plain attire (in the ordinary sense of the word) was, as it is at all times, evidence of sobermindedness and a valuable testimony against extravagance (of fantastic attire in the early days of Quakerism mention has been made)[1] but before long "plainness" came to be identified with the wearing of an antiquated (and therefore conspicuous) coat or bonnet, as if such were in itself inherently good. Any assimilation of the dress to that which at the time was generally worn was branded as "a following of the world's vain fashions."[2] Of this degeneration into empty ritual of what, in its beginning, had been valuable testimony other examples might be given.[3]

But more serious still was a certain line of evasiveness or self-deception which at times came dangerously within sight of hypocrisy. An extraordinarily able pamphlet

[1] P. 122.
[2] P. 294 note.
[3] See R. M. Jones, *Quakers in the American Colonies*, pp. 168–70. The writer is speaking of America, but everything he says is true of England. This story of Quaker attire is continued on p. 293.

issued anonymously in 1859, describing with deep insight the conditions of the Society and condemning the exclusion from office, and even from social fellowship, of those who would not conform to the conventions, calls attention to the harmful outcome of this. A "consistent" Friend must, on his ordinary coat, wear a "plain," that is a stand-up, collar, or no collar as it might be described, and no lapel in front, but to his great-coat the usual turned-down collar and lapel were permitted, the reason given for this being, that they could be turned up as a protection against inclement weather. Hence the writer says, "there are those who find themselves glad to have their great-coats over their plain collars, and sometimes retain the outer garment far into the spring; those who will not take off their hats in the usual way, but who are generally found at the right time without them." Of this evasiveness he gives other examples.[1]

The interests of historical accuracy, necessary to the completion of our picture, have demanded mention of the less happy side of Quaker development, but Quakerism, though weakened, still possessed too large a measure of truth and strength to be stifled. Arrested as was the growth, and meagre the fruit, the tree was of God's planting and

---

[1] *Nehustan, a Letter Addressed to Friends on their Peculiarities of Dress and Language.* For a savage attack on this see the *British Friend*, 1859, p. 245. The author was Edward Fry (1827–1918), in later life a Lord Justice of Appeal and eminent as an international jurist. He remained a Friend all his life, but in his later years he records that the rigidity which he had witnessed, "the miserable questions about dress and address . . . produced a chasm in my feelings between myself and systematic Quakerism which I have never got over" (*Memoir*, p. 168). The extreme of ritualism pure and simple was seen in the coat, worn by some, which, though indistinguishable from most points of view from the ordinary coat, technically satisfied the convention of "plainness" in that at the back there were a few inches of collar which stood up straight, not turning over. An uncle of mine, in 1853, at the age of eleven, went to Ackworth School wearing a coat which had a lapel and turned-down collar; these were cut off by order of the authorities.

in His earth it was rooted. The undue absorption in the outward did not supersede the good thing of which it was an exaggeration, the concern of the Friend to follow, in all parts of life, the guidance of his Lord. His "faithfulness in the little," often to his own loss, might slip into triviality, and his conscientiousness into over-scrupulousness, but when once he was convinced of the right thing for him he simply did it.[1] The rigid peculiarity might drive numbers from the Society, but to many who remained, crippled as they allowed themselves to be, it imparted sturdiness of character. The man or woman determined to pay deference to the world's conventions, in terror of differing from them, is useless for moral enterprise, and the indifference of Friends to the world's censure trained them to step out as pioneers of worthy causes without waiting to make sure of any large band of followers. In fact, the Christian, whether Quaker or another, is ever called on to bear himself in the world of men as a citizen of the heavenly country, not in the isolation of indifference to the world, and still less of scorn, but in the isolation of love continually misunderstood. "We love all men and women," wrote Fox, "simply as they are men and women and as they are God's workmanship and so as brethren."[2] Not necessarily in outward garb is the Christian called on to be marked off from others, but certainly in his service, and, deeper still, in his attitude of mind. A pioneer, not satisfied with confirming his community in the level which it has reached, but calling it to a higher plane, he will be in a minority, drawing on

[1] An example of extraordinary scrupulousness is seen in the action of a Friend whom I remember. Whenever he sent a note by hand, in order to be above suspicion to himself of defrauding the Post Office, he tore up a penny stamp. (At that time the stamp on a letter was a penny.) He it was who wrote the letter to John Bright mentioned *post*, p. 285. Another in his diary records his apprehension of having, on a certain occasion, made too low a bow on greeting some of his acquaintance.   [2] *Gospel Truth Demonstrated (Doctrinals)*, p. 521.

himself hostility as soon as his purpose is apparent. The speech of the pilgrims on their way to the Celestial City is always strange to the dwellers in Vanity Fair.[1]

When, as will be shown later, the outward conventions of Quakerism were rather suddenly broken down and the usages of ordinary society came flooding in, a natural reaction from artificiality and strictness led to an impatience of what was distinctively Quaker, sometimes, even, when this was good; often an over-keen desire for conformity with the world claimed credit for the avoidance of narrowness. Whittier, the American Quaker poet, knew better than this as he gave counsel to a youth asking what he should do in life: "Join thyself to some unpopular but noble cause." As a matter of fact Quaker philanthropic and social activity, soon to be described, has often had an instinct for passing by movements that were popular or fashionable, and addressing itself to needs that were otherwise being overlooked. In this department of life, as in their business enterprise, Friends have often been among the first in the field.[2]

The eighteenth century was not, as is sometimes supposed, devoid of spiritual activity; on the contrary, there was a certain amount of propaganda, books were published and old ones reprinted, ministers travelled throughout the country, Friends from several counties would come together at one place and hold meetings to which the public were invited. At the conference of the four Northern Counties held at Chester in 1717, nearly four thousand people met together on a week-day afternoon. At the

---

[1] "The true peacemaker . . . must be an active and resolute guardian of the peace, who so bears himself in the world that all the powers of evil are sure to try to bear him down both by violence and by misrepresentation" (Oman, *Grace and Personality*, 2nd edn., 1919, p. 103; 3rd edn., 1925, p. 109).   [2] See *post*, p. 215.

"Circular Meeting" of the Western Counties held at Coventry in 1749, nearly two thousand people were present at three meetings held simultaneously; and continually the reports of these assemblies make mention of the attendance of the townspeople and of their satisfaction with the proceedings. It would seem that at these times Friends made collections for the poor of the place in which they met, this was done at Rugby in 1735 and at the meeting of the north-western counties held at Penrith in 1757, twenty-five pounds was collected and paid "to the parson and parish officers" for the relief of the poor "in these dear and scarce seasons."[1] At these gatherings Quaker literature was freely distributed. But while all this activity advertised the existence of Friends and (apart from some unsatisfactory features) gained respect for them, it had small success in winning converts. There was no concentration of effort; the "Circular Meeting" referred to was held in each county but once in seven years, and the thought of following up the work by means of shepherding or teaching was alien to the genius of eighteenth-century Quakerism. Before the end of the century these meetings were given up.[2]

An indication of the slightness of the Quaker impact on the outside world—a valuable piece of contemporary evidence—comes from Joseph Gurney Bevan, a Friend possessed of classical scholarship and literary ability who

[1] Minutes of Strickland Monthly Meeting, 4, v, 1757; information given by T. Hall Thompson.

[2] For these "Circular Meetings" which played so large a part in the life of the eighteenth century see Braithwaite, *Second Period*, pp. 546–49; R. M. Jones, *Later Periods*, i. 118–20; Brown, *Evesham Friends in the Olden Time*, pp. 149–68; the *British Friend*, 1851, pp. 73, 81; and my chapter in *Handbook to Birmingham Yearly Meeting*, 1908, pp. 56–60. The failure of Friends to follow up the pioneer work, due to their dread of organization of spiritual activity, has often been a cause of weakness. See, concerning pastoral and missionary work, *post*, c. xvii., and R. M. Jones, *Later Periods*, pp. 871–77.

was one of the Society's leaders. Writing in the year 1800, he says:

> We are certainly, compared with the millions of our countrymen, but few in number; the world in its pursuit of fame, of wealth and pleasure, takes little account of us, and the tracts which on particular occasions have been published by our authors, either to elucidate our doctrines or to defend them, seldom attract notice enough to be much purchased out of the pale of our Society. . . .
> We are just considered as a good sort of people in the main who refuse to fight and swear and to pay tithes; and while the improved manners of the age allow that for these and other singularities we ought not to be molested, the public in general cares little further about us and seldom enquires a reason of the hope that is in us.[1]

The reason for the failure is not far to seek. The Quaker message, so far as it was given in its purity at all, was, as we have seen, clogged by the tradition of the elders concerning matters of outward observance; the would-be convert was virtually required to cut loose from old ties of relationship and friendship, and take up his dwelling behind the hedges enclosing the strange Quaker territory. If he were a "consistent Friend" (and from all who would enter a rigid standard of "consistency" was demanded), his attire and that of his children called down on them the cry of "Quack, quack!" in every street.[2] Pathetic are the

---

[1] *A Refutation of Some of the More Modern Misrepresentations of the Society of Friends*, Introduction and section iii. In 1724 John Bellers wrote: "Not one book in ten of ours is sold to any but Friends" (*An Abstract of George Fox's Advice*, p. 17).

[2] The experience recorded by William Sturge (born 1820) could have been recorded by hundred of others: "I and my brother Henry were dressed as little Quaker scarecrows with collarless jackets and broadbrimmed white beaver hats; we were followed and hooted after in the streets by troops of rude boys crying, 'Quack, quack, quack.' On my complaining of this to my father the only comfort he gave me was that 'it was our duty to suffer persecution for righteousness' sake.' I confess I was not convinced. After a while we were permitted to wear caps such as were then worn by boys of our own age so that our appearance was less peculiar." *Some Family and Personal Records* (privately printed 1896), p. 16. See *post*, p. 298 note.

stories which are still told of the difficulties of Quaker children when they passed beyond the seclusion of their homes.[1] The worship to which he was invited was a meeting of not less than two hours in length, probably held in silence unbroken by word of ministry or prayer. And such ministry as he might hear was often of a rhapsodical nature, verging upon incoherence, if not actually passing over into it, of great length, and marked by strange mannerisms of tone and demeanour which in many quarters had come to be demanded as the sign or outcome of divine inspiration (p. 258). At times, indeed, he might hear a tender or powerful appeal to be faithful to his inward Guide, but, as is said later (p. 223), the element of teaching was absent, and for this no provision was elsewhere made. The story of Quaker ministry is told in later chapters (xv. and xviii.).

But in the darkest days of the Church there has never failed the living remnant. Throughout this time of which we are speaking, the eighteenth century and the first half of the nineteenth, the labours and the lives of thousands of holy men and women saved the fire from dying out.

> The over-emphasis on the outward could not, so long as the Friends' meeting was maintained, altogether supersede the inward way of direct access to God. Side by side with prosy speaking and drowsy silence there was much true waiting upon the Lord, and the fountain of prophetic ministry was not wholly quenched. The inward way could strengthen and illuminate the earnest soul apart from outward helps. Had it been otherwise, the state of the Society, in its Quietist days, would have been destitute indeed. But here was a power that made for growth, in spite of the most adverse environment.[2]

[1] See *post*, p. 298 note.

[2] Braithwaite, *Second Period*, p. 540; and for the power of the Friends' way of worship to save the situation in difficult times see pp. 225 (quoted *ante*, p. 176), 228, 637 of the same.

Chapter XIII

THE EIGHTEENTH CENTURY: PHILANTHROPY: WORK FOR SLAVES: INTERNAL AFFAIRS: THE PEACE TESTIMONY: SOCIAL LIFE

ALTHOUGH there was little success in giving to a sceptical and shallow age a message of spiritual life, the philanthropic activity of Friends never ceased. Such activity was a necessary outcome of their central principle, although in their minds the connection between the two seems to have been subconscious rather than explicit. So far as anyone is convinced that in all men there is a "divine principle," so far is it to him intolerable that grinding poverty or other avoidable cause should put special difficulty in the way of obedience to that principle. A recent work on Church history records the tendency of eighteenth-century thought in the direction of humanitarian feeling,

> but [it continues] the Methodist and Evangelical movement greatly strengthened this and gave it force and direction; and we find the men who represented it, along with members of the Society of Friends, leaders in the attempt to mitigate the poverty and miseries of human life.[1]

Earlier on the writers say: "It was Voltaire, with Fénélon and the Quakers, who was the first apostle of modern humanitarianism."[2] As early as 1653 James Nayler

[1] Bartlet and Carlyle, *Christianity in History*, p. 547.

[2] *Ibid.*, p. 543. Sydney Smith, near the end of an article on the iniquity of sending small boys up chimneys to sweep them, unless the chimneys could not be swept otherwise (*Edinburgh Review*, 1819), says "humanity is a modern invention" (*Works*, i. 279). "Nor were churchmen very prominent in the new humanitarian movement which awoke the sympathies of unbelievers like Voltaire. . . . The humanitarian movement began in the eighteenth century outside the range of clerical influence." W. R. (Dean) Inge, *Christian Ethics and Modern Problems*, p. 275 (edn. of 1930); p. 281 (edn. of 1932).

spoke burning words concerning the oppression of the poor:

> God is against you, you covetous, cruel oppressors who grind the faces of the poor and needy, taking your advantage of the necessities of the poor, falsifying the measures and using deceitful weights, speaking that of your commodities which is not true and so deceiving the simple and hereby getting great estates in the world, laying house to house and land to land till there be no place for the poor, and when they are become poor through your deceits then you despise them and exalt yourselves above them, and forget that you are all made of one mould and one blood and must all appear before one Judge who is no respecter of persons.[1]

Ten years later William Smith, a Nottinghamshire Friend, in an appeal "To Such as Buy and Sell in Markets or in Any Other Places," condemns the hurt caused by covetous dealers:

> . . . forestalling things before they come into a market, and many times engrossing things into their hands which they have no need of, but to lay them by and keep them for advantage; and this wrongs the poor and the needy, that when things are at a reasonable price then the rich engross them and by that means keep them at a dearer price in plenty than otherwise they would be; and then in scarcity the poor must either buy at their dear prices or be in want; and this grinds the poor every way.[2]

Those who thus act covetously, he says, "are always in the thronged part, and in the cumber about many things."

Many times does Fox exhort friends and others to care

---

[1] *A Discovery of the Wisdom which is from Beneath and the Wisdom which is from Above*, p. 25; in Nayler's *Collected Works* (1716), p. 93, and in the same see pp. 27, 95.

[2] Collected works entitled *Balm from Gilead*, p. 18, the third of the pages so numbered. Some trifling grammatical alterations have been made above. "Ingross" or "engross" had the meaning (now obsolete) of buying up at wholesale price as much of a commodity as possible in order to sell it again at a monopoly price. "Cornering" is the modern word.

for the poor, himself setting the example. Even in his early life he says that he had enough to keep himself and something over for those who were in need. When engaged in his shoemaking trade at Mansfield we read that "he wrought as much as two men and what he did reserve he gave to the poor and did give all his clothes but one suit to the poor when he was in prison."[1] True to his instinct for finding appropriate service for each one, he saw the place of women in the Church's care for the poor, one of the institutions which he set up, the Box Meeting, lasting to the present day. It meets monthly to administer poor relief to women Friends of London and Middlesex Quarterly Meeting. His appreciation of women's work in this direction is seen in the following passage written in 1676:

> There is no believing husband will hinder his believing wife, being heirs of life, to administer some of their temporal things to them that are in necessity; he will not have all the earth to himself, but let her have the disposing of some of it, as well as himself, whilst they do enjoy it; and ministering of outward things is the least love. And women many times know the condition of poor families and widows and such as are in distress more than the men, because they are most conversant in their families and about such things (*Epistles*, p. 387).

This counsel of Fox, relating especially to the care of Friends for their own members, was no more than commendation of a practice already well established. William Crouch, writing of the year 1660, tells of "some ancient

[1] This refers to his imprisonment at Nottingham in 1649. When Fox was working at Mansfield certain slanders about him were current and John Camm and Francis Howgill made investigation into the matter. They reported that "some did confess it who are enemies to him that they could not in all that time hear an idle word with him, nor take him with a lie," then follows the passage above quoted. *An Answer to a Book which Samuel Eaton Put up to the Parliament* [*entitled*] "*Quakers Confuted*," pp. 52–53; 1654.

women Friends" meeting to consider the needs of the poor particularly of the families of imprisoned members:

> They sat not still until the cry of the poor came to their houses, but where they did suppose or discover a want of help their charity led them to enquire into their conditions, and to minister to their necessities (*Posthuma Christiana*, p. 23.)

When Fox was thirty-three years old he told the "priests and professors,"

> . . . that costly apparel with the lace that we formerly had hung upon our backs that kept us not warm, with that we could maintain a company of poor people that had no clothes (*Cambridge Journal*. i. 286).

Thirty-six years later Penn wrote: "The very trimming of the vain world would clothe all the naked one."[1] And the same writer, when he was but twenty-five years old, addressing those who claimed that expenditure on their pleasures was a matter for themselves alone and no concern of others, sets before them a larger view:

> . . . that the sweat and tedious labour of the husbandman, early and late, cold and hot, wet and dry, should be converted into the pleasure, ease and pastime of a small number of men, that the cart, the plough, the thresh should be in that continual severity laid upon nineteen parts of the land to feed the inordinate lusts and delicious appetites of the twentieth, is so far from the appointment of the great Governor of the world and God of the spirits of all flesh, that to imagine such horrible injustice as the effect of His

[1] *Some Fruits of Solitude in Reflections and Maxims* (1693), Pt. i., No. 67 (in some editions, 73). In 1776, Goldsmith (*Vicar of Wakefield*) wrote: "The nakedness of the indigent world may be clothed from the trimmings of the vain." For other quotations from Fox and references to the works of him and of Penn see my *Personality of George Fox*, pp. 48, 49, 51 (edn. of 1918–19); pp. 96–97 (edn. of 1933).

determinations and not the intemperance of men, were wretched and blasphemous.[1]

Elsewhere we find concern for the poor and warning against oppression; from Thomas Lawson, a Westmorland schoolmaster, a proposal for the setting-up of a labour bureau for the unemployed; from Somerset Quarterly Meeting a protest against the payment of wages in kind and not in money.[2] Irish Friends called on shipowners not to send out vessels ill-provisioned and overloaded; and on masters not to bind their apprentices to refrain from setting up in business near them when their time was out.[3] Other similar examples might be given.

It was in this spirit that John Bellers of London, born in 1654, "the first of the long line of great Quaker philanthropists and the pioneer of modern Christian socialism," devised schemes for his country's welfare. Of the children of the street, the "Black Guard," as they were called, he says:

> . . . they are our neighbours, our flesh and blood, our relations, our children, however mean and contemptible they may now appear. They are capable of being saints on earth, and as angels in heaven. How much is owing to birth and education that hath made the difference between them and us? (*Epistle to London and Middlesex Q.M.*, 1718).

Further on he speaks of "the labour of the poor being the mines of the rich."

In 1695, a time when bad harvests and foreign wars were causing stagnation of industry and distress among the labouring classes, he put forth his scheme for "A

---

[1] *No Cross, No Crown*, edn. of 1669, pp. 61–62, or, with wording slightly altered, edn. of 1682, and subsequent edns., Pt. i., c. 18, § 10. The edition of 1682 (the form in which later ones are printed) contains large additions to the work of 1669.

[2] The Truck Act of 1831 made this practice illegal.

[3] Braithwaite, *Second Period*, c. xx.; see the whole chapter.

College of Industry," a labour colony which should also maintain sick and incapable people and educate children. It was found impossible to carry out the scheme on the scale which he planned, but about the end of the century Friends of London and Bristol established in their respective cities "work-houses" for the reception of their own members who were in need, and work was provided for those who were able to do it. In these houses children were educated, and the London institution survives in the boys' and girls' school at Saffron Walden, in Essex.[1]

It was in the eighteenth century that the reputation of Friends for philanthropy and an upright way of life became firmly established. We have already noticed (p. 196) their characteristic act of making a collection for the poor at the time of the "Circular Meeting" held at Rugby and of a similar gathering at Penrith. In days of highway robbery, while the banking system was yet in its infancy, people, rather than carry their money with them, insisted on leaving it in the hands of Friends from whom it was due; others also entrusted money to them, and gradually in this way many Quaker banks grew up.[2] Enjoying the confidence of their neighbours, Friends were continually appealed to by those who were in need, and they showed themselves ready to answer to the call. It may be noted that their philanthropic activity has never been

[1] Concerning John Bellers (1654–1725) see Braithwaite, *Second Period*, Index; *John Bellers, Quaker, Economist and Social Reformer*, A. Ruth Fry; *Authority in Church and State (ante*, p. 165), Belasco.

[2] William Stout records in his *Journal* (p. 8), under the year 1680, concerning his Quaker master, Henry Coward, a grocer and ironmonger at Lancaster, "His credit was so much that any who had money lodged it with him to put out to interest or make use of." This was in a time of persecution, when Coward was at any time liable to imprisonment or to have his goods distrained. Most of the Quaker banks have been amalgamated with others; but the Quaker names Barclay and Lloyd survive.

undertaken with the object of drawing converts into the Society, and only to a small extent has it done so.

It must, however, be recognized that at this time there was but small knowledge of economic science, and while Friends were eager to alleviate poverty, they had little concern to investigate the causes of it. In this respect they appear to have had less insight than was shown by Fox, Penn and Bellers of an earlier day. Toward the end of the eighteenth century the social reformer may well have felt himself bewildered by the new conditions of life, and helpless to stem the tide of misery due to the dislocation of industry caused by the introduction of machinery and the rise of the factory system, but in their efforts for alleviation Friends showed no slackening of activity, giving liberally of their money and of their personal service. In the earlier part of the nineteenth century some of them were the helpers of Elizabeth Fry in her work for prison reform,[1] and of Joseph Lancaster (also one of their number) in the establishment of a system of public elementary education; they were interested in the abolition of capital punishment in the foundation and work of the Bible Society and in various movements directed to the uplifting of the people.[2]

[1] Much as Elizabeth Fry's work was admired, it stirred, in certain quarters, ridicule and hostility, as all good work does. Sydney Smith, having on one occasion accompanied her to Newgate, spoke in one of his sermons enthusiastically of what he had seen, but in a letter he says that with most of the clergy she was very unpopular: "we long to burn her alive" (*Life*, by Russell, p. 85). This was in 1818, and in 1819 he speaks of those "into whose heart Mrs. Fry has struck the deepest terror," scenting, as they did, revolution in all attempts to raise the condition of the poor (*Works*, i. 279, and see 331). In the earlier editions of this present work a certain cartoon of 1824 is wrongly stated to be an attack on Elizabeth Fry. It is described and put in its right place in the footnote on p. 206.

[2] "In 1819 there were 180 crimes punishable by death, but from 1838 the death sentence was executed practically for murder only. There are numerous references to the work of Friends in the card catalogue in the Friends' Library" (*Journal of the Friends' Historical Society*, xiv. (1817), p. 190). Samuel Gurney (1786–1856), a brother of

Nevertheless, at this time Friends became unpopular by reason of a widespread belief that in the wholesale market they manipulated the price of wheat to their own advantage and to the impoverishment of the community at large. In 1800 the Meeting for Sufferings put out a denial of these charges, expressing a hope that Friends might be freed "from the insults which they have long patiently borne." It would seem that the suspicion was not allayed; in 1816, J. S. Fry published a pamphlet, *Letters on the Corn Trade*, denying that there was any manipulation of prices and pointing out that, as the law of import duties then stood, large fluctuations were likely to occur. This pamphlet called down further indignation, notwithstanding a certain passage in it, expressed, as the Quaker custom was, in the way of cautious understatement:

> How far as Christians we ought to compensate that class of our fellow creatures to whom we are indebted, not only for the bread we eat but for every luxury we enjoy, at such a rate as will barely keep them in existence, is a question that I hope will hereafter be both better considered and better understood than it is at present.[1]

Joseph John Gurney, a banker, became extremely unpopular and was in danger of a prosecution for letting a forger go free, knowing that conviction would involve the death penalty. His action had great influence in bringing about an alteration of the law (Mrs. Geldart, *Memoirs of Samuel Gurney*, pp. 36–37).

[1] P. 25 note. In 1824 there appeared a cartoon (a copy of which is in the Friends' Library) which in earlier editions of this work is wrongly stated to be an attack on Elizabeth Fry. It clearly refers to this pamphlet of J. S. Fry; it depicts a woman in Quaker dress behind the counter of a pawnshop into which wretched creatures are coming. A man, clad only in his shirt, offers a pair of torn trousers, saying, "My poor Wife and Fry have not had a bit of victuals these two Days"; a child asks for sixpence on a Frying pan. The cartoon is entitled, "The New Combination Pawnbroking Company, Dedicated to the Quakers, Jews, Heathens, Incendiaries, Usurers and Monopolists, a goodly Fry." In the Friends' Library see in the card index, "Corn Trade, Friends," and also Isabel Grubb, *Quakerism and Industry before 1800*, pp. 124 ff., and Braithwaite, *Second Period*, p. 564 note.

But although their training disposed Friends to various works of mercy, the Society officially took no cognizance of their doings except in one direction—the suppression of the slave trade and of slavery. As will be shown later, their work in his direction had its far-reaching effect by reason of its bringing them into contact with the wider world beyond their own borders.

Before they were enlightened as to the iniquity of the system in itself they were concerned for the well-being of the slaves. In 1671, George Fox, visiting the West Indies on his way to America, gave counsel to treat them with kindness, to give them religious teaching, to admit them to worship and after thirty years to set them free. For admitting them to their meetings Friends were heavily fined, and on account of their general attitude towards the slaves some of them were expelled from the islands in which they lived. In 1688, some German Friends of Philadelphia urged upon their Yearly Meeting the inconsistency between the principles which they professed and slave-holding in any form. In the eighteenth-century the labours of John Woolman, Anthony Benezet and others brought about the decision of the Society in America to disown any member who held slaves, and to educate the children of those who had been set free. Beyond this, before 1760 many Friends of Pennsylvania paid compensation to their freedmen for years of unpaid work and that State was the first to pass an abolition law. This was done in the course of the War of Independence after political power had passed away from Friends. By the end of the century Friends in America stood clear of slavery.[1]

In 1727, London Yearly Meeting condemned slave-trading, and in 1761 decided that all members concerned

[1] See "Slavery," Index to *The Quakers in the American Colonies*, R. M. Jones; and *Southern Quakers and Slavery*, by S. B. Weeks.

in the traffic should be disowned. In 1783, Friends formed among themselves a society for the abolition of the trade the first to be formed in England for this purpose, and in the same year, at the instigation of Philadelphia, they presented to the House of Commons the first petition which it received on the subject.[1] Lord North, the Prime Minister, while expressing sympathy with their object, said that the trade had become "in some measure necessary to almost every nation in Europe," and that "it would be next to an impossibility to induce them to give it up and renounce it for ever." Four years later a public society was founded, the executive committee consisting of twelve members, nine of whom were Friends. Among the leaders outside the borders of Quakerism were Granville Sharp, President of the Society, Thomas Clarkson and Wilberforce, whose influence won the support of many English churchmen. The Nonconformists, particularly John Wesley and the Methodists, also took keen interest in the movement, Wesley himself being strengthened in his protest by a book written against slavery by Anthony Benezet, the American Friend already mentioned.[2] It was this same work, *Some Historical Account of Guinea*, that drew the attention of Clarkson also to the iniquity of the traffic so that he became the first outstanding English leader of the campaign for its abolition.[3] In

[1] Concerning the large part taken by American Friends in inducing English Friends to enter on a campaign against the traffic see a pamphlet (reprinted from "The Friends' Quarterly Examiner," Seventh Month, 1933), *Colonial Quaker Antecedents to British Abolition of Slavery*, by Henry J. Cadbury.

[2] *A New History of Methodism*, Townsend, Workman and Eayrs, i. 225. "Nonconformists generally—though in this matter Quakers wear the brightest crown—supported the crusade of Clarkson and Wilberforce for the abolition of the slave trade" (H. W. Clark, *History of English Nonconformity*, ii. 320). In 1780, Wesley induced the Methodist Conference to pass a resolution severely censuring any member who had an interest in the trade.

[3] Brookes, *Friend Anthony Benezet*, pp. 100–101. For the influence of the book on Wesley see pp. 84–85.

1807, an Act of Parliament was passed forbidding British subjects to be concerned in the slave trade, and Friends and others then turned their attention to the abolition of slavery itself in the British dominions. Another thirty years were to pass before victory was won.

The internal history of the Society during this period presents few points of interest, but one constitutional enactment of far-reaching importance claims our attention.

In 1737, the Society adopted a policy which came to be known as that of "birthright membership." From its earliest days it had cared for its poorer members in order to save them from seeking relief outside its borders, and naturally this practice brought applications for help from some who, if not actual impostors, had small claim to it. In 1659, Fox cautioned Friends to "keep in discerning, that ye may not be ensnared nor made a prey upon."[1]

From the beginning, and particularly from the time that they had been more distinctly marked off from the world, there had been a certain understanding as to who were "Friends," but at last (after several attempts to meet the difficulty) there were drawn up definite rules concerning membership in order that each meeting might have knowledge of those whom it was bound to help in time of need. Registers of birth had always been kept and now it was provided that the membership of children should follow that of their parents, the children being thus admitted into the Society without having in later life to make any further application or profession. One result of this policy has been the retention of a merely technical membership by many who for years have ceased to join with Friends in worship or to show any interest in the Society. Some, in fact, have never done

[1] *Epistles*, p. 136; and see pp. 75, 290 of the same.

O

so in their lives. Hence, when any statement is made about a "Quaker," (as, for instance, that he has joined the army)[1] it is necessary, in order to reach a just conclusion, to know whether or not his "Quakerism" consists, solely or mainly, in the fact that at his birth his name was put on the list of members and has never been taken off.[2]

Of the events of the eighteenth century two in particular demand mention, the founding of the school at Ackworth and of the Retreat at York. From early days Friends had been concerned for the education of their children according to their own way of life, and numerous schools were kept by private individuals. In 1671, there were at least fifteen Quaker boarding schools in England, care being taken for girls as well as for boys. Three years before this, Fox had had set up a boys' and girls' school at Waltham, and also one at Shacklewell, Hackney, "to instruct young lasses and maidens in whatsoever things were civil and useful in the creation."[3] Though himself a man of little education, he says:

[1] This point turned up frequently in the time of the Great War, 1914–18, but besides the birthright Friends who joined up there were a number who of their own accord had come into the Society from outside. See *post*, p. 328.

[2] See *post*, p. 215, concerning the French War. On the establishment of "birthright membership" see *London Yearly Meeting During 250 Years*, pp. 34–37, and *Historical Notes on Membership in the Society of Friends*, by W. C. Braithwaite, also the attitude of John Stephenson Rowntree, *post*, p. 289. With regard to the membership of children, these rules of 1737 did little more than ratify existing custom. For the benefit of those who ask (as many do) why the names of those who for years have appeared to set no value on their membership are not removed from the list, it may be stated that not only do the individuals themselves generally object to be "dissociated" (the technical term), but their relatives, who may themselves be active Friends, often show reluctance to the proposal, cherishing the hope that the tie, formal as it has become, may keep the way open for the individual to come back.

[3] Cambridge *Journal*, ii.119 and (in less racy wording) *Journal* bi-cent. edn., ii. 89.

. . . I would not have any to think that I deny or am against schools for the teaching of children the natural tongues and arts whereby they may do natural things,

but he goes on to say that, beyond this, "all must come to the spiritual school of Christ " (*Gospel Truth Demonstrated*, p. 653).

In 1695, the assembly known as "Bristol Yearly Meeting"[1] set forth a noble ideal of education:

> This meeting do desire that where Friends can they would get such schools and schoolmasters for their children as may bring them up in the fear of the Lord and love of His truth, that so they may not only learn to be scholars but Christians also, and that all parents will take the same care at home that such reproof, instruction, counsel and and example may be constantly continued in their respective families, that so from the oldest to the youngest truth may flow itself in its beauty and comeliness to God's glory and all His people's comfort.

In the same year London Yearly Meeting encouraged the setting up of as many schools as possible and recommended that "schoolmasters, as much as may be, sometimes correspond one with another for their help and improvement in such good and easy methods as are most agreeable to the Truth and the children's advantage and benefit." In 1704, Lancashire Quarterly Meeting gave similar advice. And even after the lapse of more than two hundred and fifty years since they were written certain counsels of Penn, himself among the men of highest learning in England, cannot fail to bring inspiration to educationists of the present day.[2]

[1] This was a meeting similar to the "Circular Meetings" described *ante*, pp. 195–196.

[2] *Address to Protestants*, Part i., sect. 9. *Maxims*, Part i., Nos. 4 ff., and his letter written to his wife and children just before his first voyage to America, 1682; see Janney, *Life of Penn*, p. 197.

In the course of the years 1700 to 1738 the Yearly Meeting impressed on its members no fewer than twenty-seven times the duty of greater attention to the education of youth,[1] and at last, in 1779, John Fothergill, a Friend of wide philanthropic activity and an eminent London doctor founded at Ackworth, in Yorkshire, for boys and girls, the school which became the model for a number of others, either reconstructed or newly founded in later years.[2]

The Retreat, of which mention has been made, was opened in 1796, for the reception of the insane, the first asylum in England, almost the first in the world, where these were treated with humanity and where enlightened effort was made for their recovery. Its founder was William Tuke, a York tea-dealer, who had stood by Dr. Fothergill in his work for Ackworth School. More than twenty years later, when close upon ninety years of age, he proposed the establishment of the boys' school at York. In his work of commencing the Retreat and of watching over its early years he received help from his son Henry and his grandson Samuel, the son of Henry. In 1811, Samuel Tuke wrote an account of a visit paid by himself to a workhouse in the south of England where in narrow cells he had found insane women without clothes, and men chained to posts. In 1814, Sydney Smith gave a description of the Retreat and of the methods used in it as if they were peculiar to Friends:

> . . . The great principle on which it appears to be conducted is that of kindness to the patients. It does not appear to them [the Quakers] because a man is mad on one

---

[1] Taken from the second of five papers prepared by Samuel Tuke of York for the Friends' Educational Society, 1838–42, bound up in *Sketch of the History of Education in the Society of Friends*, p. 31 (edn. of 1871); and see pp. 32–34.

[2] See *Dr. John Fothergill and his Friends*, by Dr. R. Hingston Fox.

particular subject, that he is to be considered in a state of complete mental degradation, or insensible to the feeling of kindness and gratitude.

*   *   *   *

They have set an example of courage, patience and kindness . . . which we are convinced will gradually bring into repute a milder and better method of treating the insane.[1]

In 1669, Fox advised Friends "to provide a house for them that be distempered, and not to go to the world" (*Epistles*, p. 287).

In certain ways during the eighteenth century Friends came into conflict with the law. We have noted (p. 163) that in early days a number were fined or imprisoned for keeping a school without a bishop's licence, and in the early part of the new century this form of persecution was continued. In 1714 there was passed the Schism Act apparently intended to define more precisely or otherwise strengthen the laws already existing. It confined secondary education to Anglican teachers licensed by the bishops and with keen interest Friends watched the passage of it through Parliament. A minute of the Meeting for Sufferings[2] stated that inasmuch as the teaching of Latin and Greek was in itself no crime, the Act could have no object but to harry the Nonconformists, and, after stating that many Friends were employed in teaching, the minute continues:

> Whereas in these employments our Friends were sometimes disturbed both before the Act of Toleration and since,

[1] From an article entitled "Mad Quakers" in the *Edinburgh Review* of 1814; *Collected Works*, i. 228, 233. Sydney Smith was at the time vicar of Foston, near York, but before the parsonage was built he lived at Heslington, York, near the Retreat. The history of the Retreat is told in *A Retired Habitation*, by H. C. Hunt.

[2] 19th of Fifth month, 1714: at the time July was the fifth month (Old Style).

yet the Lord was pleased to support them as we hope he will all such now who shall have faith to stand in the day of trial, and therefore we cannot advise any for fear of the penalty to decline [give up] their schools for that seems to us dishonourable and not a just vindication of our natural rights and liberties in directing the education of our own children.

Nevertheless, shortly after the death of Queen Anne the Whigs came into power, the Act was never enforced, and was repealed in 1718. Even after this, however, there were a few prosecutions on the strength of certain other Acts that remained in force. Furthermore, the refusal to pay tithes caused many to suffer distraint of goods and a few to be imprisoned; others, again, were imprisoned for refusing to serve in the militia. Of this some instances occurred even after an Act of 1762, which provided that for a Friend who refused to serve, the authorities might hire a substitute and reimburse themselves for the expense by distraint on the Friend's goods.[1] Apart from legal prosecution on these accounts, the determination not to comply with the custom of putting lights in windows on the occasion of naval or military victories brought down on Quaker houses the attacks of the mob. A minute of the "Morning Meeting" of March 1760 sets forth the position in referring to the testimony of the early Friends:

As they could not join with others in shedding the blood of their fellow-creatures, neither could they be one with them in rejoicing for the advantages obtained by such bloodshed; as they could not fight with the fighters, neither could they triumph with the conquerors.

[1] An Act of 1778 provided that anyone claiming to be a Quaker must procure a certificate to that effect signed by two Quaker householders. In 1809 John Donbavand and another Ackworth Master, along with two Pontefract Friends, suffered a month's imprisonment at Wakefield for failure to provide substitutes.

Their testimony for peace was many times sorely tried, and it was not surprising that in the French wars some of them joined the army. It is not known how many of them did so, but probably the membership of most who took this course was no more than nominal, being simply due to their Quaker parentage.[1] The Yearly Meeting Epistle of 1804 contains an uncompromising statement of the Society's position:

> It is an awful thing to stand forth to the nation as the advocates of inviolable peace, and our testimony loses its efficacy in proportion to the want of consistency in any.

In the commercial life of the country Friends came to play an important part, their shrewdness and their ability to take an independent line of action leading them to become pioneers in many important enterprises. Of this perhaps the most conspicuous example is the support given by members of the Pease family to George Stephenson in the early days of his railway career. Edward Pease (1767–1858) has been called "the father of railways."[2] The reputation for strict uprightness deservedly survived some financial failures (such failures involving expulsion from the Society), but an over-absorption in business, coupled with the Quaker isolation from the world in other respects, led to a narrow outlook on life.

Throughout all this time there was within the borders

---

[1] See *ante*, pp. 209–210, on birthright membership.

[2] See *The Diaries of Edward Pease*, edited by Sir Alfred Pease, and *Journal of the Friends Historical Society*, xvii. (1920), 132. In the same number are given other examples of Friends being pioneers, p. 113 note 1; and p. 118 "Benjamin Huntsman (1704–76) and the Casting of Steel." See *ante*, p. 184 note 4, George Bradshaw; and p. 204, and also a set of articles entitled, "Leading the Way," begun in *Journal of the Friends' Historical Society*, xix. (1922), 49, and continued in later (not always consecutive) numbers.

of the Society itself a deep social fellowship widespread; a *camaraderie*, a "free-masonry" it might be called, born of a common tradition deep rooted in the past and of associations formed by many and complicated relationships. At all periods of its history, the present included, this social life had been fostered by the coming together of Friends from different places in order to attend the Monthly, Quarterly and Yearly Meetings, and, in recent times, the lecture schools of which mention will be made later. It is part of the normal life of a Friend, whatever his position, to have frequent intercourse with those who come from meetings, towns or villages other than his own. The effect of this has been described by a writer speaking of America, but in words entirely applicable to England and Ireland:

> The reader who has imagination will easily see the social importance of these gatherings. Friends from widely sundered regions, persons of different social standing, of all stages of education and spiritual experience, thus came together . . . were entertained at the homes in the locality where the meeting was held, interchanged ideas, and formed, almost without knowing it, a "group consciousness" which played a powerful rôle in the life of the Society.[1]

These gatherings, instrumental in frequently bringing together relatives from different places, contributed to a delightful family affection. Clarkson, the leader against the slave trade, being often brought into intimate social relations with Friends, wrote, in 1806, his *Portraiture of Quakerism*, presenting them in the most favourable light, and not infrequently he touches upon the home life. He notes that they, more than others, recognized relationships

---

[1] R. M. Jones, *Quakers in the American Colonies*, p. 143; and see *London Yearly Meeting During 250 Years*, pp. 62–63. Concerning the social influence of the lecture schools see *post*, p. 317.

to distant degrees, calling one another "Cousin" if no nearer word were appropriate.[1] He admits that their manners were not those of polished society, but he says much of their simple courtesy to guests, its *sincerity* putting them at ease to a rare extent. Their custom, he says, was to invite their guest "to be free," and they were "particularly gratified" when he, by asking for what he wanted, and in other ways, took them at their word (i. 362–63).

> No Society [he wrote] has probably so many of the comforts of life in its power, number for number and rank for rank, as that of the Quakers; none, probably so wholly domestic; none where the members of it have such frequent intercourse with each other or where they are so connected in the bonds of brotherly love; and none, as far as I know men, who have such constant employment for their time (iii. 305).

It is true that their interests were confined within narrow bounds: like other Nonconformists, they were shut out from the universities and practically from public office; from their lives they banished art and music and a large part of literature; but, nevertheless, there was in certain families a good level of literary culture and even of classical scholarship. The instruction was gained from tutors resident in the homes of Friends. More particularly in the pursuit of natural history and of science, many of them found recreation, so that "even among those in moderate circumstances it was common to find an intellectual man of high scientific attainments serving behind his own counter."[2] In these branches of knowledge and in

---

[1] Vol. iii. p. 304. Concerning Clarkson, see *ante*, pp. 187 note, 208.
[2] Godlee, *Lord Lister*, p. 9. Isaac Sharpless, speaking of the mediocre standard of education among Pennsylvania Friends in early days, says: "The number of self-educated mathematicians and naturalists (chiefly botanists) who grew up among them was rather

medicine the Society has contributed to England far more than its fair quota of eminent men, though it is necessary to complete the story by recording the fact that a number of these, as they found their place in the wider world, passed out from the conventional and narrow Quakerism of their day.[1] The fact of their intercourse with distinguished persons outside the Society exposed them to a suspicion which virtually excluded them from it.[2]

This seclusion was bound to come to an end. But before beginning the story of barriers broken down, we

remarkable" (*A Quaker Experiment in Government*, p. 36). Concerning the tree-planting activity of Thomas Story, see Braithwaite's *Second Period*, pp. 424-25.

[1] On this subject see *Dr. John Fothergill and his Friends; Chapters in Eighteenth Century Life*, by Dr. R. Hingston Fox; and *The Life of Peter Collinson*, by N. G. Brett-James. Collinson (1693-1768) was one of the leading botanists of England, and was partly responsible for the rapid growth of Kew Gardens. Mention may also be made of Lord Lister (1827-1912), the pioneer of antiseptic surgery, and of Thomas Young (1773-1829), eminent as a writer on medical subjects and as a physicist, his researches in optics doing much to establish the wave theory of light. He was also an authority on life assurance and was one of the first to decipher Egyptian hieroglyphics. Both Lister and Young ceased to be Friends. Luke Howard (1772-1864, *post*, p. 226 note), who first classified clouds (*cirrus, cumulus*, etc.), "the father of meteorology," was a Friend, but left the Society under strong evangelical influence. John Dalton (1766-1844), eminent in chemistry as establishing the atomic theory, remained a Friend all his life. William Philips, a Fellow of the Royal Society, was one of the founders of the Geological Society (1807). For a list of Friend members of the Royal Society from its beginning up to the year 1910 (there have been subsequent additions) see *Journal of the Friends' Historical Society*, vii. 30, 45. For eighteenth and early nineteenth century family and social life see *Records of a Quaker Family, the Richardsons of Cleveland*, by Anne O. Boyce; *The Diaries of Edward Pease*, edited by Sir Alfred Pease; *Unhistoric Acts*, by George Baker; *The Gurneys of Earlham*, by Augustus J. C. Hare; the early part of *J. Bevan Braithwaite, a Friend of the Nineteenth Century; My Ancestors*, by Norman Penney; *The Eliot Papers*, by Eliot Howard; *Isaac and Rachel Wilson, Quakers of Kendal*, 1714-85, by John Somervell; the latter part of *Life of William Savery of Philadelphia* (1750-1804), by Francis R. Taylor; *A Quaker Journal, The Diary of William Lucas of Hitchin; Mary Howitt*, an autobiography edited by her daughter; and *Dr. John Fothergill*, above mentioned.

[2] See Rufus M. Jones, *Later Periods of Quakerism*, ii. 770.

may read the description of this middle period on its
more attractive side given by a modern writer:

> The English Friend in the latter part of the [eighteenth]
> century was educated, sometimes cultured; a man of truth,
> whose sober integrity in business was proverbial, and led
> to the acquisition of wealth. Debarred from public life, he
> was active in works of benevolence; and although he had
> little missionary zeal, yet the preaching of "public Friends,"
> alternating as it were with the frequent silent meetings,
> sought and found an audience amongst the public outside
> his borders. He did not add to his numbers, nor did he
> seek to do so, but he exercised an influence in the growth
> of spiritual religion. Many yet prize the memories of the
> old-fashioned Quaker household—for the type lasted into
> the next century—with its atmosphere of calm and sweet-
> ness, due to an indefinable sense of reserve and of quiet
> stability in its members; the outsome of what was called
> "recollection" in silence, of habitual prayer and of faithful-
> ness in little things. The garb and the language were sym-
> bols of a type of spiritual refinement unique in its way.[1]

[1] *Dr. John Fothergill and his Friends* (pp. 259–60), by Dr. R.
Hingston Fox. The word "recollection" or "re-collection" is
expressed by the French *recueillement*, a collected or "gathered"
frame of mind, as Friends expressed it.

Chapter XIV

THE NINETEENTH CENTURY: EMERGENCE FROM SECLUSION: RELIGIOUS TEACHING: THE EVANGELICAL MOVEMENT: JOSEPH JOHN GURNEY [1]

THE new world ushered in by the French Revolution, the quickening of commercial life, the advent of railways, set in motion currents of thought and energy from which the Quaker community could not stand aloof. But the emergence from their generations of monastic seclusion was fraught with difficulty and, even, pain. Many Friends were uneasy at the mixing of their fellow-members with others outside their borders, even in social and philanthropic enterprises; [2] and the entrance of some into public life caused widespread alarm. [3] The political activities of John Bright and Joseph Sturge called forth from the

[1] Chapters xiv, xv and xvi, as originally prepared for this edition, were found to be too long for insertion in it; they have been typed as they were first prepared and one copy is deposited in the Friends' Library, Friends House, London, another in the Woodbrooke library, Selly Oak, Birmingham, and a third in the library of Bootham School, York.

[2] This fear, of which mention is elsewhere made (*ante*, p. 178; *post*, pp. 221, 300), is seen in a record of the concern of the Yearly Meeting of Ministers and Elders in 1815. "Some tender cautions were given with respect to those benevolent associations in which members of our Society are now so conspicuous. There was a fear in some minds, even while they rejoiced in the spreading of knowledge, the distribution of the Scriptures and the instruction of the poor, lest a danger might secretly lurk in the pleasure received from eloquent speeches and flowing language at the public meetings of these associations; especially lest our dear young Friends should thereby lose their relish for simplicity, and be gradually drawn from the love of silent waiting in our meetings for worship" (*Memoir of Mary Capper*, p. 175).

[3] Concerning the entrance of Joseph Pease into Parliament (*ante*, p. 189) see *The Diaries of Edward Pease*, edited by Sir A. W. Pease, pp. 64–65.

Yearly Meeting of 1843 the caution to its members to "desire ever to be found of those who are quiet in the land; a condition favourable to true Christian patriotism, and in which services highly valuable and useful may be rendered to the community." Those, who, even from philanthropic motives, joined with others in "various objects of a popular nature," some of which "are calculated to bring with them great excitement," were "tenderly invited" to consider the danger of being drawn "into that assimilation with the world which is unlawful to a follower of Christ." After this there follows a warm commendation of private charity toward the poor in the distress then prevailing. In 1852 the *Epistle* expresses its concern that Friends may be a "retiring people."[1] We have already noted (p. 178) the bitter attack on Elizabeth Fry made by an American Quaker journal, and endorsed by the *British Friend*, by reason of her intercourse with highly placed individuals outside the Quaker Church. The Society had travelled far from its early day of joyous adventure. For five generations its outlook had been dominated by fear, and its avowed object had been to make sure of *safety*. It is, however, to be observed that the passages here quoted show a retrogression from the counsel given forth in 1836, cautiously as it is worded:

> The position of our members in connection with the laws which have rendered them eligible for civil offices

[1] The Yearly Meeting Epistle of 1841 contains an exhortation to "watchfulness . . . when taking a public post with others in associations for the purpose of lessening the mass of vice and misery . . . or in work of more extended philanthropy. When we consider the seductive influence of popularity and the self-satisfaction consequent upon the successful efforts of the intellectual powers, even in a good cause, we feel bound, with affectionate earnestness, to caution our Friends against being led to take an undue part in the many exciting objects of the present day." (See the *Epistle* of 1846 and *ante*, pp. 178, 188; *post*, p. 300.

from which they have long been excluded has excited our concern. We are not about to discourage anyone from taking his proper share in those services which, as a member of the community, he may be rightly called to perform, and which do not require or involve a compromise of our, Christian principles. . . . Be especially careful not to yield to the temptation of indulging the love of distinction or of seeking to promote a party.[1]

The cause of the set-back was doubtless the growing agitation of the Chartist movement, particularly the riots of 1842 in Lancashire, Yorkshire and Staffordshire.

Into the religious life also of the Society a new stream began to flow. It has to be admitted that along with all the philanthropic activity there was widespread spiritual lethargy; the maintenance of even essential Quaker testimonies was often little more than acquiescence in tradition, and a bondage to the public opinion of the community paralysed initiative. The early Quaker conception of "Christ within," as giving inward and final assurance of truth, degenerated into such *excessive* stress on the "Inward Teacher," to the exclusion of all outward spiritual help, as to sanction a barren introspectiveness, a "somewhat lazy mysticism" as it has been called;[2] it obscured, as we have seen, the man Jesus of Nazareth and shut out the sense of historic Christianity.[3] In this atmosphere there was a tendency toward neglect of the Bible, notwithstanding repeated official commendation of the private and even family reading of it. A Friend, writing in 1783, said that it was to be desired "that the *frequent* reading

---

[1] This is part of the advice issued by the Yearly Meetings of 1836 but not in "The Epistle." This refers to the repeal in 1829 of the Test Act, passed in the Restoration period, which enacted that members of municipal governing bodies should make profession of conformity with the Church of England.

[2] Graham, *The Faith of a Quaker*, p. 404.   [3] *Ante*, p. 50.

of the Holy Scriptures mentioned in our queries should be understood by us to mean oftener than on one day in the week."[1] In Ackworth School for more than thirty years from the beginning it was read publicly only once a week and many boys and girls had no copy of their own. In 1816, Joseph John Gurney arranged for a copy to be given to each one on his entrance into the school instead of on his departure, as the custom was. It seemed to him that, whilst the pupils were "remarkably sheltered from evil," they were "not positively enough led to good." Accordingly he drew up a scheme of religious teaching, expressing his disapproval of forms of catechism in his desire to encourage attentive reading on the part of each one. "Nor can I," he says, "see the advantage of doing anything superficially."[2] The staff warmly seconded his concern, and a satisfactory increase of Scripture knowledge was the result.[3] A Friend who visited the school in 1819 expressed his uneasiness at what was going on, "these devices of theirs . . . like a great idol . . . set up," giving it as his opinion that regular systematic teaching of Scripture doctrine was incompatible with Quakerism.[4] Another, a personal friend of Gurney, wrote to him concerning a visit which he also paid about the same time in order to

[1] *Letters and Memoirs of Richard Reynolds*, p. 142. Mary Howitt (*post*, p. 226), speaking of the early years of the nineteenth century, says that the Bible was read daily in her home, and her father was appointed to induce other families to adopt the habit: he was unsuccessful (*Autobigraphy*, i. 48).

[2] *Memoirs*, i. 168, 176.

[3] *John Stephenson Rowntree, his Life and Work*, p. 311.

[4] The letter (written by John Barclay) is printed in the *British Friend*, 1853, pp. 196–97. It accords with the attitude of that periodical toward the systematic teaching of Scripture doctrine; see vol. of 1853, p. 67 ("if people cannot understand the Bible and especially if they cannot understand 'certain books' illustrating Bible doctrines and duties, how are they to be so marvellously affected by *oral* 'religious instruction,' on the basis of the Bible though it be?"), also see 1854, p. 178; 1856, p. 146 (top of second column); 1858, p. 292.

see "the thing [that] is very much new among Friends." He confesses to a fear that in injudicious hands this teaching "might have the tendency of drawing our young people from the root of religion in their own experience, to become satisfied with their acquaintance with the principles of Christian Truth stored in the memory," but on seeing it, as it was carried on, he gives it his cautious approval.[1] When the "evangelical" thought of later years gave prominence to the devotional use of the Bible in *united* study the conservative Friends were alarmed at the prospect of human learning and teaching coming in as interference with the Divine leading. At Ackworth in 1858, in accord with a concern of the Yearly Meeting, a company met together for the consideration of (among other matters) "obscure and difficult passages of Scripture," and a letter in the *British Friend* expressed the writer's suspicion of this proceeding as a slight upon the Holy Spirit who, in His own time, would reveal to the faithful reader such meaning as He saw fit.[2] Another writer, "A Young Member" as he signed himself, thus expressed his alarm at the oncoming of Bible study, "if the instructions of the Holy Spirit, as revealed in the secret of the heart, are not sufficient for salvation; if 'the anointing' which abideth in us does not obviate the necessity of human aid, the apostles and our early Friends were manifestly in error."[3]

Nevertheless, a new day was dawning; as early as 1856

[1] *Memoirs of William Forster*, i. 236.

[2] *British Friend*, 1858, pp. 218 (an account of the reading meeting at Ackworth), 307–308 (the objection above mentioned). It was the Yearly Meeting of 1855 that felt the concern alluded to. In Dublin Yearly Meeting of 1859 a Friend said that those who read the Bible in a right spirit would need no teaching of man. For an expression of uneasiness at consultation of commentaries in order to ascertain the meaning of a Scripture passage, see *The Friend*, 1862, p. 189.

[3] *British Friend*, 1861, p. 278. See a reply to this, p. 298, and continuation of the correspondence, 1862, pp. 17–20.

the Yearly Meeting Epistle in cautiously apologetic strain asserted that it might "be freely admitted that the powers of the understanding were given to be employed," not only "upon worldly pursuits and engagements," but also upon "the things of God." In 1861 a large conference called to consider the subject of "Scriptural instruction" could allow a place for group meetings in which the Bible should be read and studied with a view to religious edification, but none for united study of it on the critical or expository sides.[1] This was the attitude of the "progressive' Friends; to the others the very coming together for Bible reading caused alarm as being "devastating inroads" on the religious standing of the Society. One of them speaks of these gatherings as "this new kind of meetings unknown to our fathers in the truth," expressing his belief that they would "directly and indirectly promote the officious meddling of man in his own time and will, with spiritual and Divine things."[2] The objection was due to fear of uninspired intellectual study, particularly united study; a Friend who could speak of these meetings as "a beginning of sorrow" could also advise his son to be regular in his own reading of the Scriptures.[3] Nevertheless the practical working out of this line of thought which has been described was a neglect of the Bible and, not infrequently, a subtle strain of depreciation of it as being "outward" and, therefore, inferior to the "Inward Teacher." It will be impossible for future generations to

[1] From a private letter written by one who was present. The conference was held at Ackworth at the time of General Meeting: *The Friend*, 1861, p. 195; *British Friend*, 1861, p. 183.

[2] Daniel Pickard, *An Expostulation*, etc., p. 101. For more about this book see *post*, pp. 280, 299.

[3] *Diary of John G. Sargent* (1813–83), p. 124 (1863), and p. 285 (1881). This dread of intellectual study of the Bible found considerable expression in the Yearly Meeting of 1861, *The Friend*, p. 141, *British Friend*, 1861, p. 135; and see pp. 69, 91, 112, 173, 183, 200, 297.

realize the intense indignation aroused by any reading of it in a meeting for worship.[1]

This conception of the work of the Holy Spirit as limited to "immediate" inward guidance of the individual (i.e. without human aid) naturally affected the training of the young. Even before the rise of Friends there were those who held that parents ought not to give religious instruction to their children, but to leave them to God alone, since any effort of theirs was interference with Him.[2] To Friends themselves Fox had to give warning of the disastrous effects of their neglect of teaching.[3] The length to which this doctrine could be carried is described by Mary Howitt, the well-known writer, in her story of her

[1] Although the first Friends would use the Bible in public (*ante*, p. 109), a certain uneasiness on this point soon arose. Early in the eighteenth century Samuel Bownas, reporting to a Friend that he had attended a funeral and spoken with his Bible in his hand, received the answer that such a proceeding was in danger of having in it "more of imagination than revelation" (*Life of Bownas*, pp. 26–27). In 1827, Luke Howard, a prominent minister, applied to Tottenham Monthly Meeting for permission to use his Bible in preaching. A Friend in a letter reported that discussion on the matter was twice adjourned but that he did not know the decision. He concludes: "I am surprised they should deliberate so long about it; I think they might soon have decided in the negative, for I believe the Friend is deranged" (*Journal of the Friends Historical Society*, xvii. (1920), p. 104). On one occasion he went into meeting preceded by his negro servant carrying a Bible. His daughter-in-law, the mother of my informant, fainted. He afterwards left Friends. For more about him see *ante*, p. 218 note. This supicion of the Bible in worship was a survival from pre-Quaker times; John Smyth, the Baptist, in 1608, wrote: "We hold that, seeing prophesying is a part of spiritual worship, therefore in time of prophesying it is unlawful to have the book as a help before the eye" (*Works*, ed. Whitley, i. 273; and see 282). Bunyan tells of a woman Friend (whom Quaker records speak of as being injudicious) "who [he says] did bid me in the audience of many 'To throw away the Scriptures.' To which I answered, 'No, for then the Devil would be too hard for me' " (*A Vindication of Gospel Truths*). [2] Edwards, *Gangraena* (*ante*, p. 111), pt. i., p. 34.

[3] *Epistles*, pp. 309, 372, 498, 547, 548, and see an address delivered by Samuel Fothergill in 1769 printed at the end of *A Voice from the Wilderness*, by Sarah Alexander, p. 57; also "Five Papers" written by Samuel Tuke (1838–42) on Quaker Education.

early life. She was born in 1799, and she says that her parents did not allow their children to receive religious instruction either from themselves or from anyone else; they did not, even, teach them the Lord's Prayer, but they required them to learn Robert Barclay's "Catechism and Confession of Faith." This was a compilation of Scripture texts applied to the tenets of Friends and was learned by rote without any explanation being given.[1] In 1802 a Friend called attention to the low standard of education in the Society. He asserted that in this respect it had gone backward, notwithstanding the establishment of Ackworth School, which, after all, made provision for no more than one Quaker child in ten; and he gave it as his opinion that "the present state of schools in the Society, in a general view, is deplorable." To this lack of education he attributed "*the poor and low state of the Society* in a religious sense," of which complaints were being heard from all quarters. He pointed out that Friends' children, as young as four years of age, were compelled to sit in meeting for two hours "without one word of instruction to their receptive minds," and that nowhere else was instruction given, with the result that they were more ignorant of religious knowledge than others were. He added that it was not owing to lack of outward means that Friends were "so listless and supine on the subject of a general plan of education," since at no time had the Society been more opulent.[2] In the succeeding forty years, nine schools were

[1] *Autobiography*, ii. 46–47. Mary Howitt and her husband left Friends and became interested in spiritualism, and later she became · a Roman Catholic. It was doubtless this "Catechism" of Barclay to which Gurney was making reference as mentioned above, p. 223. The story of the resignation from Friends of William and Mary Howitt in 1847 is told by R. M. Jones, *Later Periods of Quakerism*, pp. 769–74; it is instructive as giving a picture of the depressed state of the Society at the time.

[2] George Harrison, *Some Remarks Relative to the Present State of Education in the Society*. It is a short but interesting history of

officially established, some of them reconstructions of older ones, but most of them new.

The story of the effect on ministry of this emphasis on the "Inward Teacher" demands a chapter to itself; for the present we continue our study of the new influences which were modifying the Quaker society.

Early in the nineteenth century the contact of Friends with others, particularly in their work for slaves and prisoners, bringing them within the influence of the Evangelical and Methodist movements, began to open the eyes of many to a sense of Christian felllowship, to the value of the Scriptures and to a new conception of Jesus Christ. This uprising from spiritual inertia into life naturally took the form in which the life had been shown forth, the Evangelicalism which at the time was the most living religious influence in England; and we cannot wonder that many earnest-minded Friends, breaking away from Quakerism as they understood it, embraced the "evangelical" view of the work of Jesus Christ and of the written word of Scripture as in itself the final authority for their faith.[1] One of the most powerful influences to recommend this line of thought was Stephen Grellet, the son of a French nobleman, brought up in a spiritually minded Roman Catholic family and highly educated in the colleges of his religious community. In 1791, at the age of eighteen

Quaker education: the writer says that the Yearly Meeting would be better occupied in seriously facing the problem than in hearing reports from all over the country as to whether Friends were punctual in their attendance at meetings and whether they were drowsy in them. He concludes by saying that the Government ought to concern itself with the right education of every boy and girl.

[1] The story of this change of thought and of the influences that brought it about is told by Rufus M. Jones in *The Later Periods of Quakerism*, c. ix., "Development of Divergent Quaker Views," and by Edward Grubb, *The Evangelical Movement and its Impact on the Society of Friends*, a pamphlet reprinted from the *Friends' Quarterly Examiner*, January 1924, and contained in *Quaker History and Thought*.

he fled from the French Revolution and, after various adventures on the Continent of Europe, he made his way to America. Becoming acquainted with the writings of William Penn, he was drawn to Friends and in Philadelphia he joined the Society. Turning away from attractive business prospects, he occupied himself in teaching French; but at the age of thirty-two he paid the first of four visits to Europe, each of them lasting over some years. In the course of these visits he had interviews with the Pope, with crowned heads and with princes and nobles, he gained access to prisons, hospitals, orphan asylums and schools; and, travelling throughout the British Isles, he brought to Friends a knowledge of the outside world wider than they had previously possessed. His influence everywhere was heightened by great charm of speech and manner. By the religious service of others also on the Continent of Europe in the early part of the nineteenth century was a larger view set before Friends, notably by William Allen, who several times accompanied Stephen Grellet. The travels of Elizabeth Fry, Daniel Wheeler, Thomas Shillitoe and others contributed to the same end. In England also Grellet went beyond the borders of Quakerism: he joined with Elizabeth Fry in her work for prisoners; he persuaded the Meeting of Ministers and Elders to arrange in Westminster meeting house a gathering of depraved men and women; he paid visits to Jews, and in the West End he held meetings among "people of high rank and the nobility." He also met not only with Friends but with those who, for various reasons (unhappily numerous at that time) had been separated from the Society. His influence, particularly his attitude to a division among Friends in America, gave a marked impetus to the Evangelical movement among those in England.[1]

[1] See "Grellet, Stephen," and other names here mentioned, in the Index to R. M. Jones's work, *The Later Periods of Quakerism*.

This American separation of 1827–28, "Hicksite" as it is called, was due to the uneasiness felt by many at the teaching of Elias Hicks, minimizing, as it seemed, the import of the work, and particularly the death of Jesus Christ. He pushed to its farthest extreme the doctrine of the Inner Light, severing it from the rest of man's knowledge and experience, and so far isolating the individual as to hold that to each human being God had given "a complete and sufficient rule of faith and practice without the aid of books or men."[1] A counter-movement in England found expression in *A Beacon to the Society of Friends*, a small book issued in 1835 by Isaac Crewdson of Manchester. He regarded the Scriptures as the final and only authority on religion, counting the Inward Light as a delusive "notion" and denying its universality. Finally he and about three hundred others left the Society, maintaining for a time a separate existence as "Evangelical Friends" but gradually passing to the Plymouth Brethren or the Evangelical Church. The meetings most affected by the movement were Manchester, Kendal, and some in the West of England.[2] It is at first difficult to understand why they left the body which, under the leadership of Joseph John Gurney, was, as we shall see immediately, prepared to adopt a thoroughgoing "evangelical" declaration of faith. It would seem that their reaction against the teaching of Elias Hicks led them to a complete repudiation of the

[1] Taken from R. M. Jones's *Later Periods*, p. 450, and see the whole of c. xii. concerning what was enlightened and what defective in Hicks's teaching. Also see H. G. Wood, *Friends and the Scriptures* (a pamphlet), pp. 15 ff., Grubb, *The Historic and the Inward Christ*, pp. 58 ff., and Mekeel, *Quakerism and a Creed*, Index, "Hicks," "Hicksite."

[2] For an account of this division see Grubb, *Separations: Their Causes and Effects*, and his pamphlet, *The Evangelical Movement and its Impact on the Society of Friends* (*post*, p. 233 note); also R. M. Jones, *The Later Periods of Quakerism* (Index, "Beaconite Movement"), and Mekeel, *Quakerism and a Creed*.

doctrine of the immediate guidance of the Spirit, seeing as they often did, its degeneration into a futile introspectiveness which ignored historic Christianity. An ardent young Friend who speaks of "the great differences among evangelical Friends leaving very little hope for an ultimate union,"[1] caught by the current of the new thought, thus challenges the teaching of early Quakerism, the teaching which, as already stated, was in its day a protest against a merely external standard of spiritual truth:

> With them everything was inward. Their hope was within, their righteousness was within—the blood by which they were cleansed was within—the water by which they were washed was within—their Christ was within—and George Fox even declares that their heaven was within.[2]

As a matter of fact the founders of Quakerism would have repudiated this description, accurate in large measure as it was of eighteenth-century preaching. Isaac Crewdson, weary of exclusive insistence on the doctrine of inward guidance, went so far as to protest against the phrases "sinking down," "centering down," "digging deep," "dwelling deep," "turning inward," pointing out that they were "not the language of Christ and His apostles."[3] Gurney, admitting that these phrases were "somewhat awkward," replied that they were capable of a deeply scriptural meaning, adding that "the want of more depth" and of "a more frequent descent to the wellspring of life" was "one of the greatest and most characteristic dangers of [his] day." Looking back a few years later to his own part

[1] *Life of J. Bevan Braithwaite*, p. 73.
[2] *Ibid.*, p. 71. Braithwaite (1818–1906) contemplated leaving the Society, but attendance at the Yearly Meeting of 1840 changed his views and he became its foremost leader in its definitely "evangelical" period (the 1830's to the 1880's). See Grubb, Introduction to *A Mirror for the Society of Friends* (Hine) p. 19.
[3] *Beacon*, Sermon vi., 2nd edn., p. 112.

in causing Crewdson and his friends to leave the Society, he wrote: "I could not sacrifice the doctrine of the immediate and perceptible guidance of the Spirit as I think they have done practically" (*Life*, ii. 130).

In view of the publication of the *Beacon* near the beginning of 1835 the Yearly Meeting Epistle of that year, along with reiteration of evangelical doctrine, emphasized the teaching of Friends from the beginning.

> [They called] away their fellow-men from a dependence on outward forms to invite their attention to the witness of God in their own bosoms and to set forth the immediate and perceptible operations of the Holy Spirit. It was given them to testify that this divine influence was to be experienced not only in connection with the outward means of religious instruction, but in the striving of the Spirit with a dark and unregenerate world; and in those gracious visitations to the mind of man which are independent of every external circumstance.

This excellent Quaker statement was the occasion of many pamphlets put forth by the *Beacon* party, who were not reassured by the thoroughgoing "evangelical" doctrine of the Scriptures contained in the *Epistle* of the following year. Near the end of that year the separation took place.

Unsatisfactory as was the Society, to those who thus departed, it now, under the leadership of Joseph John Gurney, definitely adopted the orthodox "evangelical" position which it was to retain for half a century. By reason of his social standing, his learning and his Christian character Gurney became the chief influence among Friends in England, Ireland and America. In this atmosphere London Yearly Meeting from time to time officially put forward the "evangelical" view of the total depravity of man, of the work of Jesus Christ for man's salvation, and of the Scriptures as a final authority for religious faith. The doctrinal part of *Christian Discipline* issued in 1861, and again in 1883 as the official declaration of Quaker faith is mainly composed of quotations from the documents of this period and says little of the distinctive message of early days. The few early Quaker passages that are there quoted are selected from such as conformed to the type of thought approved by Gurney and those who held with him.[1] It is, however, important to remember that certain crude or repellent features which have at times been associated with "evangelical" doctrine and preaching have not to any great extent been found among Friends.[2]

There were, however, Friends whose opposition to the *Beacon* was based on more definitely Quaker grounds than those taken by Gurney, and with them also he conducted an animated controversy, claiming that he was taking the right position between repudiation of Quakerism on the one hand and of evangelical Christianity on the other. But the conservative Friends, those who laid the essential Quaker emphasis, not on external authority, but on the supremacy of the Light of God in the soul of man, were unable to put their case clearly. Fearful of "carnal wisdom" as they said, "they could only express themselves in cloudy imagery drawn mostly from the prophets and the Apocalypse. . . . The evangelical message was at least intelligible; the mystical Gospel, though deeper and more penetrating, was expressed in a language that few could understand."[3] At the same time the two sections were united as against the "Hicksites" in their hold on what they regarded

---

[1] Concerning these passages, Fox's statement to the Governor of Barbados, 1671, and the official statement of 1693, see Braithwaite, *Second Period*, pp. 378–79; and on "Formulation of Faith" see all of c. xiv. and the Introduction by R. M. Jones, also Mekeel, *Quakerism and a Creed*, Index, "Barbados." For a criticism of the issue of 1861 see *post*, p. 299.   [2] See *ante*, p. 49 note.

[3] Grubb, *The Evangelical Movement and its Impact on the Society of Friends*, pp. 31–32 in the pamphlet form. See Backhouse concerning allegorical preaching, *post*, p. 258.

as the fundamental doctrines of Christianity. Each of them (the conservative Friends no less than the "evangelical,") believed in the total depravity of man through the Fall, in the propitiatory sacrifice of Jesus Christ and in the infallibility of the Scriptures, equally dreading "any exercise of man's unregenerate reason for their study and elucidation."[1] Between the two, however, there was a difference of atmosphere and emphasis; the "evangelical" Friends "held broadly that the Quaker Gospel was something extra, an addition to or correction of the ordinary orthodox belief"; the conservatives stood for a "redirection of the soul from the outward to the inward."[2]

And while at first each side insisted on the Quaker "peculiarities" of dress and speech, it was an unhappy thing for the Society that the conservative party dissipated its energy by clinging to them more tenaciously and for a longer time than did the others.[3] To its hurt it attracted to itself and even encouraged the mere traditionalists who pitilessly opposed every suggestion of new adventure, disliking, as they did, the call to missionary enterprise and other spiritual service outside the Quaker society, and standing irritated at the disturbing manifestation of earnestness in general which they associated with the evangelical party. It was they whom Samuel Bowley addressed in the Yearly Meeting of 1862 concerning their opposition to home mission work, saying that he had known hours occupied with the consideration of the size and shape of gravestones, while enormous masses of vice and misery were existing all around.[4] As we have seen

---

[1] Grubb (see preceding footnote), p. 31; R. M. Jones, *Later Periods* p. 539, also 514, 531, 869.
[2] Graham, *The Quaker Ministry*, p. 68.
[3] The story of their disappearance is told in c. xvi.
[4] *London Yearly Meeting During 250 Years*, p. 59. The reader will not fully see the point of this till he has reached p. 291.

(p. 178), the early instinct of seclusion led to a habit of repression of new enterprise and thence to an excuse for indolence in the interests of which the exploitation of Quaker principles has always been easy and has often been known. It has always been open to a Friend to make profession of not having received a "call." Many years were to pass before the rise of a generation able to give adequate expression to the Quaker faith, confident in the possession of a message for its own day. The story of this is told later (cc. xviii., xx.).

Chapter XV

THE HISTORY OF QUAKER MINISTRY:
THE FRIENDS' MEETING[1]

IN an earlier chapter (vii.) of this book mention has been made of certain essential elements of Quaker worship, the absence of arrangement and of any appointed leader or conductor of "the service" (an expression not used by Friends in this connection), the freedom for any man or woman to speak or pray, the times of silent worship. Notwithstanding all the risks attendant on them, this freedom and this silence are among the most cherished possessions of Quakerism.[2] Essential, however, to the continued success of a meeting of this nature is a high degree of spiritual fellowship among some, at least, of its members; and of this fellowship of early days, in silence as well as in words, an account has been given (c. viii.). But, as had to be said, the joyous note which we heard sounded died down and, even, fell into disrepute. The excessive emphasis laid on the "Inward Teacher" discouraged spiritual intercourse and sometimes reckoned it harmful. A certain Friend in the early part of the nineteenth century, looking back on her youthful days, *esteemed it a signal favour* that for years she had no human help and sympathy, inasmuch as her poverty in this respect drove her to a closer reliance on the Holy Spirit speaking in the stillness.[3] To their immeasurable loss, Friends turned their backs on one of the ways, the way of spiritual intercourse one with another, along which God normally makes Himself known. No longer was it true, as has been said of certain meetings in early days,

---

[1] See footnote to the title of chapter xiv., p. 220.
[2] See *ante*, p. 101. [3] *British Friend*, 1849, p. 23.

that at the centre of each there was "a group of persons who had a live religion, and who knew how to share their spiritual gains with the group to which they belonged."[1] Far from this, independence of "outward" or "instrumental" help or ministry came to be regarded as a high spiritual attainment.[2] It is easy to see the depressing effect of this spiritual individualism on the ministry of the word, for while it was manifestly impossible for such ministry to be ruled out, it came to be *accepted* (certainly often with thankfulness) rather than *encouraged*. The conception, about to be described, of the Divine Spirit as working through a passive instrument had no place for "encouragement," a meddling as it seemed with the prerogative of the Divine Spirit who at His own time would give the call. If there was to be the service of speech, the call to it was conceived, not as likely to come along the ways of common life to the soul sensitively attuning itself to hear it, but always as some striking manifestation or *compelling* impulse unmistakable as the ringing of a bell and unrelated to anything already in the mind. The less it was so related, the more evidently did it seem to be divine. This quietist attitude is traceable in the first instance to the dualistic thought of early days which regarded the divine and the human as inherently separate, having nothing in common. To the human or "natural" part belonged the intellect which, certainly, differentiated man from the animals, but which had, in itself, nothing of God. In fact, Penington enraptured by the glory of the light that had dawned upon him after his long search for God in barren places ("the eternal witness awakening in me, and the eternal light

---

[1] R. M. Jones, *Quakers in the American Colonies*, p. 135. The statement is made particularly of certain New England meetings, but it is true of many others.

[2] On this point see an editorial reply to a letter in the *British Friend*, 1862, p. 39; the subject continued from 1861, p. 289.

manifesting the darkness all along unto me, though I knew
not that it was the light,") came to regard the exercise of
the intellect as inevitably a hindrance to the divine working,
saying that when the Lord began to draw him He "powerfully shut up my understanding," but that the devil, "letting that in which the Lord had shut out," "[opened] my
understanding-part (by the subtlety of temptation and
deceit)."[1] If this was the thought of Penington, who was no
Calvinist, much more was it likely to appeal to Barclay, the
Quaker "Apologist," round whom there clung the atmosphere of his Scottish Calvinism with its thought of the
immeasurable glory of God, so vast as to leave no room for
any work of man. We have already noticed (p. 52) his
conception of the divine Light or Seed as inserted miracu-
lously in the human soul, man *in himself as man* having no
more relation to the gift than is possessed by an animal or a
stone. Hence, in the presence of this operation *wholly divine*,
Barclay could find for man nothing to do except *not to resist*.[2]

This conception of a divorce between the divine voice
and the human intellect is seen in the ideal of worship
that came to be set up. It was said that the more the
worshipper could, by suppression of all feeling and thought
of his own, make his mind like a sheet of blank paper,
then on the sheet the Holy Spirit would the more clearly
write. Most disastrous of all was the conception, still
not unknown, of congregational ministry.[3] The call to the

---

[1] *Works* (edn. of 1761), i. 73–74. *The Scattered Sheep Sought After*
(1659). See also p. 345 of the same and quotation from Penington's
writings *ante*, pp. 63–64. Concerning the Light as a revealer of the
darkness see *ante*, p. 69.

[2] See Rufus M. Jones, Introduction to Braithwaite's *Second
Period of Quakerism*, pp. xxxi.–xlv., and c. xiv. of that work; and
Jones, *Later Periods*, pp. 59–60; also Grubb, *Authority and the Light
Within*, c. ix. See *ante*, p. 52.

[3] An account or description of a Friends' meeting with its times
of silent waiting upon God and its freedom for any man or woman to
take part in ministry has already been given, c. vii.

service, so far from coming along the line of love and fellowship of brethren met in the presence of their Father, was thought of as a sudden descent of the Spirit into the mind of the minister, even as a stone may, from the outside, drop into a pool, unrelated to anything already there, the pool having no power either to prevent or induce its coming. This inability to recognize a call as divine if it was linked on to anything however good, already in the mind, is seen in the experience recorded by John Wigham, a Friend of Northumberland. Writing of his early service in the ministry, about the year 1780, he says that sometimes he felt for his fellow-worshippers a love so deep as to raise in him a desire for a message to them. But he was shown that this desire was wrong as having its "origin in self-will"; and then follows the Quaker demand for ministry unmarked by any impress of the passive speaker himself, and, therefore, the more purely divine. It "should be exercised," he says, "without human labour or creaturely contrivances. Thus, I was instructed to wait in humble dependence."[1] As far as this line of thought leads away from shallowness and self-assertiveness to a sensitive perception of the divine leading it is good, but in practice it has often given rise to indolence. Easily do we find excuse for resting in the one extreme that suits our liking by claiming credit for avoidance of the other. In this manner large numbers of Friends have justified their evasion of the service of ministry by pointing out that their perpetual silence was better than shallow and un-called-for utterance. This is certainly true, but it is the argument of the spendthrift, excusing his folly on the ground of his freedom from miserliness; of the miser, excusing *his* folly on the ground of his freedom from extravagance. Miserliness and extravagance are not the

[1] *Memoirs of John Wigham*, p. 10.

only alternatives. The call to the service came to be thought of as if it were (like certain physical characteristics) an endowment or qualification possessed by only a few individuals and never to be acquired by others; it was a "gift," but the particular conception of it obscured the fact that it was a gift to be *desired earnestly* (1 Cor. xiv. 1), and a certain side of human nature found it not unpleasant to *wait*, enjoying liberty to go about its own concerns, until, through some compelling signal, it simply received its orders. For all practical purposes it could be assumed that orders never would be received. The stress was laid on passive receptiveness and against active co-operation, the one being represented as humble trustfulness, the other as impertinent self-assertiveness. There was no conception of a divinely heightened personality glad to use, in the service of its Lord, a gift which had been given to it *for its own*; on the contrary, a lowering of personality came to be regarded as the ideal state; the minister was to be the mouthpiece of the Spirit, making as little contribution of his own as might be, and thus he came to be spoken of as the "instrument," and his ministry as "instrumental means." This conception of the divine voice as speaking to man from outside himself, wholly apart from the ordinary working of his mind, showed itself in the counsel of an aged Friend, given to a young minister: "I heard thee say in meeting, 'I think.' *Now thou shouldest not have been thinking.*"[1] Another speaks of the bliss attendant on an "inward abstraction . . . even a silence from all thoughts," where no enemy can enter.[2]

Thus, the essential testimony to Divine guidance which had revolted against an arid, intellectual preparation of uninspired discourses came to include dislike of any

---

[1] This was told to the present writer by the minister himself.
[2] *A Mirror for the Society of Friends* (Hine), p. 89.

specific preparation at all. It was assumed that no ministry was truly inspired except such as appeared to be communicated in the meeting itself, the fact of a good thought or message coming to the minister in the course of his daily round being a reason why the same should *not* be spoken in the time of worship. The prevailing conception can find no better illustration that the statement once made to the writer by a Quaker minister, that if before meeting a passage of Scripture came into his mind, he would not look it up in the Bible lest he should seem to be "preparing a sermon." A friend has been known to engage in conversation when on his way to meeting by way of diverting his thoughts from the meeting to which he was going, in order that any ministry which he might have in it should come from the inspiration of the moment, free from taint of "premeditation." The Yearly Meeting of 1840 definitely pronounced against any preparation by a minister of matter to be communicated by him to an audience met for worship.[1] As far as the present writer is aware, this is the only official pronouncement on this specific point that has been made by London Yearly Meeting. Hence there grew up among some Friends a habit of assuring their hearers that what they were about to say "has occurred to me unexpectedly since taking my seat here this morning." As a matter of fact, it is owing to misunderstanding that stress has ever been laid on the unessential question of preparation beforehand, the true Quaker position being that the minister, with mind neither torpid nor assertive but calmly alert, shall, in the quiet, feel the fresh uprising of concern for his message, whether he has given previous thought to it or not, and that, if he has done so, he shall understand clearly his temptation to uncalled-for utterance, and in the absence at the time of a living con-

---

[1] This document was not the annual "Epistle."

Q

cern remain silent. If he is content to abide in this spirit, his words, when they come, will have about them a quality which could not have been prepared beforehand. Most abhorrent of all was the idea of any intellectual study carried on with a view to this service. The "opening" of George Fox, "that being bred at Oxford or Cambridge was not enough to fit and qualify men to be ministers of Christ,"[1] might, up to the end of the nineteenth century, be heard quoted in disparagement, not of intellectual equipment in itself for various purposes of life, but of such equipment as having any right bearing on ministry. This undervaluing and, in fact, suspicion of it came to be a source of weakness.

It is of interest to note in passing that the words of Fox, just quoted, find an echo a few years later in the writings of Milton:

> It is a fond [foolish] error, though too much believed among us, to think that the university makes a minister of the Gospel; what it may conduce to other arts or sciences I dispute not now, but that which makes fit a minister the Scripture can but inform us to be only from above.[2]

It was but natural that the first Friends, weary of the overmuch and uninspired ministry[3] which had profited them nothing, should in the holy silence of their meeting, where they met with *one another* in the presence of God, find a rare refreshment of soul. Richard Davies of Welshpool thus tells of one of them:

---

[1] *Journal*, bi-cent. edn., 1, 7 and 11. Concerning disparagement of the intellect and of teaching see Braithwaite, *Beginnings*, pp. 278, 294, 510–11, and *ante*, c. xiv. Also *The Friend*, 1859, pp. 186–7.

[2] *Considerations Touching the Likeliest Way to Remove Hirelings out of the Church* (1659). From John Saltmarsh (d. 1647) there comes the same warning. "Surely it is not a university, a Cambridge or Oxford, a pulpit and black gown or cloak, makes one a true minister." Taken from article "Saltmarsh" in *D.N.B.*, pointed out to me by Geoffrey F. Nuttall.   [3] *Ante*, pp. 31, 104.

> Though it was silent from words, yet the word of the Lord God was among us; it was as a hammer and a fire; it was sharper than a two-edged sword; it pierced through our inward parts; it melted and brought us into tears, that there was scarcely a dry eye amongst us: the Lord's blessed power overshadowed our Meeting, and I could have said that God alone was Master of that assembly.[1]

Of many passages that are to be found in early writings the following from Barclay is typical:

> Yea, though there be not a word spoken, yet is the true spiritual worship performed and the body of Christ edified; yea, it may, and hath often fallen out among us that divers meetings have passed without one word, and yet our souls have been greatly edified and refreshed, and our hearts wonderfully overcome with the secret sense of God's power and Spirit which, without words, hath been ministered from one vessel to another (*Apology*, xi. § 6).

This note of *one another*, which we have already seen to be characteristic of the earliest days (c. viii.), shows the conception of the Divine word as coming to the individual not only direct from the Holy Spirit, but also *as mediated through the fellowship*, even in silence. And while there was no occasion for justification of ministry in itself (it could be taken for granted), the Quaker writings are continually concerned to justify the silent worship in view of the challenge to it that was thrown out. Hence, it is possible to discern in them the beginning of the exaltation of silence over ministry which has dominated the Society throughout the greater part of its existence so far. But at first this was in small compass, and, whatever may have occurred at times, the *continually* silent meetings of a later day were but little known in the beginning.[2]

---

[1] *An Account of the Convincement of Richard Davies*, p. 34 (edn. of 1771). The meeting referred to was at Shrewsbury in 1657.

[2] See the testimony of Barclay and Keith, *ante*, p. 106. Concerning the silence of Quaker worship the reader is referred to Barclay,

As a summary of the story about to be told in detail it may be here said that in the seventeenth century the ministry of the word was held in high esteem, along with the silent worship; in the eighteenth century there set in a quietism which threw the emphasis on the in-speaking voice of the spirit in the stillness and on the "awfulness" of the call to the spoken message; by the middle of the nineteenth century this had led to a positive disparagement of ministry. From that time to the present there has been a concern for the right exercise of the service.

In view of widespread and long-continued misconception concerning the Quaker worship and ministry of early days, it is of the highest importance to note that Fox and other leaders were not afraid to commend explicitly the service of the spoken word, but after the first two generations, for close upon two hundred years, this counsel was rarely given. We have already seen (p. 102) Fox's perception of the harm done by those who in time of worship "quenched the measure of the Spirit of God, and after became dead and dull"; and elsewhere he says:

> . . . where it is quenched it cannot try things. So if any have anything upon them to speak, in the life of God stand up and speak it, if it be but two or three words, and sit down again.[1]

Apology, xi.; George Keith, The Benefit, Advantage and Glory of Silent Meetings (1670), and to modern writers, L. Violet Hodgkin, The Surrender of Silence (a pamphlet) and Silent Worship: The Way of Wonder; Joan M. Fry, The Communion of Life, pp. 50 ff.; Caroline E. Stephen, Quaker Strongholds, c. iii., and Light Arising ("What does Silence Mean"); T. Edmund Harvey, Silence and Worship; John W. Graham, The Faith of a Quaker, c. vii.; Edw. Grubb, What is Quakerism, c. iii.; R. M. Jones, The Faith and Practice of the Quakers, chap. iv., and parts of Christian Discipline and other official pronouncements of the Society of Friends. See also The Fruits of Silence and The Fellowship of Silence, by Canon Hepher, and list of works, ante, p. 102.

[1] Epistles, p. 116.

He counted it the privilege of everyone to have, at one time or another, a part in this service, *"in the light everyone should have something to offer"* he says after quoting the aspiration of Moses, "Would [God that] all the Lord's people were prophets," and he thus continues:

> Friends, you see how men and women can speak enough for the world, for merchandise, for husbandry, the plough-man for his plough, but when they should come to speak for God they quench the Spirit.[1]

At the end of the Epistle from which these words are taken he makes one last mighty appeal:

> Come fishermen, what have you catched with your nets? What can you say for God? Your brethren Peter and John, fishermen, could say much for God . . . shepherds and herdsmen, where are you? what can you say now for God, whose abiding is much in the fields . . . Come tradesmen, tent-makers, physicians and customs men, what can you say for God?[2] . . .

From his prison in "York Tower" William Dewsbury wrote:

> And thou, faithful babe, though thou stutter and stammer forth a few words in the dread of the Lord, they are accepted.[3]

And although Barclay speaks of his wonderful experience in "silent assemblies of God's people" (a passage which is often quoted by way of insinuating a depreciation of ministry), we saw his satisfaction in recording the fact of few meetings being held entirely in silence.[4] George Keith near the end of his tract, *The Benefit, Advantage and*

---

[1] *Epistles*, p. 306. The whole page and the following one are good to read.

[2] *Ibid.*, pp. 307–8 and see bottom of p. 330 of the same.

[3] *Works*, the former of two pages each numbered 185.

[4] *Ante*, p. 106, quoting Barclay's *Apology*, xi. 9; the last part of this passage is repeated in xi. 17.

Glory of Silent Meetings, says the same.[1] In line with this Barclay says elsewhere:

> . . . For though God do principally and chiefly lead us by His Spirit, yet He sometimes conveys His comfort and consolation to us through His children whom He raises up and inspires to speak or write a word in season whereby the saints are made instruments in the hand of the Lord to strengthen and encourage one another.[2]

In view of later developments, it is important to remember that Barclay, though laying the emphasis on silence (in reaction from much lifeless preaching of his time), did not fail to *commend* ministry.

And Penn, writing toward the end of the seventeenth century, after saying that the Church had "been gathered and built up by a living and powerful ministry,"[3] makes appeal for successors in the service, addressing himself especially to those who, he says,

> . . . content yourselves only to know truth for yourselves, to go to meetings and exercise an ordinary charity in the Church and an honest behaviour in the world, and limit yourselves within those bounds, feeling little or no concern upon your spirits for the glory of the Lord in the prosperity of His truth in the earth, more than to be glad that others succeed in such service. . . . Your country folks, neighbours and kindred want to know the Lord and His truth and to walk in it. Does nothing lie at your door upon their account.[4]

---

[1] In the early part of Fox's life (1651) on one occasion when travelling in the North Riding of Yorkshire, he "sat of a haystack and spoke nothing for some hours for I was to famish them [the people] from words." It is widely, but erroneously, believed that this was a typical or constantly repeated act of his and it is often caught at to exalt silence over ministry. But at last he spoke "and there was a general convincement among others," Cambridge *Journal*, i. 28; *Journal* bi-cent. edn., i. 94.　　　　　　　　　　　　[2] *Apology*, iii. § 5.
[3] Preface to Fox's *Journal* (1694), bi-cent. edn., i., p. liii.
[4] *Ibid.*, lv.

This was written in 1694 and three years later in a meeting held at Norwich there was read an Epistle "for the preservation of a living ministry."[1] In the last three-quarters of the eighteenth century and the first sixty years of the nineteenth a meeting held for this particular purpose would have been impossible, but in 1711 it was still possible for Somerset Quarterly Meeting to bear testimony:

> It is a living ministry that begets a living people; and by a living ministry at first we were reached and turned to the Truth. It is a living ministry that will still be acceptable to the Church and serviceable to its members.[2]

Thomas Story, writing of the closing years of the seventeenth century, thus makes record:

> Our meetings in the north in those days were frequently broken and melted in silence as well as under a powerful living ministry by the word.

There is here no setting off of silence against ministry as if one were inherently superior to the other, a practice which, in later years of lowered spiritual vitality, has wrought untold harm.

The seventeenth century care for the ministry, in contrast with the later depreciation of it, is seen in the concern of Fox and others for the orderly distribution of ministers among the meetings in the London and Bristol districts, so that they "might not go in heaps"[3] to one meeting and

---

[1] Arthur J. Eddington, *The First Fifty Years of Quakerism in Norwich*, p. 58.

[2] "Testimony" concerning John Banks (1638–1710).

[3] Fox's words; this is taken from *John Stephenson Rowntree, His Life and Work*, p. 158, and see p. 269 of the same. In this book three chapters in particular ought to be read by all who would understand the history of Quaker thought, namely, c. ii., "Micah's Mother," c. v., "Gospel Ministry in the Society of Friends," c. vi., "The Work and Maintenance of the Vocal Ministry."

leave others unprovided for. They met on the Monday morning to take counsel together as to which meeting each should attend on the following Sunday and on the morning of the Sunday they again came together to complete the plan. They went forth, each one as he felt himself guided, not in pursuance of any order or dictation from a superior but, "according to their concern or freedom" which did not exclude consultation with one another as to the harmonious and effective service of all. It need not be assumed that they had a vocal ministry in every meeting that they attended, and although at times some of them took too much upon themselves[1] yet for the most part they laid full stress on the importance of the silent worship and they encouraged the work of the ministry in others.

In a previous chapter (vii.) mention was made of meetings in early days in which the ministry and the silence each found its right place, and elsewhere we read of silence being regarded, not as the superior of the two but, as the preparation for a divinely inspired ministry. We noted (p. 129) the loving fellowship spoken of by George Whitehead as existing between those who, in the mainly silent meetings, at times spoke a few words, and he says that it was out of these meetings, "frequently silent," that "the Lord was pleased to raise up and bring forth living witnesses, faithful ministers, and true prophets in early days in Westmorland and other northern parts in the years 1654 and 1655 etc." Christopher Story speaks with holy enthusiasm of the meetings in his house in 1672—"glorious and heavenly times we had when no words"—"the fame of truth spread and our meetings were large and the exercise of the faithful was to draw nearer and nearer to the Lord . . . and this was that which made us beautiful,

[1] Braithwaite, *Second Period*, p. 293, referring to pp. 544–45.

though not come so far as to have a word given us to speak unto others by way of testimony publicly."[1]

But from early years of the eighteenth century until past the middle of the nineteenth it is almost exclusively commendation of silence that we hear, at the expense of ministry and even to its disparagement. In 1765 John Fry speaks of the change which he saw to be setting in, "as if," he says, "the situation of things were altered and that Church which was at first principally and mostly gathered by a living and powerful ministry, and has ever since been favoured with the continuance of it, could *now thrive and, grow and become fresh and green without it!*"[2] Upon the story of this change and of its consequences we now enter, inasmuch as a knowledge of it is essential to an understanding of the subsequent course of the Quaker society. It is, however, necessary to say at the outset that commendation of ministry and insistence on the need for it are not to be taken as any undervaluing of the living silence essential to the right holding of a Friends' meeting for worship.

We have already noticed the depressing effect on ministry of the *unbalanced* stress laid upon the doctrine of the "Inward Teacher," so that, contrary to Barclay's outlook, there came about an untroubled acceptance of the fact of many meetings being continually held wholly in silence, and, while there was encouragement to earnest waiting upon God, there was seldom a hint that the spoken word was needed or any counsel to seek ability to supply it. So far were Friends from valuing the privilege offered to

---

[1] *Life of Christopher Story*, p. 27. The italics are mine. Compare Barclay's words (*ante*, p. 105), "Silence necessarily follows . . . until words can be brought forth."

[2] This letter of John Fry is in the Reynolds MSS., Friends' Library; it is in part quoted (not quite correctly) in *The Inner Life of the Religious Societies of the Commonwealth*, by R. Barclay (not the "Apologist"), p. 534. For further quotation see *post*, p. 257.

each one of putting his power of speech at the disposal of God for the conveyance of His message, that great ingenuity was exercised in finding reasons for failure to exercise the privilege. The beginning of this way of thought which was to dominate the Society for at least five generations may be detected in early days. Isaac Penington, in his "Brief Account concerning Silent Meetings,"[1] gives a fine description of the attitude of mind demanded, and excellently does he treat of ministry: Friends are to wait upon the Lord,

> to watch for the stirrings of His life and the breakings forth of His power amongst them. And in the breakings forth of that power they may pray, speak, exhort, rebuke, sing or mourn, etc., according as the Spirit teaches . . . But if the Spirit do not require to speak . . . then everyone is to sit still.

The writer has, moreover, the glowing conception of fellowship, characteristic, as we have seen (c. viii.) of the seventeenth century (the worshippers "are like an heap of fresh and living coals, warming one another"), but at the last, he says, "the ministry of the spirit and life is more close and immediate when without words than when with words." It was upon this that the Society fastened to the exclusion of all else.[2] Typical of the individualistic advice which for a century and a half was put forth is the following sentence from the Yearly Meeting Epistle of 1724:

> Though meetings are sometimes held in silence, we tenderly beseech all Friends not to neglect their attendance;

[1] This is the final section of *A Further Testimony to Truth Revived out of the Ruins of the Apostasy* (*Works*, edn. of 1761, ii. 352).
[2] This passage is printed in italics in a reprint of this work of Penington issued by a body of conservative Friends. On this matter see a reply in the *British Friend* (1851, pp. 144–45) to a statement in *The Friend* (1851, p. 39) that meetings would seldom be wholly silent if there were greater religious vitality in the Society.

for the hungry soul will labour for bread, and the thirsty for the water of life; and the diligent hand will make rich in that treasure which is of an enduring substance.[1]

There can be no understanding of a Friends' meeting on the part of any who neglect this counsel, dealing as it does with the essential principle of silent worship, but it was not supplemented *and reinforced* by any appeal to the worshippers *to help one another*, either silently or by words. From the eighteenth century there comes, as we shall see,[2] evidence of weakness in the ministry both as to quality and sufficiency, but the Church, while giving counsel, mostly in the way of caution, to those already engaged in the work, only rarely invited others to hope that it might be theirs. The Friend went to meeting to meet with God, and innumerable times his quest was rewarded, but he met *alone*, and of his fellow-worshippers as *a united company* there was little or no thought, the conception of "membership one of another," so vivid in early days, having faded to a minimum. It was, of course, assumed that he would attend public worship, and continually was he exhorted to bear faithful testimony to his own way of meeting, but of any reason why he should come forth from his room to sit in the company of others, mediaeval Quakerism gave little account. Nevertheless such account might have seemed to be peculiarly necessary in view of the repeated insistence on the privilege, open to every soul, of communion with the Father at any time and place apart from minister or building. Barclay, in the seventeenth century, met the challenge in no unsatisfactory way, saying that as long as men were in the body "God hath seen meet . . . to make use of the outward

---

[1] This is the form as given in the *Book of Discipline* of 1883, in the first part slightly altering the original.
[2] P. 257; and for the nineteenth century see p. 316.

senses . . . as a means to convey spiritual life as by speaking, praying, praising, etc., which cannot be done to mutual edification but when we hear and see one another" (*Apology*, xi. 17). He also speaks of the fellowship known in the silence of a gathered company. Fox also asserts that one reason for the meeting of Friends together is the opportunity it gives them of hearing the words which one and another may speak. Concerning the attempt to suppress Friends' meetings by means of the Quaker Act of 1662, he writes:

> And if we must not meet together, how must we stir up one another and edify one another and provoke one another unto love and to good works, if we must not meet together to speak one to another?[1]

He is clearly referring to *ministry* in the usual sense of the word. George Fox the younger, speaks of attacks made upon Friends "when we have been peaceably met together to wait on the Lord and to hear *and declare* the everlasting truth."[2]

To the eighteenth and to a considerable part of the nineteenth century neither of the aforesaid reasons for coming together in worship made appeal, the explicit commendation of ministry being impossible and the sense of fellowship obscured by the stress laid on the immediate communion of the soul with God *alone*. It was, however, not wholly lost, and sometimes it received slight recognition, but the reason most commonly given (as Barclay himself gives it) for meeting in public worship was the injunction contained in the Epistle to the Hebrews, *not for-*

---

[1] *Gospel Truth Demonstrated* (*Doctrinals*), p. 261.
[2] *A Noble Salutation* [to King Charles] (1660), p. 13. The italics are mine. George Fox the younger, an Eastern Counties Friend, was so styled because, though older in years than Fox the founder of the Society, he was younger in convincement.

saking the assembling of ourselves together as the custom of some is (x. 25). The assembly was an open profession of religious faith. Whittier, in a beautiful poem entitled *First-Day Thoughts*, gives a description of a meeting as Friends came to understand it[1] Certainly, mention is made of the worshipper taking his accustomed seat among his brethren, but otherwise it is wholly concerned with individual striving and search for guidance in silence; it is the aspiration of private devotion, not of united worship.[2]

Although, as has been already said (p. 198), "the fountain of prophetic ministry was not wholly quenched," so strong was the emphasis laid on silence as to render it difficult for any official pronouncement or for any individual Friend to raise a call to the work of ministry as Fox and other leaders did in early days. While there was thankfulness expressed for the service of certain individuals, of *ministry itself* there was little commendation except by way of throwing into relief the greater excellence of silence. In 1749 a Friend records his disapproval of the desire to secure the presence of a minister on the occasion of weddings and funerals,[3] and thirty-six years later another was concerned to warn ministers against exposing themselves to the temptation to undue words by overmuch attendance at such meetings.[4] Again and again do we come upon counsel such as may be quoted from the Yearly Meeting Epistle of 1740:

[1] "First Day" means Sunday. See also the *British Friend*, 1855, p. 283 (bottom of col. 2). Whittier's poem, *The Meeting*, contains more of the element of *united* worship than *First-Day Thoughts* does.
[2] See R. M. Jones, *Later Periods of Quakerism*, pp. 83–85.
[3] *Journal of John Griffith*, p. 137, edn. of 1779.
[4] *Diary of Samuel Scott*, p. 149. Thomas Story, writing in 1719 before this uneasiness had set in, tells, without any blame, of a request made to him to be present at a funeral at Glastonbury and of the fixing of a day to suit his convenience (*Journal*, p. 629). In later years we read of meetings for worship at weddings and funerals held wholly in silence.

> The immediate teaching of the Holy Spirit is the founda-
> tion of all gospel worship and ministry, and those who
> depend entirely thereon shall not be disappointed through
> the failure or absence of instrumental means.

Thus it came about that *for years together* many meetings
were held wholly in silence except on the occasion of a
visit paid by some ministering Friend who felt a "concern" to travel. Nevertheless there was no certainty that
even the visitor would speak; in fact, the hope and expectation of his doing so was often felt by him to be a hindrance
in his way. It was not for him to provide gratification for
"itching ears." The suggestion that the meeting was
hungering for a message of life would have been taken as
a slight upon the "Inward Teacher." A Friend visiting
Rawdon in 1792 records that she "had deep wading at the
meeting . . . but after a considerable time of starving
that thirst for vocal ministry which is painful to rightly
exercised ministers, Truth arose." This meant that, at last,
she spoke.[1] John Griffith speaks of his attendance at meetings crowded with "the public," (to whom a special invitation had been given), but in the absence of anything that
he could recognize as a "call" he would remain silent,
troubled by what he knew to be the wonder or disappointment at his restraint, particularly the disappointment of
Friends themselves who, to his thinking, ought to have
known better.

It is not easy for us to understand the conception of
ministry of which this was the outcome. The minister did
not think of his service as a happy one, as a message of
glad tidings called forth by love of human souls met (he
and they together) in the divine presence that through
them to him in his service, as well as through him to them,

---

[1] *Memoirs of Sarah Stephenson* (1738–1802), p. 116. The expression "deep wading" is elsewhere found in Quaker writings of this
time; it meant heavy or difficult travail of spirit.

divine help might flow. He thought of himself as sitting in silence till he had come to a deep place ("centering down," he called it) where he discovered and entered into the condition of those with whom he had met and where, through divine assistance, he might raise into life and power the "suffering seed." It was the thought of *suffering* that was always with him, of the agonizing labour of opening stopped-up channels (many of them unwilling to be opened) through which life was meant to flow; he believed that he "could receive impressions from God to suffer in spirit, and that by divine grace this suffering could work effects in the hidden lives of others."[1] At times we read of the minister knowing a sweet peace when his hard labour was over; and sometimes we are told by others that he had spoken to satisfaction but rarely, if ever, do we hear of his call to minister meeting with joyous response.

Though we cannot but think of these ministers as dwelling overmuch on the note of mourning ("in a deep sense [of] the great desolation which overspreads our Society," as one of them said)[2] it is a shallow life that knows nothing of their sorrow for the world's sin. Our demand for the note of "joy," and our often excessive praise of the preacher who sounds it, may act upon us as a temptation to be satisfied with ministry that is shallow, and to hear with impatience of the grief of John Woolman as he saw human souls *separated from the divine harmony*. It was the sorrow of which George Fox spoke when the priest asked him why Christ cried out, "My God, my God, why hast Thou for-

---

[1] R. M. Jones, *Later Periods of Quakerism*, p. 92. This passage is the conclusion of an account (beginning on p. 85) of the silent travail of ministers; from this account most of the early part of the above paragraph has been taken, sometimes as to the exact wording.

[2] *Ibid.*, p. 88, and see similar examples there given. This note of discouragement or mourning was sounded over and over again; it was prominent in Quaker ministry for about a hundred years, 1760–1860. See, for example, *post*, p. 260.

saken me?" And the young man, twenty-three years old, made answer: "I told him that at the time the sins of all mankind were upon him, and their iniquities and transgressions with which he was wounded." "This," he continues, "I spoke *being at that time in a measure sensible of Christ's sufferings and what he went through.*" If our demand for "joy" or "optimism" or "the bright side" makes us call upon the preacher, "Prophesy not unto us right things, speak unto us smooth things,"[1] or if it makes us resentful of ministry that calls us to be partakers, as these Quaker preachers were, of the sufferings of Christ,[2] we have not gone with our Lord into the deep places of life. Nevertheless, the absence of the note of joy or happiness had a disastrous effect on the life of the Society.[3]

Going back to our story of the widely travelling ministers, we note that they were men and women not "uneducated," but, for the most part, of no great education, who did not go forth in pursuance of any plan arranged for them, but each of them, when he felt the time had come, laid before his "Monthly Meeting" his "concern" for visitation at home or abroad, and, strengthened by the approval of his fellow-members, he went out relying on the divine leading, timidly, but sensitively alert to the faintest intimation of service required of him. Their work of binding the Society together and inducing uniformity throughout its borders resembled that of their predecessors in the preceding century. Their range of experience was not wide, but of holiness of life they knew a wonderful depth, and to a certain type of mind they made a profound appeal. Men saw in them a strange purity or whiteness of soul.[4]

[1] Is. xxx. 10.   [2] 1 Pet. iv. 13.
[3] See an article, "Early Friends and Modern Practices," in *The Friend*, 1862, p. 98, by William C. Westlake, one of the Friends who did much to lead the Society to a wider outlook; *post*, p. 296 note 2.
[4] See R. M. Jones, *The Later Periods of Quakerism*, c. i. "Typical Leaders During the Eighteenth Century."

Their close intimate knowledge of Friends personally and of the Quaker mind, endowing them with the keenest perception, made them abnormally sensitive to the slightest of indications that revealed the thought or attitude of others. Hence they were often able to address meetings and speak to individuals with singular (and sometimes embarrassing) appropriateness. This was called "speaking to states," (or "to conditions"). It would at times seem that their insight was of the nature which we call "psychic."[1] They were, however, too few in number, and one who was, perhaps, the most gifted of them looked with uneasiness on the condition of the Church. Writing to a Friend about the "Circular Meeting" held at Warwick in 1756, Samuel Fothergill says: "Between ourselves, I had a painful prospect and feeling of the present state of the ministry amongst us, yea more so than ever before."[2]

Unhappily, there is ample evidence to justify Fothergill's misgiving concerning the Quaker society of his day. We have already noticed (p. 249) the lament of John Fry (uttered in 1765) at the undervaluing of ministry such as had gathered the Church in its beginning; "Are we ashamed," he asks, "of the foolishness of preaching which was so effectual in the primitive times?" "There had come about," he says, "lukewarmness and indifference, with a

[1] R. M. Jones, *Later Periods of Quakerism*, pp. 92 ff., Grubb Introduction to *A Mirror for the Society of Friends* (Hine), p. 18. To our readers this Introduction is commended, giving, as it does, accurate insight into the state of the Society at different periods of its existence.

[2] From a letter written to John Churchman, *Memoirs of Samuel Fothergill*, 1st edn., p. 275. On p. 414 is a letter written by Fothergill to a Friend who, by his speaking had unprofitably taken up the time of a meeting. He speaks of "a noisy, floating ministry," and says "I have feared thy branches are too large for thy root." This was in 1761. For Fothergill's unhappiness at the state of the Society see an address delivered by him in 1769, printed at the end of *A Voice from the Wilderness*, by Sarah Alexander.

R

want of love and brotherly affection," so that there was little or no help being given to the young and inexperienced. "If," he says, "young ministers are not properly encouraged to be faithful in their gifts and not to despise *the day of small things*, from whence shall the Church be supplied with able ministers?"[1] It would seem that already there had set in the belief, which was to hold sway for another hundred years and more, that the taking of thought for the supply of ministry was alien from the spirit of Quakerism. From others we get confirmation of John Fry's misgivings and the outcome of all this was a passive acceptance of the situation leading to an adulation of silence and a disparagement of ministry. Nevertheless the supply never failed, but much of it lost its force by reason of certain conventional mannerisms which accompanied it, at times an excessive slowness of delivery, at others a sing-song or chanting tone which came to be looked on as evidence of the divine message speaking through human agency.[2]

In the late 1840's James Backhouse, one of the company of able ministers of his time, uttered a caution against allegorical preaching, saying that some ministry was "beclouded through unduly mystical expression,"[3] and he speaks of overmuch reading in the Old Testament, "and of allowing the mind unduly to dwell on prophecy" instead of diligent reading in the New Testament.[4] Some

[1] Concerning this letter of John Fry see Braithwaite, *Second Period*, pp. 543–54.
[2] See Bownas, *A Description of the Qualifications Necessary to a Gospel Minister*, pp. 41–42 (edn. of 1750); pp. 37–38 (edn. of 1767), and see *The Friend*, 1856, pp. 128, 172, 210, 224; 1867, p. 130; 1868, pp. 28, 217; also *The Society of Friends, its Strength and its Weakness*, Fry (published anonymously, 1859), pp. 28–30.   [3] *Ante*, p. 233.
[4] MS. Collection of letters, Friends' Library, dated 30. vi. 1848, and see Letter Book No. 5, 1842–68, pp. 233–41 and 260, and *The Friend*, 1861, p. 74, near the bottom of the second column, an important contemporary account of the state of the ministry.

of the sermons of this time were very long (occasionally two hours or more) and some consisted of a stringing together of Scripture texts which had between them little connection that was apparent to the hearers.[1] A large share of the ministry (two-thirds, it was said[2]) came from women, in fact as early as 1811, in the Yearly Meeting of Ministers and Elders, a woman accused the men of unfaithfulness to the divine leading.[3] In 1859 a Friend ventured to call attention to the need for ministry, "especially from among our young men.[4] In the 1860's, however, more men, both younger and older, began to take their right part in this service,[5] and in the latter half of the nineteenth century the stream of able ministry (of both men and woman) which, after all, had never ceased to flow, broadened into a river.

The writer would again remind his readers, as he has already done in another connection, that this story is being told, not primarily as a matter of antiquarian or historical interest, but in order to give understanding of the career of the Quaker Church, that those who labour for its welfare may gain wisdom from a knowledge of its past. In the light of what has been said and of what is to follow we can understand how it came about that, notwithstanding much philanthropic service (it was from 1783 to 1807 that Friends were doing their great work for the abolition of the slave trade) and many saintly lives deservedly gaining respect for the Quaker name the meetings for worship themselves came to have little power and in England, Ireland and America very many

---

[1] See Grubb, Introduction to *A Mirror for the Society of Friends* (Hine), p. 18. The present writer can, out of his own recollection, bear the same testimony.

[2] *The Friend*, 1868, p. 68 and see p. 112 (at the end).

[3] *Pen Pictures of London Yearly Meeting*, p. 131.

[4] *The Friend*, 1859, p. 99.

[5] See *The Friend*, 1868, pp. 28, 112 (at the end).

of them faded out. The decline was attributed to deadness and the prevalence of a worldly spirit, but of the need for right ministry and teaching no one seems to have been aware.[1] A certain Friend, himself a minister, wrote in 1783: "Silence seems to be the dispensation of the present day; at least among us as a religious society, peculiarly called from a dependence on the teachings of men, and to that worship which stands not in word, but in power."[2] Twenty years later another minister writes in a letter: "But my dear friend! is not this a day wherein the true ministers have rather to mourn in silence than to proclaim glad tidings?"[3] Of this note of *mourning*; sounded almost to the exclusion of every other, mention has already been made.[4] The ministers themselves often laid stress on the value of silence. The thought of the time is seen in a passage from the Yearly Meeting Epistle of 1806:

> Instrumental ministry in the life and power of the Gospel is a great favour to the Church, but the distinguishing excellence of the Christian dispensation is the immediate communication with our heavenly Father through the inward revelation of the Spirit of Christ.[5]

This was repeated in the Epistle of 1832, and about

---

[1] In the annual reports, known as "Answers to the Queries," sent up to the Yearly Meeting, mention is continually made of drowsiness in meetings. See *ante*, p. 228 note and *post*, p. 269 note. In those days windows were not usually made to open.

[2] *Diary of Samuel Scott* (1719–88), p. 81.

[3] *Memoir of Mary Capper* (1755–1845), p. 129. About twenty years later it is recorded that on each of three occasions, addressing special audiences, none of them in a Friends' meeting, she spoke for an hour and a half (pp. 204, 211, 261). [4] P. 255.

[5] Typical of entries that occur in Quaker diaries is the following: "Our meetings both silent; I thought that something was to be felt excelling words; my own mind was bowed in sweet inward stillness with a precious, renewed sense that the Spirit of the Lord teaches in the secret of the soul more powerfully than any vocal sound communicated to the ear" (*Memoir of Mary Capper*, p. 141, in the year 1805). Concerning the perpetually silent meetings see *post*, pp. 266 ff.

ninety years after this it was said in London Yearly Meeting by a survivor of the older school of thought that it did not matter whether there was much or little ministry or none at all, provided only there was life. This utterance, characteristic of mediaeval days, overlooks the fact that if there is life there will not be long-continued failure of right ministry, and that such failure indicates absence of life.

The result of all this was that round the idea of ministry there clung an atmosphere of unnaturalness and even of weirdness. As already stated, there was little official commendation of the service, but in course of time it became not infrequent for a minister in an address or prayer to hint that there were present one of more on whom the Lord was laying His hand. Terrified or encouraged, according to temperament, the young man or maiden who had been facing the prospect and shrinking from it took the message home as a personal one. There is also record of private encouragement, but throughout the greater part of the Society's history such counsel has been generally disliked as being impertinent interference with the delicate operation of the Spirit, so small has been the understanding of spiritual help given by one to another. The prevailing conception of worship laid so great stress on the *danger* of disturbing the silence or of "exceeding the measure" or "outrunning the Guide," that most Friends, once and for all, ruled the service of the spoken word out of their lives. Those on whom the awful compulsion had descended came to be regarded as a separate order of men and women, for ever marked off from others. Mightily against their will they had been borne across a chasm, wide and deep, into an awesome land from which there was no return; they had joined the ranks of those who *spoke in meeting*. In fact it came to be widely held opinion that no one was justified in entering on the service unless he could truthfully say, "Woe is me if I preach not the Gospel."[1] A Friend, writing about the year 1865, deploring the convention of restraint which the Society was cherishing, calls attention to the absence from Quaker family worship of any word of counsel or of prayer, the worship being rigidly limited to a Bible reading followed by a silent pause except, possibly, on the rare occasion of a visit paid by a ministering Friend. The writer names some of the reasons in which this lifelong silence found refuge, the fear that the utterance of the good word "would be taking too high ground for myself," "everyone would say I was becoming a minister."[2] And although a deep peace was usually the reward of obedience to the divine leading, there was no conception of any joyous leaping forward to welcome the call, and still less of any longing that it might come. Self-revealing in curiously minute detail as are the numerous spiritual journals of this time, I have found no record of parents either praying or hoping that their children might be ministers. The writer of the tract to which reference has just been made, passing on from the subject of family worship to speak of worship in public, points out that in her day the free and willing service of the early Friends

> . . . has been exchanged for a reluctance, a hesitation, nay, even a direct and urgent desire to be excused from the service, in some cases expressed in terms which would lead

[1] See *British Friend*, 1866, pp. 207, 232. At a later time when this extreme opinion came to be questioned a Friend satirically observed (not without a measure of truth) that it seemed to be thought that no one should undertake the service of ministry unless he had received a call of sufficient urgency to justify him in publicly denouncing a city for its wickedness. This is not the inevitable alternative to shallow ease of utterance.

[2] Anna D. Peet, *The Constraining Influence of the Holy Spirit*, one of fourteen tracts of "The old Banner" series, 1864–66. Later on the writer left Friends. See also *Seven Letters to a Member of the Society of Friends* (p. 21), by Dr. Edward Ash of Bristol (1855).

the casual reader to suppose that, far from regarding the office of minister as one of privilege and blessing, the writer looked on it as one of personal shame and humiliation (p. 10).

Further on she says that it is impossible to conceive of either Peter or Paul sitting in an ordinary Friends' meeting for worship,

> . . . adopting the language so lamentably frequent within the past hundred years in the published journals of our members, so often heard even now in private, or from the gallery itself,[1] the earnest entreaty and desire to be spared from labour, to be allowed to keep silence in the face of this multitude of famishing souls (p. 12).

There is no lack of evidence to justify the statements concerning this dread which have been quoted. A Friend in terror at the prospect of a call to the ministry, no longer to be evaded, could speak of himself (or herself) as being "accounted a fool for Christ's sake," or as being "made a gazing-stock," or as becoming "a poor despised Quaker preacher." One of them, writing in 1768, speaks of the call as if it were a grave affliction; "I have," he says, "been much troubled of late and exercised in my mind concerning the ministry which I sincerely desire to be excused from, but may my soul say, 'Thy will be done'."[2] A few years later a certain Friend, a year after she had first begun her ministry, tells how, one day as she sat in meeting, she heard the call to speak—"after a deep labour of mind, there felt something to gather about me"—but she continues:

---

[1] The gallery, or "ministers' gallery," is a raised seat occupied by certain of the elders and those who speak fairly often. Most modern meeting houses are built without it.

[2] Samuel Dyer, manuscript diary.

> . . . with it came *my deep-rooted dislike to the work* which
> so strove with the other that, for a time enduring a state of
> agony, the meeting broke up.[1]

John Yeardley, looking back to the year 1804, when he
was eighteen years old, and describing his first impression
of a call to ministry, says that he took it as a temptation
of the devil:

> I have often [he continues] secretly said, "Get thee
> behind me, I will not be tempted with such a thing." . . .
> *Such was my dislike to the work* that I suffered myself to be
> lulled into a state of unbelief as to the rectitude of the
> concern.[2]

It would seem that this attitude of mind became conventional among Friends. Elizabeth Fry, in 1809, beginning her service at the age of twenty-nine, records her fear
that what she supposed to be a call might be a temptation;
and thirteen years later Thomas Pumphrey, afterwards
headmaster of Ackworth School, entering on his ministry
at the age of twenty, says that he "struggled against the
call, fearing it was a suggestion of Satan to bring dishonour on the precious truth."[3] It was with reference to
this way of thought that a Friend wrote, "It is one of
Satan's devices to suggest wickedness of heart as a
warrant for disobeying the divine command.[4]

[1] *Life of Sarah* [Tuke] *Grubb* (1756–90), p. 12. This was in 1779
She was a daughter of Willaim Tuke, the founder of York Retreat
(*ante*, p. 212). The italics are mine, otherwise the passage is quoted as
it stands.

[2] *Memoir*, p. 24. Although John Yeardley did not technically
become a member till 1808, before the year 1804 he had been
"convinced," i.e. he had thoroughly adopted the Quaker outlook and
general attitude of mind. The italics in the quotation are mine. As
early as 1655 William Edmundson records that when he first began
to say a few words in ministry he was in fear lest a wrong spirit, in the
likeness of an angel of light, should deceive him (*Journal*, p. 15). See
also *Memoirs of John Wigham*, p. 10 (about the year 1780).

[3] *Life*, p. 9.

[4] *Memoirs of Elizabeth Dudley*, p. 265, under the year 1839. See
The Friend, 1862, p. 99, article by W. C. W[estlake].

In all this we see the concern of the true minister that his life shall commend his words; but Quakerism has suffered from over-cautiousness, slipping at times into lethargy and under the cloak of humility, into excuse for drawing back from service. A genuine desire for correspondence between life and ministry will be more concerned with elevation of the former than with suspicion of the latter. Unworthy the preacher may feel himself to be (in fact, what preacher does not?); grieved at his inconsistency in his falling short of the ideal which, having seen, he sets forth; and strong (and not always unwelcome) is the temptation to withhold his offering under plea of avoidance of hypocrisy. But it is an abuse of language to charge with "hypocrisy" the preacher, or any other, who, notwithstanding failure, is honestly set in the right way, pressing toward the goal even though he cannot count himself to have attained. Inconsistency is not the same as hypocrisy.

Of other holy men and women also, the journals reveal this paralysing fear of the call, shutting out the response, "Here am I, send me." Only rarely do we hear of willing co-operation with the Divine leading, the service was conceived as forced upon them. "Preaching will indeed be of necessity, not of choice," wrote one as she dreaded the call awaiting her.[1] Thomas Shillitoe (1754–1836), in his *Journal*, writes: "about the twenty-fourth year of my age my mouth was first opened in this awful work" (i. 5). William Allen, eminent in the world of science and known throughout the country, and beyond it, for enlightened philanthropic leadership in many directions, describes his state of mind on being recorded as a minister in the year 1820, shortly before his fiftieth birthday:

[1] Manuscript diary of Mary (Bowen) Burtt (1800–85.)

I am now placed in an awful situation. May the Great Preserver of men be near to support and sustain under every trial, and prevent me from doing anything which may injure His great and good cause. I am indeed very low and in much fear (*Life*, ii. 172).[1]

Lydia Ann Barclay, in the early part of the nineteenth century, making frequent mention of her distress at the prospect of ministry, on one occasion writes: "I feel now ill with conflict, and the dread of meeting days."[2] Another Friend who, after twenty-five years' struggle, at last yielded to the call by quoting a single text, wrote a few weeks afterwards in her diary: "My heart is saddened by the recollection that to-morrow will be meeting-day again."[3]

It is in the first half of the nineteenth century that we begin to find expressions of doubt, not at all as to the right place of silence in the Quaker worship, but as to the excessive or unbalanced emphasis that was being placed on it. This misgiving, in its turn, called forth a stream of positive disparagement of ministry, the desire for it being

[1] The "recording" or "acknowledging" of a minister (man or woman) in theory meant that his Monthly Meeting officially recorded the fact that Friends, having for some time heard his offerings and believing him to be rightly engaged, encouraged him to continuance in the service. This custom, however, fell under suspicion of setting apart a separate order of ministry and after (for the most part) falling into disuse, it was officially ended in 1924.

William Allen (1770–1843), a wholesale chemist and druggist, was also a lecturer in chemistry and physics at Guy's Hospital and the Royal Institution, a Fellow of the Royal Society and a member of other learned bodies. He was a leader of the anti-slavery cause and a promoter of philanthropic enterprise in England, Scotland, several parts of the Continent of Europe and in other parts of the world. See R. M. Jones, *The Later Periods of Quakerism*, Index.

[2] *Letters*, p. 41. The reader who does not understand the situation might not always realize that the conflicts described by the writer were due to the prospect of ministry; she seems to have feared the very word. On p. 7 the Editor of the *Letters* (*anno* 1862) speaks of ministry as "this awful engagement." See *post*, p. 270.

[3] Manuscript diary of Mary (Bowen) Burtt.

represented as *dependence* on human aid when, all the time, the divine teaching in the silence was available. Of course, this contrast or rivalry, wholly contradictory of the thought of the earliest Friends, would never have been set up had there been understanding of the fact that the word spoken is *one* of the modes of expression of the Christian fellowship by means of which the divine word is mediated to man. The misgiving of which we have spoken is seen in a letter written in 1834, by one Friend to another, saying that if silent meetings had been the most effectual way of bringing men to Jesus Christ, this blessed consequence "would be more apparent in places where our fellow professors assemble together from childhood to old age without hearing vocal ministry except when occasionally visited by strangers." The writer goes on to say that every good thing is liable to abuse, and that the testimony to silent worship "has been abused to purposes of indolence, self-love and an increase of that carnal mindedness which is death."[1]

In Yearly Meeting two years later there were some who ventured to question the desirability of perpetual silence, but they were met with indignant remonstrance, one Friend saying that he had enjoyed more consolation in silent meetings than under the most powerful ministry.[2] Elizabeth Fry, also, expressed her sense of the need for "more external aid," "though," she says, "I do not see how it is to be given," adding that she felt "the want of each openly uniting in some external act of worship."[3] The conventional depreciation of ministry is seen in an editorial article in the *British Friend* of 1860. After the writer has pointed out the undeniable truth, "Much speaking is no

[1] *Memoirs of Elizabeth Dudley*, p. 211.
[2] From a report of the Yearly Meeting of 1836 published by the *Christian Advocate*.   [3] *Memoirs*, ii. 188.

more an evidence of *general* vitality in a meeting than habitual silence is of torpor" (the usual presentation of "much speaking" and "habitual silence" as the only alternatives) he thus sets the emphasis according to the way of his school of thought:

> While a living gospel ministry is a precious blessing, it is not unaccompanied with a snare—even that of leading to a *dependence upon instrumental help*, more than to trusting on the Lord for the immediate teachings of this spirit.[1]

Nevertheless, a new tide was beginning to flow[2] and the Yearly Meeting of 1855 made an appeal to the Quarterly Meeting to take into consideration the spiritual needs of their younger members, and to make report in the following year. Certain of the Quarterly Meetings, notably Yorkshire and Bristol and Somerset, which, in the following year, published their reports, interpreted this as a call to take a survey of the whole situation, and among other matters they ventured to draw attention to the undue withholding of ministry in meetings for worship.[3] In the atmosphere that was thus being generated the Yearly Meeting Epistle of 1860 expressed its "renewed Christian

[1] *British Friend*, 1860, p. 218, the italics are in the original. On p. 119, beginning at the bottom of col. 1, there is a similar passage in a letter signed "W."

[2] The story of this is told in the following chapter, p. 278.

[3] In 1854–55 a Report of a Committee of Yorkshire Quarterly Meeting for visiting the meetings and families of Friends had to some extent anticipated the above-mentioned report of 1856. It shows the difficulty that was felt in the way of open commendation of ministry in that the hints as to the need for this service are so timidly expressed that present-day readers may fail to recognize them for what they are, e.g. "Far be it from the Committee to encourage an undue reliance one upon another in spiritual concerns, or any dependance upon mere arrangement; but human instrumentality has its proper place," etc. Concerning the Report sent by Bristol and Somerset, see *post*, p. 296; the Yorkshire Report, *post*, p. 296. In the Yearly Meeting Epistle of 1810 we come on a solitary instance of exhortation to take thought for the ministry; it was probably due to the Gurney influence, but many years were to go by before the call was repeated.

interest" toward Friends who met in small meetings or in
others where ministry was seldom heard, pointing out
that the fact of a meeting having usually been held in
silence afforded no reason why this should always continue to be so, and calling upon Friends to realize their
own responsibility for service. "A self-imposed silence
in man's will," so runs one sentence, "may be scarcely
less formal or hurtful than words wanting fitness or
power."

In the *Epistle* of 1862 this uneasiness concerning the
continually unbroken silence of many meetings again
found expression. This was largely the outcome of an
appeal which in one of the sittings had been made by Isaac
Brown, a Friend who, by means of his powerful ministry
and intellectual endowments, was a leader of the fine
company of men and women who brought a new stream of
life into the Society. He said that in his youth he had
passed ten years, part of the time as a pupil and part as a
master, in a school of sixty or seventy boys and that, in the
meeting which they attended, months together might pass
without a word being spoken. He also mentioned the
deficiency of ministry in the meeting attended by three
hundred children at Ackworth, where he was then living.[1]
At that time each meeting would be not less than an hour
and a half in length.

The fact of this misgiving as to continual silence finding
expression in official pronouncements of the Society called
forth lively indignation. One Friend wrote of it as "tend-

---

[1] *The Friend*, 1862, p. 130; *British Friend*, 1862, p. 139. The report
of a subsequent address shows that he had been taken to task for what
he had said, *The Friend*, p. 135; *British Friend*, p. 142. In 1864 a
Friend wrote, "Often has the mother of a large and interesting family
told me, with tears, that she hardly knew how to keep on taking her
children to meeting where, most often, not a word was heard and
where some at the head of the meeting were habitually overcome with
drowsiness," *The Friend*, 1864, p. 277.

ing to the disparagement of a mode of worship already too much despised and undervalued especially by the younger members."[1] Another writer took objection to what he described as "an un-Quakerly and unscriptural exaltation of the 'ministry,' as the public preaching of the Gospel is now somewhat conventionally called." He speaks later of public ministry as an "awful service."[2]

In the following year a writer in *The Friend*, in no way disparaging the silent worship but calling attention to the right place, both of it and of the ministry of the word, spoke of the easy excuse by which at that time (as at many others) Friends sought justification for their refusal to face disquieting facts; "the gifts of the Spirit," he says, "have died out or been withdrawn through want of faith—and so, in order to fill up the void, we have stretched a truth beyond its proper dimensions, and tried to comfort ourselves with holding up this 'power beyond words' as the one great object of our meetings!"[3]

In 1868 it was officially reported that there were more than a hundred meetings in which there was no vocal ministry except from visitors.[4]

---

[1] *British Friend*, 1860, p. 250.

[2] *Quakerism, Catholic and Evangelical*, Anonymous (1863), pp. 20–21. The writer holds firmly the essential inward principle of Quakerism and at the same time the doctrines of the Evangelical party, the "progressive" party, as it is elsewhere called. He expresses thorough agreement with its principles but objects to its "mode of manifestation" (p. 18), i.e. where it clashed with his opinions, above expressed, concerning ministry, and in a certain "evangelical" enthusiasm, not to say exuberance, of new life. Curiously enough, however, from the conservative Friends who, on this matter, were in full agreement with him he parts company in his whole-hearted commendation of the "evangelical" party for bringing about "the present 'revival' among us," "new life into the torpid system," as he puts it. For more about this part of the pamphlet, see *post*, p. 297.

[3] *The Friend*, 1863, pp. 117–118. The other two articles in the series of which this is the third are on pp. 68, 94.

[4] *The Friend*, 1868, p. 155. On the same page see the address of Isaac Brown.

In 1862 there appeared in *The Friend* (p. 307) a curious allegory entitled "After Bunyan." Christian and Hopeful, on their way to the Celestial City, fall in with a solitary pilgrim, who tells them that his name is Silent, and that he has come on pilgrimage "from the village of Respectability, which is a place a little way out of the City of Destruction where many of the richer citizens do have their abode. [His] father's name was Love-the-Truth." Although he would for a time converse with them on certain topics, when they wished to take counsel concerning their way or otherwise to speak of their pilgrimage he withdrew from them, saying that in order to avoid the sin of Talkative he had made a promise to God that in regard to spiritual matters, until he "should stand within the pearl gates of the City, [his] lips should be silent." Accordingly, refusing to get or give spiritual help by means of intercourse with them, he went on his way solitary, but when all three of them were safe in the City they raised the song of the redeemed and "the song of him that was lately named Silent was the loudest and most joyful of all."

The *excess of fear* of the call to the ministry of which we have spoken (as distinct from a holy sense of responsibility) is not the necessary or only alternative to the lightmindedness from which comes a shallow utterance of words, but it has left its unhappy mark on succeeding generations. To this day in many quarters the very mention of responsibility for ministry arouses embarrassment and an attempt to blunt the edge of the appeal for the service, but of positive disparagement of it in itself there has been less heard in the present century than in the preceding one. There may, however, at times be caught a hint or insinuation that the spoken word is an intrusion on the silent teaching of the Spirit, a suggestion that the dwellers on a high spiritual plane have got "beyond words." This way of thought characteristic of the middle period of the Quaker Society rather than of the earliest has, under the guise of aesthetic or spiritual culture, continually led to indolence and deadness, even if it was not in its beginning prompted by them. Spiritual luxuriousness is destructive of spiritual life. In 1867 a leading Friend, himself an able minister, made his protest against this pseudo-Quakerism: "We do not," he says, "find in the New Testament that disesteem of 'words' which some have supposed to be a mark of superior spirituality."[1] A Quaker writer has left on record the fact of his hearing a Friend say in Yearly Meeting that "the only thing the ministry amongst us required was universal repression," and that he was "happy to say that in the meeting to which he belonged they had had no resident minister for above fifty years."[2] In all this we see the chief reason for past and present decay of hundreds of meetings in England, Ireland and America. Friends of keen philanthropic and public activity, of spiritual power and saintly life, have deplored the dying away of their congregation and have never sought the gifts of ministry, teaching and pastoral care which might have saved it. The silence of each generation in turn has heaped up difficulty for the next. The weakness has, at times, been accentuated by so great an insistence on the fact of ministry being but one service among many, as to depress it (being but "words") *below* the rest. It is seldom a profitable pastime to arrange in scale of value things which are all *necessary*. At one time it became conventional

---

[1] William Ball, *The Friend*, 1867, p. 31.
[2] *Gospel Ministry in the Society of Friends* (p. 14), by Joseph John Dymond (1825–1907), a series of articles which appeared in *The Friend* of 1892. They give insight into the curious attitude of mind which prevailed round about the middle of the nineteenth century. See an Editorial article in the *British Friend*, 1860, pp. 193–94.

to point out that *minister* meant *servant*, and that, besides the service of words, there was the "ministry" of a man in his business and of a woman in the home. This is, of course, true, but the effect, if not intention of this way of talk was to damp down the ministry in the meeting for worship by furnishing excuse for abstention from it. For lack of watchfulness and honest self-examination we may, half-unconsciously, find ourselves framing excuses for our withholding of that which we ought to give, allowing "inertia to put on the garb of humility, commendation or even exercise of 'faithfulness in the little' to serve as evasion of faithfulness in the great, insistence on 'diversity of gifts' and on 'all service ranking the same with God' to justify our selection of the easiest."[1] The mistake which the Quaker society has made throughout a great part of its history has not been its essential testimony to the striving of the Inward Teacher speaking in the silence, but its neglect and, even, disparagement of religious teaching and of the ministry of the word: "The eye cannot say to the hand, I have no need of thee."

From this it will be seen that this historical record of misunderstanding or depreciation of ministry is not intended as depreciation of silence, *an essential element in Quaker worship* (equally essential being the *liberty* to speak), or of the helpful spontaneous utterance, longer or shorter, given forth by the worshipper alert to receive and transmit the message. Well has it been said, "The real question for a Friend to answer about any meeting is not 'Did you speak?' or 'Did you keep silence?' but, a far deeper one, 'Did you obey?'" And the same writer draws attention to a forgotten truth, "to go to a meeting determined to speak or determined to keep silence are both

---

[1] The passage in quotation marks is repeated (slightly altered) from my Swarthmore Lecture, *The Things that are Before Us*, p. 54.

unquakerly."[1] Equally unquakerly, it may be added, is the indifference which never gives thought, one way or the other, to personal responsibility for ministry.

A testimony to the power of the silent worship, similar to that of Robert Barclay, will be given later when we come to the work of Caroline E. Stephen in the latter part of the nineteenth century.[2]

And inasmuch as the purpose of this book is to give understanding of present-day conditions, a digression may be permitted in order to say further concerning ministry that while it is a joyful service, it should be neither a casual nor even an easy one, nor apart from travail of soul is it to be exercised. A Friends' meeting is a coming together for the worship of God, and is no place for the airing of opinions by those who are unable to find an audience elsewhere. A Church, alive to the all-round welfare of its members, will welcome and, if possible, provide opportunities for discussion and intellectual study, but its united worship, as distinct from these, arises in response to the spiritual needs of man, and it is toward these needs that ministry will be directed. It will have no narrow range, it will neither discard the intellect as an instrument nor will it turn aside from a view of the world's sickness, but, inasmuch as the greater part of this is due to man's evil, the ministry, and in fact, the whole of the worship, will have as their concern the nurture of the spiritual life both of individuals and of the congregation at large. It is this life that will animate and make permanently effective the schemes that may be devised and the good work that may be done for the healing of the sickness.[3] As we thus under-

---

[1] L. Violet Hodgkin, *The Surrender of Silence* (a pamphlet), pp. 7, 9. [2] P. 322.
[3] The writer takes leave to refer to his Swarthmore Lecture, *The Things that are Before Us*, pp. 18 ff.

stand the Friends' meeting for worship we shall know that
it finds no room for debate or for the answering (still less
for the contradicting) of one speaker by another; if this is
desirable, it will be left for another occasion. And if anything should seem to be spoken amiss, the spiritually
minded worshipper will have the wit to get at the heart of
the message, overlooking crudity and lack of skill in its
presentation, and so far from giving way to irritation at
what seems unprofitable, he will be deeply concerned for
his own share in creating the right spiritual atmosphere
in which the harm fades out and the good grows. Many a
meeting has known this power, transforming what might
have been hurtful into a means of grace.[1] Each Monthly
Meeting appoints "Elders," whose main function is the
help of the ministry and of ministers. They give counsel,
not as spiritual superiors or (still less) as infallible guides,
and the minister who, it is to be assumed, has wished to
speak for the help of the congregation, not for the airing of
his own ideas, and not for the advertisement of himself,
will be willing at least *to consider* the suggestions of those
whose concern for the meeting's welfare is as deep as his
own. The hard assertiveness which is determined to have
its own word, resenting kindly counsel even if such seems
to be mistaken, is wholly out of place in a Friends' meeting,
being alien to the spirit in which alone right ministry can be
exercised. The true message, however plain-spoken it be,
will win its way, not by truculence and discourtesy, but by
persuasiveness and love. And, notwithstanding difference,
there will in practice, be no strain between minister and
elder, each of them seeking to serve the congregation
in the mind of Christ; and each of them will help the
other.

Concerning the attitude of the worshipper toward the

_____
[1] *Ante,* p. 104.

minister himself there comes a fine word of counsel, a refreshing air, from the eighteenth century:

> [I] would beseech Friends when it may please God to raise up and qualify any for the work of the ministry that they do not slight it nor despise the instruments who may be so concerned how mean so ever they may appear in the eyes of men; for it is the Lord's work who is able to qualify; *but be diligently exercised in your minds that they may feel the help of your spirits for their strength and encouragement; for the exercise and concern of the true ministers is of more weight to them than some are aware of.*[1]

Another word from the eighteenth century, spoken by a son of the seventeenth, is also to be heeded in our own. Samuel Bownas, who, more than other Friends, gave attention to the ministry, records his service in 1726, when he was fifty years old, at a meeting of ministers in Pennsylvania,

> . . . wherein was shown the danger of murmuring at the seeming weakness of our gifts to a degree of dejection and neglect to exercise ourselves in them, showing that every gift of the ministry was of great service though but small in comparison [with the gift] of others and had a great beauty in it, and that we ought by no means to slight and neglect it, but to think well and to be thankful that the Father of spirits hath given us a gift though but small.[2]

[1] John Bell, "Testimony to James Dickenson" (1659–1741), Dickenson's *Journal*, pp. xxi.–xxiii. The italics are mine. It was Dickenson who, in 1726, started the movement which led to the compilation, *Sufferings of the Quakers*, by Joseph Besse (1753). *J.F.H.S.* (xxiii.), 1926, p. 1. See *London Yearly Meeting During 250 Years* (1668–1918), pp. 42 ff.

[2] *Life of Samuel Bownas*, pp. 159–60. In 1750 Bownas issued a book, *A Description of the Qualifications Necessary to a Gospel Minister* (see *ante*, p. 258). He was an English, not an American, Friend. Concerning the subject of this chapter see *The Quaker Ministry*, by J. W. Graham (1925), pp. 42–65, and an article entitled "A Few Thoughts on the Present State of the Ministry in the Society of Friends," by J. G. [Jonathan Grubb], *The Friend*, 1868, pp. 27–28; also by the same writer an article in *The Friend*, 1864, p. 276.

This story of Quaker ministry remains to be completed when we speak of the changes which came about in the middle of the nineteenth century, and particularly of the work of John Wilhelm Rowntree at the end of it (p. 320).

Chapter XVI

PHILANTHROPY AND SPIRITUAL LIFE:
BREAK WITH TRADITIONAL OBSERVANCES[1]

IN our telling of the emergence of Friends from their seclusion into the life of their time it has been necessary to describe the condition of the Society during the eighteenth century and part of the nineteenth, and to show the influences that were shaping it. We saw the flow of a new stream into its religious life which had become circumscribed owing to a one-sided stress on the profoundly important fact of the inward teaching of the Spirit. The philanthropic genius, which never failed it, also began to enter on new fields of activity, and it was here that the new life began to come into conflict with the old. We have already noticed (p. 178) the alarm of the bewildered conservatism which exercised a pitiless repression on all new adventure. The insistence on the need for some extraordinary sense of "call" (a protest, it must be remembered, against its opposite extreme of superficiality and lightness) gave rise to the assumption that anyone undertaking religious or philanthropic work outside the traditional or usual lines, or appearing in ministry without certain conventional mannerisms, was acting without a call, "running before he was sent" and thereby rendering himself liable to be "consumed with sparks of his own kindling." Other expressions, catchwords as they might be called, which came into use were "creaturely activity" and "unsanctified zeal," and these, for long years, acted as a blight on many an upspringing of life. The former of them was used to stigmatize good works

[1] See footnote to the title of chapter xiv, p. 220.

lightly undertaken without divine leading, and the indiscriminate misuse of it by way of repression called forth a plain-spoken and much needed protest. The *British Friend*, the organ of the conservative party, printed the challenge addressed to it, but repudiated the accusation:

> I should be truly glad if many of our dear timorous Friends—and the Editors of the *British Friend* among them —would cease so unreasonably to alarm themselves about *"creaturely activity."* I believe it will be found as the heart is honestly searched, that this favourite expression is a term that is often used as a cloak to hide *much spiritual sloth.*[1]

A suggestion of any new line of corporate action could always be dismissed by some "weighty" Friend saying that "the time had not come," or that the matter must be "left to individual faithfulness." In the early days of the Adult School movement, to be described later (p. 308), there certainly was considerable encouragement given to the young men who taught reading and writing, this service being in line with the tradition of philanthropy, but there was alarm at their giving direct religious instruction. In the late 1840's the work of Sunday-school teaching, which for many years had been carried on by some Friends, received a great impetus under the guidance of many of the finest minds in the Society,[2] but an undercurrent of dislike to it at times showed itself on the surface. In 1861 a Friend expressed his fear "that the Sabbath Schools and Bible Classes may lead Friends away from their principles and into great activity."[3] Friends

---

[1] *British Friend*, 1860, p. 222. [2] *Post*, p. 295.

[3] Hine, *A Mirror for the Society of Friends*, p. 121 note, and see letters in the *British Friend*, 1860, pp. 119, 218 ("I look upon this movement as even a snare to our young people so engaged from . . . the undue putting forward of the creaturely powers which lead to . . . a display of that knowledge which puffeth up"), 249; 1862, p. 17 (see replies to this, pp. 39, 40); 1864, p. 294.

visited with at least unofficial censure one of their number
who called together his neighbours to minister to them,
or who assembled young men at his house for united
Scripture reading, and a certain one who made a
practice of reading the Bible to the inmates of a workhouse was cold-shouldered out of the Society. "They
tread on slippery ground who assume the capacity of
giving *religious* instruction," wrote one of the older school
as with fear he saw the mixing of Friends with others;
such proceeding being in his eyes "the dawnings of that
forwardness and licence of action on the part of the young
which is now so much promoted for the furtherance
of popular benevolent enterprises."[1] Those who can
remember the prevalence of this spirit in the Society are
the less disposed to be impatient at opposition to present-
day progress as they have knowledge of its ancestry (and
also of the Christian character of many of the ancestors)
and as they contemplate the progress that has been
made.

Throughout this time there is evidence of concern
for the spiritual welfare of the younger members in particular, and meetings of them were addressed by certain
Friends, but sustained, effective pastoral care was unknown. In fact, the absence of this and the poverty
of religious teaching have been a cause of weakness in the
Society throughout its history. On this conception of
each human soul standing faithful to its own Divine
leading, such *unbalanced* emphasis was laid as to result
in a hard individualism, making instruction difficult and
widespread communion of saints impossible. It was for
this reason that John Stephenson Rowntree had to point
out that the strength of Friends "has never been ade-

[1] Pickard, *An Expostulation*, etc. (1864), p. 110; see *post*, p. 299.

quately put forth towards the development of an active congregational spiritual life" on a large scale, their failure in this respect being no less conspicuous than their success in fashioning strong individual characters.[1] A profound reserve on which Friends came to pride themselves rendered inconceivable the group gathering of like-minded persons meeting for communion and prayer; the glowing spiritual fellowship of early days had no place and would have been repressed had it made its appearance. Forgotten was the loving counsel of Fox as he pleaded for gentle and not harsh judgment of the young minister: "Let it be your joy to hear or see the springs of life break forth in any."[2]

Apart from knowledge of the lines of thought here described, an understanding of present-day conditions is not to be reached; and particularly are we able to understand the contrast, so perplexing to many, between the weakness of Quakerism in setting forth its spiritual message and its strength in philanthropic enterprise. There is continual temptation to regard outward works of benevolence as an adequate alternative to spiritual life rather than as the necessary outcome of it. To this

[1] *Life and Work*, pp. 216, 272, 292. The writer, however, does not make it clear that he himself saw fully the reason for the failure which he accurately describes.

[2] *Journal* (Cambridge edn.), i. 222, *Journal*, bi-cent. edn., i. 344. Elsewhere Fox gives counsel, "Let not the mouths of babes and sucklings be stopped," *Epistles*, pp. 235, 328. For this side of his character see *ante*, pp. 39–40. The writer has good reason for believing stories told by elders claiming as a meritorious act their stopping of young Friends speaking in meeting. The Quaker conventional expression cannot be better illustrated than by the following passage in an obituary notice of a Friend of upright business life who for many years filled important posts in the organization and business affairs of his meeting. He "was a typical 'Friend,' especially in a certain reserve he maintained about the deepest things of life, but he was an example of a man whose life was 'hid with Christ in God,' and bore a silent testimony to what he believed were the fundamental principles of all true religion."

lack of clear perception John Stephenson Rowntree, in 1897, addressed a warning:

> I cannot concur in the opinion that the main place for Friends in English society is now to furnish a body of benevolently disposed persons, concerned in the philanthropic work of the nation whilst declining more strenuous issues. Rather I should say that their great contribution to the national life consists in keeping before it a presentation of Christianity—at once spiritual, ethical and practical in influencing conduct.[1]

Elsewhere the same writer observes that Friends had "gone at least far enough in the direction of . . . civil and political life" and that a caution was needed "against undervaluing the quieter and less conspicuous spheres of services wherein Christian character is formed and matured."[2] These words appeal to us with the greater force as we remember that the writer, one of the most powerful of Quaker ministers, was himself mindful of them during several years' service on the York City Council, for one year filling the office of Lord Mayor.

In face of the appalling need of the world on its material side, demanding instant attention, the self-denying, earnest philanthropic worker may overlook the fact of his losing touch with his spiritual base of action. To this danger the Society of Friends has been exposed, a danger described by a modern writer, after speaking in moving words of the poverty and misery which call for aid:

> I should not say all I have to say if I did not pass on from nobler cares to the noblest cares of all . . . what we think of as ordinary "philanthropy" is not enough. It does not touch the poverty of the soul. . . . Man does not live by

---

[1] *Life and Work*, p. 215.   [2] *Ibid.*, p. 241.

bread alone—who will acquaint him with the words which proceed out of the mouth of God? Where are the men who will tell plain people "what they want to know about God and Jesus Christ"?

*   *   *   *

Even these nobler cares may be the cause of our losing a direct touch with God. The thing has been known— perhaps I ought to say that it has often been known in our time. In the multitude of philanthropies, God Himself has faded out of men's lives. And so, not only do they never grow themselves to the full stature of a perfect man in Christ Jesus, but they fail those whom they have made their friends just when their need is greatest. They will do anything for them but the highest thing of all.[1]

The statement of doctrine put forth in 1836 (p. 230), evangelical though it was, was not immediately accompanied by any lifting of the weight of repression. From those who would serve the Church conformity to the Quaker garb and speech was yet to be demanded for another twenty years or more, and as we have seen (pp. 220, 221), there was alarm at the growing intercourse of its members with those beyond its borders. For the carrying of a spiritual message to the outside world there was but little opportunity or encouragement outside traditional lines, the service of Friends in this direction being, for the most part, confined to the giving away of Quaker literature, mainly tracts and Barclay's *Apology*, and the holding of "public meetings." It would be made known in a district that, at the request of a Friend, sometimes named, sometimes not, a meeting to which the public were specially invited would be held;[2] there was careful

---

[1] George Hare Leonard, *Nobler Cares*, 3rd edn., pp. 57, 58, 63.
[2] It is not unlikely that the giving out of these invitations to what were called "public meetings" is partly responsible for the widespread belief that the ordinary "Friends' meetings for worship" are private. Concerning these meetings see the *British Friend*, 1864, pp. 174, 293.

avoidance of any statement that he would speak and
sometimes (in the eighteenth century, at any rate, though
perhaps not later), to the bewilderment of large numbers
who had come together, he did not do so.[1] A considerable
number of Friends, in their ardour for a wider Christian
service, left the Society which could ill afford to lose any
of its spiritually active members. Unmoved and con-
temptuous, it saw them go. But although their service
ignored much of essential Quakerism, their desire to
minister to the souls as well as to the bodies of men
was more nearly akin to the spirit of the seventeenth
century than was the crushing weight of traditionalism
by which it was opposed. It was to this instinct or habit of
opposition which, as the writer can remember, had with
many Friends become a kind of "second nature," that
Samuel Tuke of York addressed himself in defending
religious enthusiasm, even with all its risk of misleading
the judgment:

> It is observable that there is nothing which the world
> more easily forgives than errors of this kind, with one
> exception, and that in regard to religion. A man may be an
> enthusiastic soldier—an enthusiastic poet—an enthusiastic
> lover—and may carry his enthusiasm on all these points
> to very absurd lengths without offence to the world; but
> he whose love for his Maker and Redeemer absorbs his
> soul, and who, acting on imperfect judgment, is led to any
> erroneous views or expectations, commits, in the court of
> the world, the sin *unpardonable*. There is, let it be remem-
> bered, such a thing as too *little* as well as too much zeal;

[1] *Ante*, p. 254. It was in the early 1890's that there first grew up the
present widely adopted plan of holding on Sunday evenings meetings
at which an announced speaker gives an address or lecture on an
announced subject, an exposition of Quakerism or other spiritual
message. They are not technically regarded as "Friends' meetings for
worship," in that there is but little time of silence or opportunity for
others to give a message. Many Friends were seriously disturbed at
this innovation.

and it is worthy of remark that where religious enthusiasm is severely censured, religious indifference does not rank in the catalogue of offences.[1]

In these words we see the dawn of an uprising against the tradition by which Friends had long been bound. Other indications of this can be found scattered up and down the writings of the time; Elizabeth Fry expressed her uneasiness at the stress laid on minor testimonies to the neglect of weightier matters.[2] In the Yearly Meeting of 1849 there was a discussion concerning the insistence on a certain mode of dress and speech as qualification for office, however humble, in the service of the Church. John Bright spoke in favour of relaxation, and to a letter which he afterwards received taking him to task for so doing, he sent a reply, charming in its courtesy and humility. It is treasured at Ackworth School, where Bright was, for a short time, a pupil.[3]

[1] Introduction to *Life of Stephen Crisp* (1628–1692), published 1824, pp. xl.–xli.

[2] *Memoirs*, ii. 5. For the indignation of the conservative Friends at Elizabeth Fry's criticism of their rigidity in outward observances, see *British Friend*, 1848, p. 70; 1853, pp. 127–28. See also *ante*, p. 185.

[3] The following is part of the letter: "Don't for a moment suppose I can be displeased with thy letter. I know it proceeds from the most honest motives, and from a real desire for my welfare, and as such I can and do receive it. . . . I often suspect that in these things we are 'teaching for doctrines the commandments of men,' and making to ourselves burdens which Christianity is intended to free us from. Simplicity and absence of ostentation in dress, and truthfulness in language, are consistent with and required by the religion we profess, and from these I hope I do not depart, altho' in my conduct they do not adopt the precise form which seems to thee to be essential." See *ante*, p. 191 note. The following account of Bright's address to the Yearly Meeting is contained in *A Quaker Journal, Being the Diary of William Lucas of Hitchin*, pp. 431–32: "An interesting discussion brought on by John Bright, on our peculiarities of dress and language, was the most novel feature during the proceedings. The weight of the meeting was all against him but I felt the truth of his remarks as I have no doubt did many more. Whilst highly estimating the testimony of the Society to plainness and simplicity of dress and sincerity in language, he condemned the formality and singularity into which we have fallen."

From this time onward letters appeared in *The Friend* advocating freedom from traditional conventionality,[1] and, on the other side, the *British Friend* and its correspondents set themselves uncompromisingly against any change. It took as its motto "Stand ye in the ways and see, and ask for the old paths, where is the good way and walk therein" (Jer. vi. 16). A certain passage written in the year 1858 shows the inner working of the conservative mind more clearly than we are usually allowed to see it: "So highly do we value the writings of our early Friends . . . that we are always rather averse to say much in favour of works of modern date lest we should thereby contribute, in any degree, to throw the former into the shade" (p. 134). Each of the two periodicals referred to was started in 1843.[2]

But notwithstanding all the good work done by Friends in the nineteenth century, there were ominous signs that all was not well with their Church. And yet the beginning of the century had seen the triumph of the campaign, to which they had made large contribution, against the slave trade; later on, largely through the efforts of Joseph Sturge, slavery was abolished in the British dominions; Elizabeth Fry had done her great work (greater than is generally realized) for prison reform, Friends in many places had taken their part along with others in providing schools for elementary education (such education not being compulsory till the Act of 1870), they had set up several boarding schools for their own children, in their own

[1] The correspondence in *The Friend* was not all on one side, and at first the paper itself on some points took the conservative stand, e.g. "we believe that the *peculiarity* of the dress of the Society has its advantages which could not be dispensed with without loss to the body" (1853, p. 147. See also pp. 91, 104-5, 128-29, 148-50.

[2] Each of them began as a monthly periodical; in 1892 *The Friend* came to be issued weekly; in 1913 the *British Friend* was given up. It had long ceased to be the exponent of immovable conservatism.

districts they were often to the fore in work for the public welfare, they were recognized as having played a fine part in the relief of distress caused by the potato famine in Ireland in 1846–47;[1] in 1848 a Friend could write, "Perhaps at no period of the Society's history, more than the present, have Friends, both individually and as a body, been more esteemed" (though he admits that the public in general were almost totally ignorant of their principles).[2] It is true that by reason of their Peace testimony they became unpopular in the time of the Crimean War, but otherwise they were held in high esteem for their good works, their simplicity and sincerity of life and their honesty in business. Nevertheless to the outside world it was becoming evident, resolute as many Friends were in refusal to face the disquieting fact, that the Society was dying down. As late as 1862 John Bright was reported as saying in Yearly Meeting:

. . . there must be something wrong when a body professing a faith so sublime, so simple and so scriptural, not only did not increase as it ought, but decreased, and threatened to become altogether soon extinct.[3]

In fact, for about a hundred years this note of hopelessness had been heard and for more than twenty years before the last mentioned date (1862) the actual membership had been declining at the rate of nearly one hundred and twenty a year. Part of this decline, however, was due to emigration.[4] A list of tracts or pamphlets published in the late 1850's furnished melancholy evidence of the weakness. One of them was entitled, *An Essay on the Cause of the*

---

[1] A full report of the work of English and Irish Friends is given in *Transactions of the Central Relief Committee of the Society of Friends During the Famine in Ireland in 1846 and 1847.*
[2] *British Friend*, 1848, p. 310. [3] *Ibid.*, 1862, p. 139.
[4] *Ibid.*, 1859, p. 25; see the letter on p. 24.

Decline of the Society of Friends, by "Quantum Mutatus," the opening sentence of which runs thus: "To regard the Society of Friends as it now is, and to remember what it was two centuries ago is something like paying a visit to the bed of an exhausted mountain torrent, or the crater of an extinct volcano." Others were issued under similar titles containing the words "Decline" or "Decadence."[1] In later years a writer looking back from outside of the Society on this period of its history and rejoicing at its subsequent recovery, has accurately spoken of its condition: "It was dying—a slow, delicious death no doubt, but dying none the less—of introspection, of self-esteem, of quietism." "Nothing," wrote a prominent Friend in 1864, "can exceed the quietness of my mind."[2]

In 1858 there appeared in many periodicals and newspapers the announcement that "a Gentleman" who believed that the Society of Friends had at one time borne "a powerful witness to the world concerning some of the errors to which it is most prone" was anxious to know the reason of that witness "becoming more and more feeble." He offered a prize of one hundred guineas for the best essay written on the subject and one of fifty guineas for the one next in merit. Three well-known religious leaders (none of them Friends), one of whom was F. D. Maurice, were invited to be judges of the essays sent in for the competition. About one hundred and fifty were submitted to them; the two to which prizes were awarded and a number of others were published. The name of the donor has never been disclosed. To Thomas Hancock, a clergyman of the Church of England, was awarded the second prize, which was increased to a hundred guineas;

---

[1] Some of these were written by Friends, others, like the one above-named, by non-Friends.
[2] Hine, *A Mirror for the Society of Friends*, p. 113.

his essay, *The Peculium*, written from the Anglo-Catholic point of view, argued that the Society was inevitably destined to die out by reason of its departure from the Church as constituted by Christ, built on the apostolic foundation which he had laid.

The first prize was won by John Stephenson Rowntree of York, at that time twenty-four years old; it was published under the title, *Quakerism, Past and Present: Being an Enquiry into the Causes of its Decline in Great Britian and Ireland*. The author was one of the fine company, of whom mention will be made later, who rescued the Society from the torpor into which it was settling down. His essay traced the causes of decline to certain internal weaknesses, neither inherent nor inevitable but due to a deadening traditionalism and to the weakness of individual members. Among the causes mentioned were: (*a*) the lack of suitable ministry (it has already been stated that many meetings were continually held wholly in silence)[1] and of religious teaching, due to the disparagement of the intellect as serviceable to the spiritual life; (*b*) the official insistence on antiquated forms of dress, speech and manners; (*c*) the ruthless "disownment" (expulsion from the Society) for marriage with a non-Friend, "marrying out," as it was called;[2] (*d*) the practice of "birthright membership," as already explained (p. 209). Concerning this last alleged cause of weakness, Rowntree subsequently changed his opinion and defended the practice in an article which appeared in *The Friends' Quarterly Examiner* of 1872.

Not unnaturally the conservative Friends took alarm.

---

[1] *Ante*, p. 269.
[2] The technical ground of disownment was not the marrying of a non-member, but the using the service of a "paid" minister, although there was no way of marrying a non-member except by resort to a minister; see *post*, p. 293.

T

For some time they had refused to face the fact of the decline in the Society's numbers and when they could no longer wholly evade the challenge they would speak of it as "the alleged decline," knowing, as they did, the reasons for it that would be put forward.[1] When the announcement of the competition was first made and when the essay was published the depth of their indignation can be seen in correspondence and in articles which appeared in the *British Friend*.[2] *The Friend*, on the other hand, while making certain criticisms, gave the essay a cordial welcome.[3]

About this time it became conventional to insist that what the Society needed for its regeneration was not more ministry and teaching but a greater faithfulness to that which was already known and a deeper spiritual life.[4] This was, of course, true as regarded the end to be achieved, but there was little recognition of the place of ministry and teaching in stirring up and strengthening the deeper life, in fact, as we have seen, they were liable to be looked on with suspicion as hindrances to it.

But a true understanding of all this cannot be reached apart from a knowledge of the background against which it is to be seen, and this will be furnished by the story of the changes in outlook and practice, the painful emergence from a conventional traditionalism, which took place in the Society shortly after the middle of the century.

In 1850 the Yearly Meeting came to a decision which

[1] Up to the present day, 1938, it is one cause of weakness, the refusal to face disquieting facts often by means of a trick of saying some pleasant thing pretending to hide the weakness, cp. Is. xxx. 10; Jer. vi. 14, viii. 11; Ezek. xiii. 10.

[2] See 1858, pp. 96 and particularly, 297 ff.; 1859, pp. 236, 256, 268; 1860, pp. 34, 51, 107, 173, 186, 203.

[3] 1860, pp. 1, 32, 35, 56, 69. Concerning this essay see R. M. Jones, *The Later Periods of Quakerism*, pp. 947 ff., part of the chapter entitled "The Awakening in England."

[4] See, for example, *British Friend*, 1858, p. 302.

some Friends regarded as a "sapping of the foundation of one of the distinguishing testimonies of our Society," namely the "testimony" against gravestones which we have already noticed (p. 186) The decision was that the placing on graves of "a small flat stone with the name and date inscribed" was not a breach of Quaker principle.[1] A certain Friend in the course of a prayer of thanksgiving for the refusal of his Monthly Meeting to avail itself of the permission thus granted ejaculated: "O foolish Yearly Meeting of 1850! what an apple of discord hast thou cast forth." Further departures from ancient custom were causing uneasiness in many minds. A letter in the *British Friend* draws attention to "the increasing practice of wearing wedding rings," calling it "the badge of an hireling ministry."[2] Another expresses regret that in certain families, instead of "Father" and "Mother," children were saying "Papa" and "Mamma" inasmuch as these were "worldly phrases," "inconsistent with Gospel simplicity" and not "according to Scripture."[3] Other letters contain warnings against Friends having their portraits painted or possessing portraits, and against the insertion of them in biographies.[4] There are two protests against crochet and other fancy work, *"little foxes,"* as they are described, "small, cunning and injurious, which creep stealthily onward to the destruction of those fruits of self-denial

---

[1] See *The Friend*, 1850, pp. 94, 110, 111. In the following year a "considerable time" of the meeting was taken up by discussion of a request from Norfolk for permission to place the stones upright instead of flat. The request was refused: "It appeared to the meeting that to entertain the proposition would be to open the door to endless diversity of practice of which no one could either foresee the end or the consequences that might result," *British Friend*, 1851, p. 135.

[2] 1847, p. 81; see *ante*, p. 184.   [3] 1844, p. 54.

[4] 1847, pp. 81, 128; 1848, pp. 77–78, 300–301. See 1862, p. 16, a review finding fault with a certain biography for containing a portrait, and more on p. 40, also 1849, p. 77 ("Barclay's Apology—Ury").

that are characteristic of the true Friend."[1] Against "the increasing prevalence of hymns among Friends" (not the singing of them but the use of them at all) "in this day of lapsing," a Friend raised his protest, fearing that they would draw away the mind from the teachings of the Holy Spirit. As to a calendar published by Elizabeth Fry, "a text for every day in the year," he can see "nothing of Quakerism about it." To him it seemed the intrusion of uninspired human contrivance into the life of the spirit. "Whither," he asks, "will all these inconsistencies in high quarters lead the people?"[2] An editorial article in the *British Friend* cordially describing a Quaker Sunday school entertainment, nevertheless expresses regret at the introduction of a Christmas tree: "Friends must be on their guard [against] . . . Popish or Episcopalian practices."[3] A Friend, writing to another in 1862, says that a recent Quarterly Meeting had been "a trying time" because it had come to be understood that the tabular statement of statistics relating to membership, which had for the first time been issued in that year, was, for the future, to be an annual production, "the fruits of the natural will," he calls it, "not productive of good or life in our meetings."[4] The increasing practice among Friends of closing their shops on Christmas Day and Good Friday (*ante* p. 184) was described as a "stumbling-block in the way of the serious enquirer after truth."[5] The Yearly Meeting Epistles of 1854 and 1860 give expression to the alarm which was being felt concerning the increasing

[1] 1854, p. 304, and 1855, pp. 48, 74, also 1857, p. 130, col. 2. The Scripture reference is to Cant. ii. 15, a favourite text with Friends at that time and earlier.

[2] *Correspondence of William Hodgson* (1850), p. 114. The Friends Tract Association had put forth a book of hymns for every day in the week.   [3] 1858, p. 43.

[4] *Diary of John G. Sargent*, pp. 115–16.

[5] Editorial note, *British Friend*, 1854, p. 314, and see p. 317.

interest taken in music.[1] But the two main centres of contention were the propositions to discontinue official insistence on the Quaker garb and speech, and to allow marriage in the Quaker way of those who regularly met with Friends in worship although not actually in membership. Up to this time it was legally impossible for a Friend to marry a non-member in his meeting house, and for giving countenance to a "paid" minister by going elsewhere he was "disowned," that is, expelled from the Society. Permission for the change was at last given in 1859. The leader of the movement in favour of it was Joseph Rowntree of York, who lived just long enough to see the success of his work.[2] In 1873 permission for marriage in the Quaker way was given to all persons whomsoever.

It is impossible for us now to understand the strenuousness of the contention against any change in the official attitude, which excluded from all service in the church those who did not conform to the conventional dress and speech. The Quaker garb was said to be a "hedge" protecting the wearer from temptation, and the wearing of it to be in itself good as being, in its humiliation, a taking up of the Cross; that any deviation from it "bespeaks the

---

[1] See, for example, *British Friend*, 1854, p. 93; 1855, p. 138; 1857, p. 212; 1858, p. 161; 1859, pp. 159–60, 160; 1862, p. 93. In her extreme old age, a Friend who had been a mistress at Ackworth in the 1840's told the writer of girls getting into trouble for singing; and as late as 1870 groups of girls would get together to sing out of hearing of the authorities with scouts posted to warn them of the approach of any. At Sidcot, however, when the writer went there in 1873 (he does not know how long before) both boys and girls sang. About 1865 a Friend went with her *fiancé* to a concert and on the day that a relative heard of it he was so much disturbed that he could not in the evening conduct the usual family worship. See *ante*, p. 186 note.

[2] In *The Friend* of 1859, pp. 214–15, is quoted a long obituary notice which appeared in the *York Herald*. It records a life, typical of thousands of others, of the Quaker citizen at his best, lives, many of them of shopkeepers, as Joseph Rowntree was, which have gained respect for the Quaker name. He was the father of John Stephenson Rowntree of whom mention has been made.

beginning of an unstable mind,"[1] that one change would only be succeeded in turn by others and "[*Friends'*] *principle prohibits a following of the fashion.*"[2] On one occasion it was said that as the Queen had her soldiers and officials clothed in her uniform, so the Quaker dress was "the livery of Jesus." On the writer being taken to task he repeated his assertion, and added to it, "I regard our outward peculiarities not only as needful but *indispensable appendages to our high profession*, as a test of our fidelity to the higher principles from which they spring, a guard and defence to our youth." [3] In other words, it was only those who wore the conventional Quaker costume who had any right to be counted as true Friends worthy to be entrusted with service for the Church. A hostile review of *Nehushtan* (*ante* p. 193) in the *British Friend* claimed that these outward "peculiarities" (the Friends' own word) "which it is now the fashion among a portion of our members of the present day to deride, are in fullest accord-

---

[1] *British Friend*, 1851, p. 229, part of an extract from Clarkson's *Portraiture of Quakerism*, in which the writer is setting forth the reasons alleged by Friends of his time (1806) against change of dress. This story of Quaker attire is continued from p. 192.

[2] *British Friend*, 1858, p. 128, and see pp. 102, 156, 301 of the same; also 1854, p. 179; 1856, p. 147; 1859, pp. 121, 269, 297. It was here that the conservative Friends chose to take their stand. Aware of the weakness of their position in an insistence on a particular costume, they asserted that it was *change*, a vain following of the world's fashions, to which they objected. Nevertheless, change had gone on slowly, see a letter, "Quaker Apparel," *The Friend*, 1851, p. 170. The writer tells of a proposal made, near the beginning of the century, at an Ackworth General Meeting for "some improvement in the dress of the boys who had been accustomed from the beginning to wear three-cornered hats and short smalls [breeches] made of leather of durable texture. This antiquated costume exposed them . . . to ridicule." The proposal met with much opposition and the question was postponed, "a fear was expressed that by taking a brick from the crown-arch of the building others might follow and the whole edifice be endangered."

[3] *British Friend*, 1858, pp. 218, 304. On this matter of "peculiarities" see R. M. Jones, *Quakers in the American Colonies*, pp. 168–70, and *Later Periods of Quakerism*, Index, "Peculiar People."

ance with both the spirit and letter of Scripture, and such as do not thus believe are not thoroughly convinced of the Truth as professed by Friends" (1859, p. 246). But the rising tide could not be kept back; in 1851 a writer in *The Friend* viewed with foreboding "the present extensive departure [as he viewed it] from the original practice of the Society";[1] as early as 1853 it was stated that several meetings had appointed to certain services in the Church some who did not wear the Quaker dress.[2] There were many Friends of fine intellectual and spiritual culture who saw with distress the critical state of the Society, though with loving patience they had for years refrained from forcing an issue upon those whom personally they held in esteem. Mention has been made (p. 168) of the Quaker way of controversy which is willing to wait (albeit sometimes overlong), seeking to persuade rather than to override a minority. It was they who met once a year at Ackworth to attend the meeting of the Friends' First Day [Sunday] School Association (p. 279), by far the most spiritually alive organization in the Society at that time. The reports of the proceedings given each year in the August number of *The Friend* and *British Friend* are evidence of the current of new life that was flowing. It has already been said (p. 279) that at times an undercurrent of dislike to the work showed itself on the surface, but those who each year met together, unhindered by the presence of opposing spirits, entered into a fine fellowship among themselves and to them the Society owes an immeasurable debt of gratitude. It was this type of Friend that stirred up interest in the formation of groups for

---

[1] P. 172.
[2] *The Friend*, 1853, pp. 91, 150, and see *Correspondence . . . of William Hodgson*, p. 196, his correspondent mourning over the declension as she viewed it: "if the leaders of the people cause them to err, what can we expect the flock will become?"

Scripture and other religious teaching[1] and gave the impetus which, as already stated (p. 224), led the Yearly Meeting of 1855 to issue a direction to the Quarterly Meetings to take thought for the religious care of their younger members.[2] Yorkshire Quarterly Meeting appointed a committee to consider the matter and published a valuable report of its conclusions; the report contained a timid hint that appointments to service in the Church ought not to be restricted to those who conformed to the official Quaker conventions of dress and speech;[3] Bristol and Somerset Quarterly Meeting spoke out more plainly; and in 1858 the Yearly Meeting arranged for the holding of a conference to take a comprehensive survey of the conditions of the Society. The official record of the proceedings states that "after a full interchange of sentiment concluded in a remarkable degree of brotherly love" it was decided that a change was called for[4] and, accordingly, in 1861 a new *Book of Discipline* was issued in which the ancient form of words "plainness of speech, behaviour and apparel" (an expression which had come to have a purely technical meaning[5]) no longer found a place. Not easily

[1] *Post*, p. 318; for the names of some of the chief leaders see *British Friend*, 1860, p. 210; *The Friend*, 1860, pp. 163 and editorial note, p. 152; also see pp. 187, 203, 204.

[2] One of the leaders of the progressive section was William C. Westlake, who wrote a series of articles giving valuable insight into the state and needs of the Society, *The Friend*, 1861, pp. 256, 284; 1862, pp. 21, 98, 173, 224, 302 (replying to a criticism on pp. 252–53). See also a letter (probably by John Stephenson Rowntree), *The Friend*, 1859, p. 69 and see pp. 187–8, concerning religious teaching: also p. 167.

[3] "Report on the Care of Younger Members," p. 10; the hint is conveyed in the last sentence, as everyone at the time would understand.

[4] Readers who are not Friends are reminded that the decision was not arrived at by means of a vote, see *ante*, p. 168.

[5] *British Friend*, 1858, p. 102; 1859, p. 121. The words were part of the "Fourth Query." Plainness of speech had come to mean the saying of "thee" and "thou" instead of "you" to single persons, the use of the numbers of days of the week or month, instead of the

was their removal brought about; they had become, as it were, the sacred flag or standard which the conservative party was concerned to defend to the last. But the outcome of all this was that, without explicit direction, the "Exhortations to Christian simplicity, moderation, and self-denial" were understood to have no longer any reference to a particular costume or way of speech. With the disappearance of these "peculiarities" others gradually came to an end.[1]

About this time the Society reached its lowest ebb in point of numbers—13,755 in the year 1864.[2]

In view of the foregoing history we can understand the pass to which the Society had come as described in 1863 by the anonymous author of a pamphlet entitled *Quakerism, Catholic and Evangelical*. While he speaks as strongly as any of the "conservative" party in his disparagement of ministry (*ante*, p. 270) and condemns the

---

heathen names (e.g. "Fifth day" instead of "Thursday," the day sacred to the god Thor) and the avoidance of "flattering titles," "Mr.," "Mrs.," "Miss," etc.; plainness of behaviour referred mainly to the avoidance on the part of men of taking off their hats in salutation or on any other occasion when men ordinarily took them off; plainness of apparel referred to a certain garb which had become conventional for men and women respectively.

[1] Three volumes of short stories written by Maude Robinson, illustrative of different periods in the history of the Society of Friends, contain some that describe the period of quietism or the emergence from it. The three volumes are, *The Time of Her Life, Nicholas the Weaver* and *Wedded in Prison*; see also *The Living Remnant* (short stories), by "K. K. K."; *Friends at Their Own Fireside* (two vols.), by Mrs. Ellis; *The Accepting of Thomas Stutterly*, by H. M. Wallis in "Friends' Quarterly Examiner," 1911, p. 246. See also *Some Quaker Characteristics of Seventy Years Ago*, by Walter Robson," *ibid.* 1922, p. 51.

[2] At the end of 1836 the membership of London Yearly Meeting numbered something over 20,300, about 1,100 of whom were resident outside Great Britain. These figures include infant children (see *ante*, p. 209 on "birthright membership") and a number who show no interest in the Society. In addition to the foregoing there are between 4,000 and 5,000 regular "attenders" of Friends' meetings not in membership.

attitude of the "evangelical" or "progressive" party toward it, it is with this party (strange as it seems) that he
takes sides in thankfulness for its earnestness in bringing
"new life into the torpid system" by its care for Sunday
Schools and for Bible study. "Then again," he says, "it is
to Friends of this turn of mind, chiefly and primarily, that
we have to look for that interest and earnestness for the
alleviation of the immense mass of physical, moral and
spiritual destitution that surrounds us, which has become
of recent years so prominent a feature in almost all the
deliberations of the body." He further says that perhaps
the work of greatest value done by the "evangelical
Friends" had been their protest against that formalism
which, during the latter half of the eighteenth and the
first half of the nineteenth century, had been draining the
very life-blood of the Society.[1]

Thus it was, as to certain outward observances, that the
time had come for a change of the old order and passionate
was the grief of many a spiritually minded Friend as he
saw it loom up before him. It had seemed to him as part
of the eternal order that he and those of his own mind
should have the decisive word, and the sight of momentous

---

[1] For an indignant review of this pamphlet see *British Friend*, 1863,
p. 204. At times the outcome of all this was evasiveness and hypocrisy;
young men, when visiting theatres or other places where they wished
to avoid recognition as Friends, would have ordinary turned-down
collars which they could button on to their collarless "plain" Quaker
coats, i.e. on to the "straight" or "stand-up" collar. Girls would keep
at places away from their homes ordinary hats to wear instead of their
Quaker bonnets when out of sight of their parents. A curious formalism was seen in the practice of some Friends wearing ordinary attire
in their everyday life, but putting on the "plain" Quaker garb when
they attended meeting for worship. There is, however, something to be
said on the other side; the garb received the respect accorded to the
costume of a nurse or nun or minister of religion. The writer knew
one of the last of the old school whom some working men on one
occasion followed into his place of business and asked to take care of
some money of theirs, though they knew nothing about him except
that he wore the Quaker dress.

change apart from his consent was like a waking up in a new world where every relation was different, every value changed. The writer remembers one of them preaching from the words of Jeremiah, "O that my head were waters, and mine eyes a fountain of tears, that I might weep day and night for the slain of the daughter of my people."[1] A small group went so far as to part company from the main Society (the "lapsed Society," they called it) and to set up, at Fritchley in Derbyshire, a meeting of their own, outside the Quaker organization, alleging that they were in the true succession from which the larger body was apostate. They left behind them a number of sympathizers who would enter into fellowship with them but who were not prepared to take the extreme step of separation.[2]

The outlook of the conservative Friends is shown in a work entitled *An Expostulation on Behalf of the Truth Against Departures in Doctrine, Practice and Discipline*, written in 1864 by Daniel Pickard of Leeds. It is a minutely detailed review of the "Book of Discipline" of 1861, containing certain justifiable criticisms of that work, both as to matter and style, but in the main it is an expression of opposition to every change. Its point of view has already been indicated (pp. 225, 280). The writer mourns over the fact of many parents

> . . . bringing up their children *from infancy* in the practice of saying "*you*" to one person; and thus exposing their little ones to become an easy prey to the corrupt fashions, vain compliments and bondage of this world.[3]

[1] Chapter ix. 1.

[2] For an account of the uneasiness of the conservative Friends leading up to the Fritchley separation see *Diary and Correspondence of John G. Sargent* and *Correspondence and Memoirs of William Hodgson*.

[3] P. 30. This quotation may give some insight into the importance attached to these "peculiarities" and the tenacity with which they were held. The present writer was once told by a leading Friend, a

He deplores the permission given for the use of grave-stones and for marriages in Friends' meeting houses of persons not in membership, he sees danger in the growing missionary zeal, in the commendation of united Bible study and the expression of thankfulness for intellectual as well as for spiritual gifts as aids to it; he is troubled at the abolition of official enquiry concerning "plainness of speech, behaviour and apparel," at the uneasiness that was being felt in regard to meetings continually held wholly in silence, and at the encouragement to service that was being given, particularly to young Friends who would in that way be brought into association with others.[1] Nevertheless, however desirable and overlong delayed we may think these changes to have been, it is impossible to withhold our sympathy from grief-stricken men and women who, circumscribed as might be their world and ill-proportioned their estimate of values, had yet (more than some of those who had stood against them) a sight of essential Quakerism,[2] whose lives had gained respect for the Quaker name, but who now, though still numerous, came to understand that they no longer held the field. Some of them had borne the outward badge of the Quaker society all their lives, others had, in adult life, taken it on

good deal older than himself, of a stiff Quaker farmer whom he remembered who said he would "rather die like a dog in a ditch than say *yow* [you] to any man." Readers may feel assured that to the present writer this anecdote does not at all seem incredible. He has had from another quarter confirmation of it.

[1] In the *British Friend* for 1848 (p. 282) there is an article containing a warning against Friends being drawn into the "false system" of ministers of other denominations by "an intimate friendship and co-operation with them in private life, and in works of public utility and Christian benevolence." The article asserts that "the more fair-seeming and goodly" the minister, the greater is the danger to the Friend. See *ante*, pp. 178, 188, 220, 221, and *Pen Pictures of London Yearly Meeting*, p. 147. For a protest against this attitude see the *Friend*, 1851, p. 139. On Friends "dwelling alone," see *ante*, p. 189; and *An Affectionate Address to the Society of Friends*, Anon., 1843.

[2] *Ante*, p. 233.

themselves with deep searchings of heart and often with pain, they had all of them "borne the cross" of derision and humiliation, and it was hard to see all this set at nought by a younger world.

But grievous would be the error of the younger world if, in its freedom, it failed in thanksgiving for the men and women who have handed down to it a goodly heritage. Still, as in Fox's day,[1] do men expect from the Quaker Society a high standard of private and public life, they praise it for its works, and to it there must come with mighty appeal the counsel of the old peasant to St. Francis, *Be as good as men think you are.* Intellectual and aesthetic wealth, from which past generations turned aside, is now open to the Friend richly to enjoy, but according to the place in his life which he gives it will it minister abundantly to his fullness of life in its bearing on his spiritual nature, life's crown; or it will be among the riches which make the strait and narrow way, the entrance into the Kingdom, hard. It needs great wisdom and great love at one and the same time to foster the refinement, the culture, the graces of life and, along with them, a mind heedful of the call, *Take thy part in suffering hardship as a good soldier of Christ Jesus.*[2]

> The Master stood upon the mount, and taught.
> He saw a fire in his disciples' eyes;
> "The old law," they cried, "is wholly come to nought,
>   Behold the new world rise!"

> "Was it," the Lord then said, "with scorn ye saw
> The old law observed by Scribes and Pharisees?
> I say unto you, see *ye* keep that law
>   More faithfully than these!"

*   *   *   *

[1] *Ante*, p. 138.   [2] 2 Tim. ii. 3, margin reading of R.V.

Ah! from the old world let some one answer give:
"Scorn ye this world, their tears, their inward cares?
I say unto you, see that *your* souls live
    A deeper life than theirs!"[1]

[1] Matthew Arnold, *Progress.*

Chapter XVII

FOREIGN AND HOME MISSION WORK:
ADULT AND CHILDREN'S SCHOOLS

ONE result of this evangelical movement and release from traditional observance was a stirring of interest in missionary work among the non-Christian peoples. In early days Friends had visited the Turks as well as the "blacks and Indians" confident in their power "to direct them to the grace and spirit of God in them which they have from God in their hearts."[1] And although Fox strenuously contended that in the heathen who knew not the Bible there was "a divine principle," a knowledge of God,[2] nevertheless, in a time when there were but few translations outside the languages of Christendom, he urged the translation into "every man's language and mother tongue" of "the Scriptures of the New Testament and New Covenant," pointing out that the Jews had their Bible in their own language. "They that are against it and do gainsay it, are they not barbarians?" (*Gospel Truth Demonstrated*, p. 742). It is noteworthy that he says nothing about the Old Testament.[3] Friends, however, had little to show for

---

[1] Fox, *Epistles*, p. 493. Fox threw out a challenge to Christian ministers as to why, instead of scrambling for comfortable benefices, they did not "go among the Turks, Tartars, Blacks and Indians and give unto them freely as Christ gave himself freely," *Gospel Truth Demonstrated (Doctrinals)*, p. 389.

[2] *Gospel Truth Demonstrated*, p. 327. "The Heathens' Divinity set upon the Heads of all called Christians, that say they had not known that there had been a God or a Christ unless the Scripture had declared it to them" (1671). See also Penington, *Works*, i. 563 (edn. of 1761), referred to, *ante*, pp. 45–47, 95–96.

[3] About the same time as this, Fox, although he continually used the Old Testament to establish his case, wrote a tract entitled *A Clear Distinction Between the Old Covenant or Old Testament and the New Covenant or New Testament*, showing that Christ abolished the former

their missionary efforts, over-estimating, as they did, the receptive capacity of their hearers and failing to realize the need for sustained educational and pastoral work. Before the end of the seventeenth century their activity in this field died down.

In the early part of the nineteenth century a few Friends became interested in this matter and twice over, in the years 1830 [1] and 1835, at the instance of Bristol and Somerset Quarterly Meeting, it was brought before the Yearly Meeting. Each time, however, and also in 1832, that assembly declined to proceed further. To many Friends the pecuniary support of the missionary seemed to be a violation of their testimony concerning the "free," that is the unpaid, ministry, but when all allowance is made for the sincerity of this objection and for the fact that much energy and money were being expended over philanthropic causes at home, it must be admitted that the refusal of the Society to enter upon this new service was mainly due to an unreasoning conservatism, incapable, as this always is, of taking any large view of the world's need. But in this, as in other matters, a wider outlook was being reached, a stream was flowing too steadily to be held back. Friends were beginning to emerge into public life (mention has been made of Joseph Pease, John Bright and Joseph Sturge) and, as we have seen, the rigidity which insisted on a particular style of dress and of speech was being dissolved away, Acts of Parliament were obtained allowing those who were not Friends

and established the latter (*Gospel Truth Demonstrated*, p. 746). It is told of Ulfilas, the apostle to the Goths in the fourth century, that he refrained from translating into their language certain historical books of the Old Testament on the ground that his people, being so warlike, would get no good from reading them.

[1] See R. M. Jones, *Later Periods of Quakerism*, p. 872.

to be married in the Quaker manner, and the disastrous practice of disownment for "marrying out" gradually came to an end. To the foreign mission cause this atmosphere was favourable, and George Richardson of Newcastle, eighty-five years of age, stepped forth as its leader.

In a letter published in *The Friend* in the year 1860 he pointed out that "brief and transient visits, though very useful for instruction and edification, are not all that is required for the conversion of heathen nations," and he anticipated the day when Friends will be "drawn to take up their residence among the heathen."[1] In 1862, at the age of eighty-nine, he passed away, and two years later the leadership of the cause was taken up by Henry Stanley Newman of Leominster, not yet thirty years old. In 1865 a provisional committee was formed, and the following year Rachel Metcalfe of Manchester went to India, the first missionary to go forth under the auspices of a Quaker organization definitely formed for the purpose. After working for a time with the Church Misionary Society she was joined by two American Friends, and together they started at Hoshangabad, in the Central Provinces, among a "people ignorant even beyond the average in India at that time," the work which continues to the present day.[2] In 1867, Joseph Stickney

---

[1] The opposition to the work is seen in a reply to Richardson's letter, *British Friend*, 1861, p. 172; to *this* there is a reply on p. 200.
[2] *Friends Beyond Seas* (p. 69), by Henry T. Hodgkin, late Secretary of the Friends' Foreign Mission Association. To this book I am indebted for most of what is here written about Friends' foreign missions. On pp. 28–29 a footnote makes mention of typical opposition and p. 29 of the evasive way in which the matter was put on one side. The same thing is seen in the *British Friend*, 1865, pp. 117–18, an article making a show of unwillingness to hinder any good work, and yet, as everyone at the time would understand, pouring cold water on the idea of missionary enterprise. For other instances of this habit of evasiveness see *ante*, pp. 193, 298 note.

U

Sewell, at one time a master in Ackworth and Rawdon Schools, went to Madagascar primarily in order to conduct educational work in connection with the London Missionary Society, but shortly afterwards, as other Friends went to the country, he and they undertook a missionary work of their own in one particular district. In 1868 the Friends' Foreign Mission Association was founded as a permanent organization, having as its first honorary secretary Henry Stanley Newman, who held the office for more than twenty years.[1] For many years it existed as an independent body, and the story of its progress to an official place in the Society is instructive as illustrating the Quaker caution or, even, timidity which for a hundred and fifty years had been dominant. Nevertheless, as has been said, when the long-delayed step is taken, controversy ceases and there is no looking back.[2]

The first annual meeting of the new association was, to the consternation of many Friends, held at the headquarters of the Society in the course of the Yearly Meeting of 1869; and three years later the relation of that body to this and other "outside" organizations was considered at a conference specially convened for the purpose.

The Yearly Meeting of 1873 declined to accede to the recommendation of the conference that it should receive reports from these organizations, but consented that a bare record of the holding of their annual meetings should be entered on its minutes. In 1882, however, a short account of the foreign mission work was read and gradually the matter came to occupy an important place in the deliberations of the assembly. Finally, in 1917, the Meeting decided to admit the Association into organic union with the Society, directing its constituent meetings to appoint

---

[1] The Friends' Foreign Mission Association has been merged in the Friends' Service Council; pp. 307, 341.   [2] See *ante*, p. 169.

representatives as members of the Board of Management. In 1927 the work of the Association was linked in one organization, the Friends' Service Council, with other overseas work of London and Dublin Yearly Meetings. (*post*, p. 341).

In the last twenty years of the nineteenth century, mission work was established in Syria, China, and Ceylon,[1] and in 1897, seven years after the British Government had taken over the islands of Zanzibar and Pemba, the Yearly Meeting itself set up in Pemba an industrial mission for the slaves who were being emanicipated.[2] From the year 1894 Friends had taken a leading part in calling attention to the existence of slavery in a British possession, but inasmuch as it was regarded as an economic necessity, they had to overcome powerful opposition before their efforts met with success. A certain decree did not, as had been supposed, abolish the system, but gave to the slaves (with some exceptions specially relating to women) the right to claim their freedom; and the efforts of Friends to inform them of this fact and to help them, ignorant as they were, to overcome the obstacles placed in their way, attracted the hostility of the British officials. This appears frequently in their despatches making the most of any mistakes into which Friends may have fallen. In the report of a certain Commissioner the efforts for emancipation are described as the work of "a rich Mission with plenty of money to waste."[3]

[1] The work in Ceylon was given up after the Great War.

[2] In 1890, in return for the acknowledgment by Germany and France of the British protectorate over these islands, Lord Salisbury's Government ceded Heligoland to the former; and in favour of the latter renounced all claim to Madagascar.

[3] *Correspondence Respecting the Abolition of the Legal Status of Slavery in Zanzibar and Pemba*, "Africa, No. 6, 1898," p. 61. There is much more to the same effect. See also "Africa, No. 2, 1897," and "Africa, No. 8, 1899," *The Friend*, 1897, Index, "Slavery," and 1898, p. 72, and Anti-Slavery Society Reports. Now that the

It may be here said that the need for vigilance in this matter is no less urgent than ever it was. Powerful financial interests, able, through Parliament and the newspaper press, to mislead public opinion, are always alert to exploit the labour of native races, bringing men and women, who have no power to make their case heard, into a condition differing little from that slavery. To this danger John Stuart Mill, writing in 1861, called attention:

> If there be a fact to which all experience testifies, it is that when a country holds another in subjection, the individuals of the ruling people who resort to the foreign country to make their fortunes are, of all others, those who most need to be held under powerful restraint (*Representative Government*, c. xviii.).

The stirring of life which led to renewed interest in foreign missions aroused also a concern for men and women of the less favoured classes in England. In the days before education was compulsory there were many who had no school education, and from the beginning of the nineteenth century groups of people came together for instruction in reading. These groups were called "Adult Schools." In most of them the interest of the teacher lay chiefly in enabling people to read the Bible and there was less concern to instruct them in writing, such instruction, in fact, often meeting with disapproval. The direct ancestor of the modern Adult School appears to be a group of women gathered together by William Singleton, a Methodist, at Nottingham in the year 1798, for the purpose of Bible reading and for the teaching of writing and arithmetic. After a time it came under the

struggle is long past, the record of it is profitable to future reformers. It is, however, characteristic of Quaker procedure that, at the time the reports in *The Friend* and elsewhere, while they could not conceal the slowness of the process, say little of the hostility that was being offered.

leadership of a Friend, Samuel Fox, a grocer, who together with his assistants, chiefly women, gave themselves to the service, closing the shop early on Saturday nights in order to be prepared for the Sunday morning work. Before long a men's class was added, and one of the features of the school in later years was the preparation of teachers for junior Sunday Schools.

In 1842, Joseph Sturge, one of the candidates at a parliamentary election for Nottingham,[1] became acquainted with the school, and after three years' consideration he called some of his younger friends together and persuaded them to begin a similar work in their own town of Birmingham. In 1848, William White, originally a teacher in a Wesleyan Sunday School at Reading but then a bookseller and printer in Birmingham, threw himself into the cause and for fifty years, till near his death in 1900, he was the beloved apostle of the movement. With the spread of education throughout the country the need for instruction in reading and writing passed away and the schools became increasingly free to apply themselves to the considerations of religious, social and other topics bearing on the life of humanity. For many years they were the chief outlet for the religious activity of Friends. In course of time the movement spread beyond the Society and in 1899 the Quaker schools and others became organized under the National Council of Adult Schools on which Friends, with the advantage of long experience behind them, continued to take a leading part, although it is definitely an unsectarian and not a Quaker institution. The schools, by their provision of libraries, savings banks and other social agencies, have

[1] Sturge lost the election by 84 votes, but though his opponent was unseated for bribery, he (Sturge), did not contest the second election, and it was won by a member of his own party against the son of the unseated member.

uplifted the lives of many and they have drawn into Christian fellowship large numbers of men and women who stood aloof from the recognized Churches. To the Society of Friends itself they have contributed a small addition to membership; but more important than this has been the opportunity which they have afforded of friendship between those who would otherwise have been separated and of knowledge of social conditions which has led many to work for their betterment.[1]

This record of work done for men and women leads on to mention of the Sunday School movement for the teaching of children. Although this has affected the Society of Friends less than the Adult Schools have done, it has a longer history than theirs. In 1793, a beginning was made in Rossendale, Lancashire; and a few years later there was a school, not far away, at Lothersdale in Yorkshire, and one at Nottingham. We also read of one at Lewes, Sussex, in 1809 and of another at Northwaite, Yorkshire, in 1834.[2] The oldest of those that still live was begun at Bristol in 1810. It would seem that the movement was not widespread; in 1847 report was made that there were only twenty or thirty schools in existence, but in that year it received a great impetus by means of the founding of The Friends' First Day [Sunday] School Association. This, as has been said (p. 295) was the concern of the most enlightened minds of the Society which under their guidance was brought out of the groove into which it had come. The work of Friends in this direction has been largely outside their own borders, comparatively few of the children whom they have taught having

---

[1] For further information the reader is referred to *A History of the Adult School Movement*, by J. Wilhelm Rowntree and H. B. Binns (1902), and *The Adult School Movement, its Origin and Development*, by G. Currie Martin (1935).

[2] *Journal of George Richardson*, pp. 22, 273.

had any other contact with the Society. Of late years, Friends have been among the first to encourage improved methods of teaching; and, mainly by means of Quaker gifts, a training institution, known as Westhill, has been established near Woodbrooke (of which mention will be made later) in the southern outskirts of Birmingham. This institution, training both men and women, is not confined to Friends, but is managed by a committee representative of the Free Churches.

The evangelical movement also showed its concern for the Society itself. In the year 1882, in view of the fact that many meetings were dying down, a Home Mission Committee was formed with the sanction of the Yearly Meeting which, however, left it to make its own arrangements and to collect its own funds. From the first it reported its proceedings to the Yearly Meeting, but it was not until 1894 that it was drawn into organic union with the body. Its main concern at its beginning, and for a number of years, was the revival of dying meetings through the spiritual influence of Friends who felt called upon to live for a time within their borders. To those whose private means were not sufficient to enable them to leave their businesses in order to undertake this work the Committee was prepared, out of money which it collected, to make up what was necessary. This plan, leading, as it seemed, in the direction of a paid ministry, stirred the keenest controversy. It is to be borne in mind that the authors of the scheme had themselves no wish to set up such a ministry, their concern being that a Friend, man or woman, a "worker" as he came to be called, should live in the meeting as one among his brethren, assuming no leadership but such as was willingly conceded to his spiritual influence, an influence exercised for the development of ministerial and other gifts among the congregation. Then, having built up a living fellowship in which each one took his own right part, he would go on his way, perhaps to similar service elsewhere. It cannot be said that this hope has been realized. By the Home Mission workers, living for the most part on very scanty means, self-denying and fine service has been given for the temperance cause and for the adult and junior schools; by means of evangelistic services and otherwise the poor have been helped and the degraded have been raised; some of the workers have taken part in the public life of their town or village; but the task of lifting a decaying meeting into a position of sturdy independence has been more difficult than was first supposed, and for the labour expended in this direction there is little to show. Of late years the Committee, without entirely giving up its earlier work, has sought other methods of making known the distinctive Quaker message; it takes a survey of the Society as a whole endeavouring to supply the needs of the various parts, and at the time of writing new fields of service are opening out. In 1927 the name was changed to the Home Service Committee.

Chapter XVIII

THE NEW THOUGHT: THE MANCHESTER CONFER-
ENCE: THE WORK OF JOHN WILHELM ROWNTREE:
THE SERVICE OF THE COMMUNITY

THE opposition to the Home Mission Committee and its methods did not proceed wholly from unreasoning conservatism or dislike of religious earnestness; a new spirit was making itself felt. No more than others were Friends able to remain heedless of the new thought now penetrating to all quarters, their standard of education was rising, to them, as to other Nonconformists, the older universities had been opened and many of them were attending the recently founded colleges in the larger towns. To the conclusions of Biblical criticism and of scientific research, particularly to the doctrine of evolution, they could not refuse intellectual assent, and along the line of strict evangelical doctrine they could find no reconciliation between "science" and "religion." In their bewilderment some left the Society or, even, felt themselves to be driven from it, and of those who remained many found themselves in opposition to the Home Mission Committee and other activities as they were then carried on. Their conviction that Quakerism, rightly understood, was not shaken by the new Biblical and scientific knowledge found expression in the Yearly Meeting of 1893, a critical moment for the Quaker body. The plea of the younger members on behalf of freedom won the assent of the meeting and thus was made possible the developments of succeeding years. John Wilhelm Rowntree, not yet twenty-five years old, the leader and spokesman of the newer life, wrote of his reception:

We have spoken out plainly at last, and have been heard with wonderful charity and sympathy. There will now be no fear of a rupture, I think, or need of aggressiveness, if only the spirit of the sittings is continued—while for those like myself it has been an immense stimulus for work[1]

At the instance of the Home Mission Committee itself, the Yearly Meeting in 1895 directed the holding of a Conference to consider the position of affairs, and this met in November at Manchester, some of its sittings being attended by about thirteen hundred men and women.

Although the company was by no means unanimous, and the meeting did not for a short time "settle down," yet, when once it had done so, the proceedings, free from noise of applause or dissent, were conducted throughout in the atmosphere of courtesy and love. Questions that were stirring in the minds of both younger and older members were definitely faced, the message of Quakerism to its own day, the attitude of the Society to modern thought, the effective presentation of spiritual truth.

To the infinite relief of many, they heard Friends, held in honour for their Christian character, openly declare that there was no need "to accept the Hebrew chronology or the Hebrew cosmogony as a necessary part of an all-rounded and infallible word of God,"[2] that modern thought, far from being an evil, was largely a blessing, that Friends would do well to accept the general principle of evolution, and that the doctrine of the total depravity of the human soul was no part of Quakerism. They heard

---

[1] *Essays and Addresses*, p. xxiii. A letter written by J. W. Graham in *The Friend* (1927, p. 643), gives an account of some of those who had been leading the new movement in the few years preceding the appearance of J. W. Rowntree. From the letter itself readers will not gain any idea of the mighty impetus which he (J.W.R.) gave to the movement, carrying it, by persuasiveness of words and personality, over a moment of great strain and uncertainty as to what might happen in the Society.

[2] Dr. Thomas Hodgkin, *Report of the Proceedings*, p. 209.

it said that Friends had a unique opportunity and, therefore, unique responsibility, and that they must regard as
intolerable all social conditions that went far toward pre-
venting the true development of character and the exercise
of responsibility.

The Conference was the visible sign of the turning-
point in the life of English Quakerism. From many minds
a cloud was lifted, and if as yet there was but little building
up, the necessary work of clearing the ground had been
done. The process of reconstruction was continued by
means of lecture schools which from that time onward have
played a large part in the life of the Society. To John
Wilhelm Rowntree the movement owes much of its first
impetus. He saw that the Society of Friends had a message
to give that was not elsewhere being given, able to reach
many who were not otherwise being reached, and he made
earnest appeal for the spiritual and intellectual equipment
of its members that would enable them to give forth the
message with power. Still, as has been said, in young life,
not in possession of normal sight and hearing, he realized
that among all the Quaker activities in so many directions
there was danger of the Society itself being overlooked,
and that if it were to fail, the good work which Friends
were doing would not long survive. It was with no narrow
sectarian aim that he pleaded with its members to give
to it of their spiritual best, as to an instrument that was
itself worth working for, in view of the use to which it
might be put. Earlier than this, his uncle, John Stephenson
Rowntree, had drawn attention to the same point. For
many years, the Society has gladly placed money, energy,
buildings and organization at the disposal of its members
and others labouring in good causes, itself showing
sympathetic interest in the fact of its power being used to
turn their mills, but not all of them have repaid it by

contribution of their own to its communal spiritual life. There is on the part of some a readiness to avail themselves of its resources, but to have no interest in it except as a source or generator of power (to which, as has been said, they themselves make no contribution) for the furtherance of some cause which they have at heart. In view of the possible slackening of this power, and the consequent dying down of the good work which it serves, John S. Rowntree, in 1892, uttered a warning no less appropriate to-day than it was then:

> It would seem as though the responsibility of larger claims and widened duties demands in some respects even a closer union with the channels through which spiritual strength largely flows. Men need to be spiritually equipped for the most secular services, and when the stream of human life and effort widens out, is there not more need than ever that the channels of communication with its source be kept free, deep and unclogged? To fulfil the outward duties of life nobly, there must be a vigorous, continually renewed and quickened inward or religious life—a vigorous Church life in the most spiritual sense of the word. . . . Not selfishly, but for the sake of worthily discharging their service to humanity, may Christian people desire, pray and labour for the continual growth and prosperity of the Church to which they belong.[1]

The strong and often-repeated concern of John Wilhelm Rowntree was for the right ministry in Friends' meetings, and, deeper still, for that spirit of which it was *necessarily* the outcome. He realized that absence of ministry, and even its confinement to very few in a congregation, indicated a low level of spiritual life.

> I think [he wrote] in 1896 that the state of our meetings generally justifies the belief that our greatest outward need is a ministry—fearless and direct—able to deal with life

---

[1] *Life and Work*, pp. 231–32.

in its various aspects, and presenting . . . the message of Jesus to the men of to-day . . . [but] we are compelled to review meeting after meeting where the pulse of spiritual life beats low, where the sense of individual responsibility is weak, and where apparently no young Friend is preparing himself for the inevitable call to the service of the ministry . . . we have shown a strange indifference to the responsibility we have voluntarily taken upon us (*Essays and Addresses*, pp. 174–75).

To the younger generation, and not to them only, he himself spoke as a prophet, but at the moment when a large prospect was opening out before him, in the year 1905, he died in America at the age of thirty-six.[1]

In 1897 the first lecture school came together at Scarborough, and from that time others have, for longer or shorter periods, been held in all parts of the country. In various directions has the movement branched out, continually adapting itself to new circumstances, and taking forms which the first promoters could not have foreseen. Like the Quarterly and Monthly Meetings, it continually brings together from different places men and women of all ages and of differing social position and degrees of education and these, united, often for several days, in an intellectual and spiritual atmosphere, come to know a corporate consciousness, to have understanding of one another's needs, and to enter into an ever-deepening fellowship.

This movement, however, showed clearly the lack of

---

[1] A knowledge of the writings of John Wilhelm Rowntree is necessary to an understanding of the turning-point years 1893–1905, viz. *Present-Day Papers*, edited by him 1898–1902, and *Essays and Addresses*, published after his death. Equally important for the same purpose is much of the writing of his uncle, John Stephenson Rowntree (1834–1907).

equipment for the new work. The need had also been perceived by certain leaders of the Adult Schools, and already there were men and women, who, with some learning, could speak effectively on Biblical and Church history and on the problems of economics, politics and philosophy. Nevertheless it was evident that the determination to avoid reliance on the intellectually trained minister had led to an undervaluing of the teacher as distinct from the minister. As early as 1831 Joseph John Gurney had seen this and, himself a man of no small learning, he gave courses of lectures in different places, "We shall," he says, "never thrive upon ignorance" (*Memoirs*, i. 440). In the years shortly before 1860 there had again been an awakening to the need for religious instruction. The Yearly Meeting of 1857 stated in an "Address to Parents": "Children continue to enter our schools very imperfectly instructed in their moral and religious duties and lamentably ignorant of the contents of the sacred volume."[1] Similar complaint was made in the years 1805 and 1818.[2] The outcome of this concern was the formation of meetings for Bible study and for the delivery of lectures on the history and doctrines of Friends;[3] and a further result was the establishment in a few towns of Friends' Institutes or of Library and Lecture Associations.[4] There was, how-

---

[1] Taken from *The Sure Foundation*, by Wm. C. Westlake, pp. 76–77. Westlake (p. 64) says that the encouragement of teaching "would tend to remove some of the dread and awfulness with which the ministry is regarded amongst Friends." On ignorance, see *ante*, p. 227.

[2] *London Yearly Meeting During 250 Years*, p. 53.

[3] See, for example, *The Friend*, 1861, pp. 92, 123, 195; and for the misgiving concerning this felt by some Friends, p. 141 and *ante*, pp. 224–5. See report of a conference at Ackworth, *The Friend*, 1862, p. 187. The new movement was on a larger scale than the short mention of it here made indicates. See also *ante*, pp. 224–5, 295–6.

[4] The Birmingham Friends' Library was begun in 1829. Institutes or Libraries (for other than "Friends' Books") were established in London, 1852 (first in Gracechurch Street, then at Devonshire House, 1862); Manchester and Bristol, 1857; Liverpool, 1860; York, 1862.

ever, little systematic or consecutive work, and much of the more definitely spiritual effort died down in the atmosphere of suspicion that was not yet dispersed. This, however, was not the only hindrance. These years mark the beginning of the period of unrest, due, as has been said, to the new scientific thought; and many Friends, conscious of dislocation between their spiritual and intellectual life, found themselves unable to give religious teaching either in their own families or elsewhere.

To meet the need at last clearly seen to be urgent, a few Friends, in the year 1903, placed at the disposal of the Society a house and estate on the outskirts of Birmingham to which men and women might, for longer or shorter periods, resort and from lecturers and teachers gain knowledge calculated to help them in all forms of Christian work.[1] It was hoped that by this means many would be qualified to give instruction in their own meetings and elsewhere, even while engaged in the ordinary business of life. Woodbrooke, as the institution is named, has attracted to its neighbourhood not only Kingsmead, the Friends' missionary training home, but also other institutions outside the Society. The group, which has its own organization, is collectively known as "the Selly Oak Colleges."

Of late years, the Society has found a place for the travelling lecturer or teacher and for the organizing secretary giving his whole time and receiving pecuniary support, but in this there is no move whatever toward the *minister* set down in one congregation. Continually is the ideal held up of development of personal responsibility on the part of each one.

---

[1] The house and estate, together with most of the endowment, have been given by George Cadbury and his family. The idea in the first instance came from John Wilhelm Rowntree, whose own family have from the beginning made large contribution.

This new presentation of truth has brought to many a firmer hold on Christian faith, a deeper understanding of the Quaker setting forth of it, and an increase both of desire and ability to make this known. Nowhere was this more evident than in the heightened loyalty of many of the younger members, largely the result of the twelve years' earnest appeal of John Wilhelm Rowntree. Groups were formed for united study, communion and service, a measure of the fellowship of early days being known among them. In 1911 a Conference attended by nearly four hundred Friends in younger life was held at Swanwick—a formative and decisive time for many. A second one was held at Jordans in 1920, following immediately on the Conference of All Friends, of which mention will be made later.[1]

Nevertheless a complete story of present-day Quakerism requires mention of the fact that some have, with uneasiness, seen the emergence of the new teaching, regarding its presentation of Christianity as inadequate and, therefore, finding themselves unable to adopt either its methods or conclusions. Like most religious bodies, the Society includes "evangelical" and other strains of thought, but although these at times find their own lines of Christian activity, there is a consciousness of underlying unity which maintains fellowship in worship and in certain forms of service.

One result in particular of this new life may be noted. Under the influence of the movement led by John Wilhelm Rowntree, the Society, breaking away from its traditional reserve, at last found itself able officially to call attention to the need for ministry in

---

[1] Reports of these Conferences were issued, that of Swanwick being a complete account of the proceedings and containing a short historical narrative (written by the present writer) of the years leading up to it.

its meetings and to exhort its members to faithful
service. To this end, a large committee was, in 1903,
appointed by the Yearly Meeting of Ministry and
Oversight (a body no longer existing), and for some years
its members visited meetings throughout the country. At
the time of its appointment, the Society was under a deep
sense of responsibility in view of the spiritual need made
manifest by the South African War. To most Friends, the
message of the Committee was comparatively new; to some
it was bewildering; and it was not easy to change the
traditional outlook inherited from six generations. Finally
the Yearly Meeting officially published a pamphlet,
Ministry and our Meetings for Worship. The revised edition
of *Christian Discipline* issued in the same year, 1911, also
invited Friends to consider their responsibility for ministry,
all the extracts which it quotes as bearing on this specific
point (as distinct from counsel to those already engaged
in the service) being taken from documents put forth in
1900 or in later years. In 1919, a "Letter from the Elders
of London Yearly Meeting" dealt with the same matter.
Calling attention to the necessity for silent worship with
its opportunity for hearing the voice of God, and warning
against assertiveness and the spirit of debate and the airing
of opinions, it thus deals with one of the elements of
Quaker worship:

> Some have a call to speak often in our meetings, having a
> gift of teaching, comfort, praise or prayer, which their
> friends are glad to recognize. To others the call comes but
> seldom, it may be only once in a lifetime, to speak a few
> words. These have as true a service as the others; the word
> of one who has seldom or never spoken may avail more than
> the familiar voice. We would not lay burdens on tender
> spirits, but we believe that very many of our members
> should use the privilege of vocal testimony, once or more,
> if they would know the fulness of Christian life for them-

selves. It is, if we may say so, a natural and reasonable service for our Lord. Sometimes human cowardice must be met by a sense of heroism, and we must dare to be called inconsistent if need be, that we may follow the call.[1]

It is impossible to speak of all those who at this time led the Society into a larger life, but of Caroline E. Stephen mention must be made. She belonged to a family some of whose members were distinguished in literature or in law, and she herself, in cultured and literary style, "was able to do a work of interpretation which few Friends of the time could hope to accomplish."[2] Weary of the controversies of the day and the noise of words, she discovered the quiet of the Quaker meeting and there found rest. In words which recall the experience of Robert Barclay more than two hundred years earlier she writes:

> On one never-to-be-forgotten Sunday morning I found myself one of a small company of silent worshippers who were content to sit down together without words, that each one might feel after and draw near to the Divine Presence, unhindered at least, if not helped by any human utterance. . . . My whole soul was filled with the unutterable peace of the undisturbed opportunity for communion with God. . . . And since that day Friends' meetings have indeed been to me the greatest of outward help to a fuller and fuller entrance into the spirit from which they have sprung; the place of the most soul-subduing, faith-restoring, strengthening and peaceful communion, in feeding upon the bread of life, that I have ever known (*Quaker Strongholds*).

To Quaker literature she made a number of contributions, the two most important being *Quaker Strongholds* (1891) and *Light Arising* (1908). In this way and by her personal influence she gave Friends a deeper understanding of the treasure which was theirs and of the

[1] Concerning inconsistency see *ante*, p. 265.
[2] R. M. Jones, *Later Periods of Quakerism*, p. 969.

possibilities before them; "and she turned the attention of many serious seekers to them as a religious body and to their way of life and worship."

Throughout all this time the philanthropic activity of Friends was maintained and in the course of the nineteenth century new service opened out before them. With ardour they devoted themselves to the temperance cause; men and woman served on boards of guardians (of the poor); in the work of public education and of municipal or other local government of their community they have taken their full share. Besides the temperance cause two others in particular, the abolition of the opium trade between India and China and of the State regulation of vice, occupied the attention of the Society, and a number of its members joined with others outside its borders to bring the campaign to a successful end. Their work lent itself to no popular cry, it won few votes at elections, it was met by the fury of vested interests and the dull opposition of officialdom, but behind it was the power of God, and, neither for the first nor the last time in history, the weak things of the world confounded the mighty.[1]

[1] See Braithwaite, Second Period, c. xx., "The Church and Social Questions," particularly its conclusion. Concerning the anti-opium campaign and its successful issue see Life of Joseph Gundry Alexander, pp. 59, 97, and also The Imperial Drug Trade, by Joshua Rowntree. For the share of Friends in the latter of the two above-mentioned campaigns see the Autobiography of Josephine Butler (not a Friend), the leader of it. Speaking of a stormy election at Colchester in 1870, she says: "on our first arrival at Colchester we went as was our wont straight to the house of a Quaker family" (p. 103; and see pp. 96, 274–76). The campaign was directed against a system introduced (by the Contagious Diseases Act) into England in 1866 designed to protect the health of profligate men in garrison and dockyard towns by providing healthy women for their use. Women of immoral life, or those supposed to be, were put on a police register, compelled to be medically examined at frequent intervals, and imprisoned if diseased. They were under the power of a special body of police and from their

Another activity of the nineteenth century, playing a considerable part in the life of the Society, was the formation and maintenance of associations for the distribution and, in some cases, for the printing of tracts. The Friends' Tract Association, which existed till 1935, was founded in 1813, and there were others in Bristol, York, Manchester, Swansea, Newcastle and Dublin. At the present time the spreading of Quaker and other literature on religious and social questions is a prominent feature of the modern "extension work," a form of service which goes back to early days. Early in his ministry, Fox was concerned that Friends beyond the seas should be kept supplied with books and pamphlets, and that Quaker books should be printed in foreign languages and distributed.[1] As early as 1655 he gave counsel to "All Friends," "None stop writing or speaking when ye are moved with the Spirit of the Lord God."[2] In the following year he also wrote, "Take heed of printing anything more than ye are required of the Lord God."[3]

In 1889, at the instance of Yorkshire Quarterly Meeting, the Yearly Meeting in a joint session of men and women[4]

ruling there was no appeal. After storms of opposition from military and naval authorities the system was abolished in 1886. The British example was gradually followed (and in this order) by Norway, Denmark, Finland, Holland, U.S.A., Sweden, Czechoslovakia, Bolivia, Palestine, U.S.S.R., Germany and Switzerland; but lately (1936) Germany has reintroduced the system in certain towns.

[1] *Epistles*, pp. 140, 143 (1659). The Report of the Friends Tract Association of 1826, signed by Joseph John Gurney, speaks of Friends travelling throughout England and Ireland, and mentions activity at Newcastle: "A complete survey of the Quayside and lanes adjoining has been made, and tracts or papers were left at almost every house." A Manchester Report speaks of the distribution of tracts among the crowd gathered to see a public execution. Concerning Quaker literature see Braithwaite, *Second Period*, pp. 280–81, 418–27, and Index, "Literature"; also Anna Littleboy, "Devonshire House Reference Library," etc., *Journal of the Friends' Historical Society*, xviii. (1921).

[2] *Epistles*, p. 85.　　　　　　　　　　　　　　[3] *Ibid.* p. 104.

[3] It was not till 1908 that all sessions were held jointly.

considered "how far our duty as members of a Christian Church is concerned in relation to the deep poverty and degradation in which large masses of our countrymen exist." Thus the Society came to take official cognizance of this matter, recognizing it as a vital concern of the Church. The interest which for many years Friends had taken in the temperance question led them to lay emphasis on excessive drinking as the main cause of poverty, but in time their growing knowledge of ecomomic and social science gave them a wider view. It came to be seen that poverty was a cause as well as an effect of drunkenness and other social vice; and attention was drawn to the ecomomic system itself as leading to the wealth of the few and the want of many. In 1889, and with increasing clearness as the years went by, the inevitable connection between poverty and vast military preparations was perceived and the crash of 1914 compelled attention to the economic causes of war. In view of the complexity of the problem a large committee— the War and Social Order Committee, as it was called— was appointed by the Yearly Meeting of 1915 to "investigate what connection there is between war and the social order, to encourage the study of the question, and to consult with those Friends who have been led, owing to the war, to feel the need of a personal readjustment of their way of life." In the following year it presented its first report, stating as one of its conclusions:

> The rush for markets, the desire for exclusive spheres of trading, the use of diplomatic intrigue to support the schemes of financiers, have been a constant source of antagonism. . . . . . This grasping rivalry, seeking monopoly advantages, is one in which only a small proportion of the nation has prospects of gain, while the majority reap no corresponding benefit. Not only does this rivalry develop armaments, but the need for armaments excites

still fiercer and more definitely national competition for the possession of mineral wealth, coaling stations and the like, and an increasing number of industries become interested in war trades.

From time to time the Committee has put forth other pronouncements, received sympathetically by the Yearly Meeting, and this meeting in 1918 adopted as the foundations of a true social order the following principles:

1. The Fatherhood of God, as revealed by Jesus Christ, should lead us toward a Brotherhood which knows no restriction of race, sex or social class.

2. This Brotherhood should express itself in a social order which is directed, beyond all material ends, to the growth of personality truly related to God and man.

3. The opportunity of full development, physical, moral and spiritual, should be assured to every member of the community, man, woman and child. The development of man's full personality should not be hampered by unjust conditions nor crushed by economic pressure.

4. We should seek for a way of living that will free us from the bondage of material things and mere conventions, that will raise no barrier between man and man, and will put no excessive burden of labour upon any by reason of our superfluous demands.

5. The spiritual force of righteousness, loving-kindness and trust is mighty because of the appeal it makes to the best in every man, and when applied to industrial relations achieves great things.

6. Our rejection of the methods of outward domination, and of the appeal to force applies not only to international affairs, but to the whole problem of industrial control. Not through antagonism, but through co-operation and goodwill can the best be attained for each and all.

7. Mutual service should be the principle upon which life is organized. Service, not private gain, should be the motive of all work.

8. The ownership of material things, such as land and capital, should be so regulated as best to minister to the need and development of man.

But while there is widespread an honest desire to carry out these principles, leading to some adjustment of both private and business life in view of their realization, there is not unanimity concerning the economic system in which they can find fulfilment. There are many Friends who see in Socialism, in some one of its forms, the necessary condition of a well-ordered communal life, while others are either not yet prepared to stand on this side or regard any such system as impracticable and agitation for it as mischievous. Nevertheless, even among these there is much anxious heart-searching as to the right ordering of society and of personal living. A committee known as the Industrial and Social Order Council is charged with the duties of making investigation and of keeping the concern before the Society.

Chapter XIX

PEACE SERVICE DURING AND AFTER THE
GREAT WAR: FRIENDS' SERVICE COUNCIL

IT now remains to speak of Quaker activity and testimony in the four years' war of 1914 to 1918, and after the conclusion of hostilities. For many years previously, and particularly since the South African War of 1899–1901, Friends had been active in setting forth their testimony for Peace; but while they were not wholly unprepared, the suddenness of the shock bewildered many. A number of young men, stirred by the call of invaded Belgium, and seeing their friends going into danger, joined the fighting forces as some had done in the French wars of an earlier day,[1] but many more promptly set to work to qualify themselves for service in other ways. A voluntary association which came to be known as the Friends' Ambulance Unit accepted from the military authorities such work as it felt free to undertake, either in relief of the French civilian population or, at the scene of battle, in aid of the wounded necessarily under military direction. After the introduction of conscription in 1916, many conscientious objectors to military service (including a number who were not Friends) were allowed to join the Unit either for help in the ways already mentioned or for work on the land in England and other forms of activity deemed to be useful. The Unit

---

[1] *Ante,* pp. 209–10, 289, concerning birthright membership. It has been stated (see *post,* p. 346 n.) that thirty-two per cent. of the men Friends of military age entered the army in one capacity or another. This refers to those whose names stood on the list of members, a high proportion of those who joined up were already mainly or entirely out of touch with the Society.

reported its doings to the Yearly Meeting, but it was not an official concern of the Society.

It has long been the endeavour of Friends to heal the wounds caused by war, particularly in the way of bringing reconciliation between enemies. In the Napoleonic Wars, at the beginning of the nineteenth century, there was work done for French prisoners in England. In the Greek war of independence (1821–29) Friends, under the guidance of William Allen, gave a lead to England (which had lagged behind other European countries and America) in organizing relief of distress.[1] In 1854, early in the Crimean War, the English fleet in the Baltic, being unable to damage the Russian battleships and naval bases, destroyed private property along the coast of Finland a country which had been annexed by Russia less than half a century previously. By this outrage terrible suffering was caused; and at the close of hostilities, Thomas Harvey, of Leeds, and Joseph Sturge visited the scene of destruction. On their report a committee collected about £9,000, sending it to a Finnish relief organization which had been set up by the two visitors.[2] More than fifty years later some Friends carried relief to civilian sufferers from the Balkan wars in the early part of the present century, and at the close of the South African War in 1902 others visited the Boers in order to make the contact of sympathy and love, the atmosphere in which the spirit of war dies down and the spirit of peace grows. During and after the war in Ireland in 1920 and 1921 English and Irish Friends set themselves to the work of reconstruction, being moved

[1] *Journal of the Friends Historical Society*, 1934, p. 39.
[2] See any *Life* of Joseph Sturge (in Hobhouse's *Life*, pp. 158-61) and two poems by Whittier, *The Conquest of Finland* and *In Remembrance of Joseph Sturge*.

by the conviction that, imperative as might be the call for material relief and repair, far greater would be the outcome of spiritual healing. True at all times are the words of Fox, after he has dwelt on the loving duty of charity to the poor:

> Your bestowing of outward things to such as stand in need is the least love, and things of little value in comparison to the things that are above and immortal (*Epistles*, p. 136; see also p. 387).

In the civil war which is now, as these lines are written (1938), being waged in Spain, Friends are taking an active part in bringing relief to the starving children and other victims of it.

But the greatest work of the nineteenth century was done at the close of the Franco-Prussian War of 1870–71, when Friends set themselves to the task of building up ruined villages and towns, and of setting farmers and others in a position to resume their business. It was, however, the World War of 1914–18 that offered the greatest challenge of all to English and American Friends. By the Meeting for Sufferings there was set up a Committee bearing the name of that which had been formed in 1871, "The Friends' War Victims Relief Committee," adopting as its badge the black and red Quaker Star of the same date. This became known all over Europe and was everywhere understood to symbolize the friendly spirit which to sufferers expressed itself in material and spiritual aid. In reply to an offer of help in the early part of the war a letter was received from the French Government recalling the service given more than forty years earlier, and gladly accepting the assistance of builders, doctors, nurses and other workers for the homeless people. Further mention of this will be made when we come to speak of the relief work of the Committee in different countries when the war was ended.

In all this it is to be kept in mind that, although English Friends began the various services whose story is being told, they received from Irish Friends and from beyond the borders of Quakerism valuable help in gifts and subscriptions and in untiring personal service both in England and elsewhere. They were, moreover, entrusted with a share of the administration of various funds that were collected publicly and not through their own agency.[1] Most especially must mention be made of the co-operation of American Friends in all departments. In the work for war victims in France they came to have a preponderating share in the direction: and one of the happiest results of their co-operation has been a closer understanding between all English-speaking Friends, particularly between the various branches into which in America the Society is divided.[2]

A third Quaker work, already mentioned, was that which was done for "enemy aliens" in England. In the same week as the outbreak of war the Meeting for Sufferings[3] met in ordinary course and, at the concern of a few Friends, a committee—the Emergency Committee as it was called—was appointed to deal with the situation. There were in this country large numbers of Germans and Austrians, many of them in receipt of weekly wages, engaged as waiters, hairdressers and in other employments; some were filling important business posts, permanent residents though not naturalized, and besides these

---

[1] E.g. *Manchester Guardian* Fund, Treasury grants, Lady Forster's Australian Fund, the Save the Children and Imperial War Relief and Russian Famine Relief Funds.

[2] See *Sixth Report of the Emergency and War Victims' Relief Committee*, March 1920, pp. 6, 11.   [3] See *ante*, p. 174

there were travellers, students and teachers. The wives of the residents, many of them English women who had never been out of their own country, now found themselves in the position of "enemy aliens," and, on their husbands being thrown out of employment and collected into internment camps, they were in desperate condition. Some of them were attacked and their houses wrecked, the guardians of the poor were often unfriendly and harsh, so that large numbers, some of whom had been in good positions, were brought within sight of starvation. The Emergency Committee successfully grappled with the vast mass of misery, facing problems many and complicated; and far beyond the material help given to thousands was the kindness and love unstintedly poured forth to those who had suddenly found themselves submerged in an ocean of hate. The story of those days will, for long years to come, be told in the home of many an "enemy."

And it is not irrelevant to our history to record the fact that in Berlin a similar committee had, quite independently, been formed for the purpose of helping those, British, French and others, who in *Germany* were "enemy aliens." The following is a quotation from the appeal issued by that Committee:

> The task is laid upon us by our own desire to undertake friendly service in these times of hatred to those who now find it difficult to obtain help. Even in war-time, whoever needs our help is a neighbour, and love of their enemies remains the distinguishing mark of those who are loyal to our Lord.

The Emergency Committee also concerned itself with the men segregated in the internment camps. In the Isle of Man alone there were at one time 23,000 of them. Tortured by anxiety concerning their families and their future prospects, having no employment to occupy their time, they began to degenerate in body and character. The Committee established workshops, provided literature, arranged for visits, and in order to meet the business difficulties of the interned men, it set up a special committee which, from beginning to end, dealt with over 9,000 requests for help. It was also allowed by the authorities to give similar assistance in the camps of German soldiers sent to England as prisoners.

> One of the happiest features of the Emergency Committee's work has been the generous help and support received, both in money and personal service, from vast numbers of sympathizers outside the borders of the Society of Friends. Many have desired to repay former kindnesses received in Germany and Austria; others have been glad of an opportunity to show practical Christianity to those who were called our enemies, and even those who have lost their dear ones in the war have again and again found their truest comfort in taking a share in this work of healing and reconciliation.[1]

At the beginning of 1916, conscription for military service was set up in England. It is probable that if

[1] Elizabeth F. Howard, *Friends' Service in War Time*, pp. 16–17; and see the story of the work of the Emergency Committee told in *St. Stephen's House*, by Anna Braithwaite Thomas. Concerning the work about to be described in nine countries of Europe see *A Quaker Adventure*, by A. Ruth Fry. The authoress tells a story of the difficulty of the military authorities in giving to pacifists permission for relief work in districts where they were in command. They made strict regulations against "propaganda." The writer says: "Exactly what this included it was not easy to ascertain, and an enquiry of the Permit Office in London as to whether reading a chapter of the New Testament to an old woman in hospital would come under this heading received the interesting reply, after careful thought, that some of that book might be very dangerous!" (p. xxiii.). Other surveys of the work done abroad are *Quakers in Action* and *A Service of Love in War Time*, both by Rufus M. Jones, and two personal journals of workers in the war zone, *With the Quakers in France*, D. O. Stephens, and *A Scavenger in France*, W. Bell. See also official reports.

Friends had pressed for it, they might, in virtue of their well-known testimony concerning war, have gained for their own members complete exemption, but the conscience of the Society, and particularly of the men primarily concerned, revolted against a way of escape which was not open to others, equally conscientious, outside its borders. There was, however, introduced into the Act a clause allowing conscientious objectors to military service to appear before tribunals which might grant them exemption from it, either absolutely or conditionally on their undertaking useful service apart from military control. It soon became clear that the power to give absolute exemption was being rarely exercised, many tribunals, in fact, refusing to be convinced that they possessed it. Friends, as a rule, declined to base their claim on the mere fact of their being Friends, but inasmuch as in most cases their position was well known, they found little difficulty in gaining permission to serve in the works of relief already described or, in some cases, to continue in their business if to the tribunal this seemed useful to the community.[1] There were, however, more than two hundred and seventy members and other regular attenders of Friends' meetings who, claiming the absolute exemption which the law had provided, suffered imprisonment with hard labour for periods varying from a few months to more than two years. It was no negative position that was taken by those who refused acceptance of an alternative to compulsory military service, such acceptance being in their eyes a compromise, not necessarily with war, but certainly with conscription for war. The value of their work is more clearly evident as from a distance it is seen in its right proportion, inasmuch as the stand taken by them and others

[1] See *ante*, p. 328, concerning conscientious objectors and the Friends' Ambulance Unit.

will in future years be a strong barrier against any re-imposition of conscription.[1] An incidental effect of their imprisonment was to make known the inefficiency and cruelty of the prison system and a beginning is being made in the training of prisoners to take their place as useful members of society on their return to freedom.[2] In this work a number of Friends take part.

While the imprisonment lasted, the wives and families of many outside the Society were cared for by Friends, either unofficially or through the agency of the Service Committee set up by the Yearly Meeting in 1915 in view of the coming of conscription, in order to help its own members and others.

Under other Acts also, hastily passed in the war emergency, about half a dozen Friends, including two women, suffered imprisonment either for disregarding censorship regulations concerning the issue of leaflets, or otherwise "creating an atmosphere prejudicial to recruiting."[3] Besides them there were others who were for the same reasons prosecuted and convicted.

During the course of the war, Friends in various parts of the country held public meetings in their meeting-

[1] An account of the treatment of conscientious objectors before the tribunals and elsewhere is given by J. W. Graham, in his work, *Conscription and Conscience*. See also *We Did Not Fight*, edited by Julian Bell, narratives of individual conscientious objectors in different countries.

[2] This is partly due to the imprisonment of a number of women of different classes of society who came under the criminal law during the agitation in favour of women's suffrage shortly before the war. Prison reform was greatly advanced by the Report of the Prison System Enquiry Committee (*English Prisons To-day*, edited by Stephen Hobhouse and A. Fenner Brockway), an unofficial body, established in 1919, in which Friends co-operated with members of the Fabian Society and others.

[3] See *ante*, p. 142, concerning a trial at the Guildhall, London.

houses in order to spread knowledge of facts and, particularly, to create a peaceable spirit. At their headquarters in London a number of these meetings were broken up by an organized mob.

In the Friends' meetinghouse in Manchester, on a day in 1918, a quiet meeting was held, under the auspices of the Society of Friends and certain other bodies, for prayer for peace by negotiation; into the room came storming a tempestuous mob, but the worshippers held their ground unmoved and the disturbers went away.[1]

On the signing of the Armistice in November of 1918, the Emergency Committee, having knowledge of the appalling condition of Central Europe, set about devising measures of relief, notwithstanding the obstacles placed in their way. Owing to the continuance of the allied blockade many thousands of infant children and others continued month after month to die of starvation, but the newspapers withheld knowledge of facts, the public for the most part were averse from hearing them, and even ministers of religion generally refused to face the odium incurred by calling attention to them. Nevertheless the Emergency Committee worked on, and after long delay they were allowed to send out food and other necessaries of life. For a long time they were the only agency to which this permission was granted.

A few days after the signing of peace, more than seven months after the Armistice, a few Friends entered Germany and everywhere found the Quaker name opening a way for them. Before long some American Friends joined them. So appalling was the abyss of destitution that the

[1] *Centenary of the Friends Meetinghouse, Manchester*, pp. 19–20, part of an account of the relief work carried on by Friends in Manchester.

British public could no longer refuse to heed it and a public subscription was opened for the "Save the Children Fund." For some time the Government made a grant equal to such part of the amount collected as did not go to relief in Germany.[1] By other countries also, and by representatives of the Student Christian Movement and of the Salvation Army, help was given, each of these bodies thus acting in accord with its international character.[2]

It is now appropriate to take up the promise made some pages earlier to describe the work of the Friends' War Victims Relief Committee. By Miss A. Ruth Fry, the untiring Secretary of that Committee, the following account has been furnished, although in the meagre space which is all that can be allotted to it there is conveyed no adequate understanding of the extent and depth of the service rendered. It is to be hoped that what is here said may send readers to Miss Fry's own work, *A Quaker Adventure*.

From very small beginnings the work grew, especially after the American Friends joined forces in 1917, till some 1,070 English and 780 American workers had taken part in it. About one and a half million pounds passed through the London books (though far more had been administered abroad) and an unknown number of civilian victims of the war, probably amounting to millions, were, in one way or another, relieved in nine countries of Europe, from 1914 to 1924.

---

[1] This fact shows the intensity of the hate that devastated England. There were private subscribers who stipulated that their contributions should not go to Germany; and there were some who, in letters to newspapers and in other ways, expressed disapproval of attempts to save the children.

[2] The Student Christian work is recorded in *Rebuilding Europe*, by Ruth Rouse.

Relief, in clothes, food or furniture was given, or sold much under cost in France, Germany, Austria, Poland and Russia, the greatest number relieved being in Germany (where a supply of food for one million children was organized by the American Friends, with funds largely provided from other sources, and for 30,000 in Cologne district fed by English Friends),[1] Russia (where 260,000 people were maintained in Buzuluk district in the famine of 1922) and Austria (where 64,000 children were provided with food in depôts, for a small charge).

Medical work was undertaken in France, where several hospitals and children's homes were maintained, and a maternity hospital was founded at Châlons-sur-Marne. In it nearly 1,000 births took place, and, finally housed in a new building, it was in 1922 handed over to a French committee.

Medical work in Poland took chiefly the form of delousing the inhabitants of typhus-stricken districts, a preventive work, dangerous to the workers, but productive of increased immunity to the district. In Russia, too, very extensive clinical and prophylactic work was, in conjunction with the Soviet authorities, undertaken after the famine.

Building was a very important activity in France during the years 1914-20. At first, repairs to houses were carried out, but before long factories for making frame-houses were organized and large numbers of them were erected, especially in a district west of Verdun, handed over by the French authorities to the Anglo-American Mission. It was here that the most extensive reconstruction was carried out, and the needs of the dispossessed inhabitants, who returned to complete desolation, were met as far as possible. Among the items provided to set them up in

[1] After the war the F.W.V.R.C. and Emergency Committees were amalgamated, so that all the foreign relief was administered together.

life were sewing cotton and rakes, bees and spectacles! Co-operative shops in the district were established and stocked.

In Holland the Belgian refugees were enabled to make portable houses transferred to Belgium after the war, and in Poland, horses were provided for the villagers to bring from the forests their ration of timber for housebuilding. The horses, which were purchased from the Army authorities on very favourable terms and let in rotation to village after village, enabled the peasants in one year alone to bring into cultivation 24,000 acres rendered derelict by the war. Such agricultural reconstruction was of vital importance and in Poland, in France, and, to some extent, in Russia, land was ploughed and seeds and tools were distributed. In France some 25,000 chickens, rabbits, sheep, pigs, and even cattle were distributed, 900 tons of grain threshed in one year, and machines and tool repaired.

Very often the work initiated by Friends was eventually handed over to other bodies; such was the feeding of students undertaken on a large scale in Germany, Austria and Poland. Also they often co-operated with other bodies, e.g. with the Serbian Relief Fund, where their representatives took important parts in rescuing refugees.

Mention must be made, too, of the industries which cheered the lives of miserable refugees and war victims in Holland, France, Austria, Russia and Poland. In the last-named country they still (1938) continue to be carried on.

At least twelve workers lost their lives as a direct result of their devotion and the hard, and often dangerous, conditions under which they laboured.[1]

---

[1] For recollection of the various ways of Quaker service in the time of war and afterwards see *The Friend*, 1934, Index heading, "I Remember."

It is also to be noted that in this war as in others, there were a number of Friends in business who, by their refusal to execute orders received from the War Department and in other ways, stood clear of making profit out of the slaughter of their countrymen and others.

To not a few in the Society of Friends the years of war, 1914–18, afforded a revelation of the contribution to the spiritual and cultural life of the world which the Quaker Society might have the opportunity of making.[1] The relief work done during the war and afterwards brought large numbers of Friends into touch with the life and problems of many races and nations, but in the permanent service which should express again, and in a fuller and deeper sense, the universal concern of the early Friends, outward relief was to take a comparatively small place. There was an earnest desire to find a means of breaking down the barriers of race and nation and religion, and of binding together men, even those who had been "enemies" of one another, in a realization of the indwelling God. To this end it was hoped to throw out a chain of centres in all the "strategic" cities of the world and, further, that each centre would come to rest, in the main, on a virile, growing Quaker society in the country where it was planted. Accordingly, in 1919 the Friends' Council for International Service (the "C.I.S.") was set up, composed of representatives of London and Dublin Yearly Meetings.

From thence onwards to 1927 this Council established a more permanent service in many European countries in conjunction with the American Friends Service Committee,

---

[1] For this sentence and for the rest of the chapter I am indebted to Carl Heath.

which had been active in relief work throughout the war. The English Quaker Relief Committee (Emergency and War Victims) had been amalgamated in 1919, and as the work of relief gradually passed into reconstructive effort a time came when the amalgamated Committee could be discontinued and its remaining services transferred to the new Council.

The European Service at this time was carried on in France, Germany, Austria, Poland, Russia, Greece and Switzerland.

New Yearly Meetings of Friends were at the same time coming into existence, both in the foreign mission fields and in Europe, and in 1927 it was decided to link together in one organization *the whole* of the overseas services of London and Dublin Yearly Meetings. For this purpose the Friends Service Council (the "F.S.C.") was established —a body at once missionary and international and working in close unity with Yearly Meetings of Friends all the world over.

In the last few years a series of Friends' International Conferences has now (1937) been held in Elsinore, Paris, Amsterdam, Geneva, Prague and again near Paris and at Jordans, having for their purpose a deepening of the international life and understanding between Friends of many nations. Fifteen nationalities have been represented in these gatherings, and thus there is in the making a world fellowship of a *society of Friends*. Another All-Friends' Conference, similar to that held in 1920 in London,[1] was held in the autumn of 1937 at Swarthmore, Pennsylvania. It took into consideration the essential message of the Society of Friends and the work of the Society and of its members individually in national and international life. For many months before the holding

[1] *Post*, p. 343.

of the Conference five international commissions had been making a study of various lines of Quaker thought and service; reports of their findings have been published and are commended to the notice of our readers. Particularly may mention be made of the Report of Commission I (in pamphlet form), "The Spiritual Message of the Religious Society of Friends." An official report of the proceedings of the Conference has been published.

Chapter XX

THE ALL-FRIENDS' CONFERENCE OF 1920 AND THE PEACE TESTIMONY: THE SOUL OF QUAKERISM

IN August of 1920 a new thing happened in the history of Quakerism. In London there was held a Conference of Friends from all parts of the world and of all branches into which the Society in America is divided. Assuming the Quaker testimony for Peace, it considered the bearing of this testimony on international, social and industrial problems; and it was the means of bringing together Friends of differing ways of thought, some of whom had for many years been separated. It was a time of understanding and of healing, sending new and vigorous life into all parts of the body. Its restatement of the Quaker position lays stress on the pre-eminent value of human personality and on the essential unity in all its parts of the Christian life.

The Christianity which makes war impossible is a way of life which extirpates or controls the dispositions that lead to war. It eradicates the seeds of war in one's daily life. It translates the beatitudes out of the language of a printed book into the practice and spirit of a living person. It is not consistent for anyone to claim that his Christianity as a way of life stops him from war unless he is prepared to adjust his entire life—in its personal aspirations, in its relations with his fellows, in its pursuit of truth, in its economic and social bearings, in its political obligations, in its religious fellowships, in its intercourse with God—to the tremendous demands of Christ's way. If Friends are to challenge the whole world and claim the right to continue in the ways of peace while everybody else is fighting, they must reveal the fact that they are worthy of peace and that they bear in their bodies the marks of the Lord Jesus.

This fundamental religious ground . . . remains to-day the primary ground of the Quaker refusal to fight. Friends are as conscious as other people are of the complications of the social and political order. They are aware that perfect conditions are not to be expected at this stage of life. The Kingdom of God has obviously not yet come in all of its extensity or intensity. But they take the way of life revealed by Christ as a divinely given programme of human action and of social relationship. They do not rest their case on sporadic texts. They find themselves confronted with a Christianity, the Christianity of the Gospels, that calls for a radical transformation of man, for the creation of a new type of person and for the building of a new social order, and they take this with utmost seriousness as a thing to be ventured and tried. That it is difficult, and that it involves living, even at this imperfect stage, as though the Kingdom of God had come, and as though love were the supreme force of life, seem to them no adequate reasons against this experiment. The only way it ever can come, they believe, is to have a nucleus of people who practise it here in this very difficult present world, who have faith enough in it to make a venture and experiment of trying it, of living by it and, if need be, of dying for it. Finally, they profoundly believe that Christ's own loyalty and dedication to it, even though it cost Him life itself, has made it for ever a way of sacred obligation.

Earlier on, this declaration of Quaker faith points out that the answer of Fox in Derby gaol to those who pressed him to be a soldier[1] shows that

. . . he proposed . . . to make the experiment of exhibiting a type of life which will finally expel war by the creation of a society that has no seeds of war in it. That experiment calls for the practice of love in the midst of hate and bitterness, and it involves the refusal to lower the ideal in the face of any external difficulty. It is not a policy; it is a conviction of the soul. It cannot be followed at one time and surrendered at another time.

[1] *Ante*, p. 42; and concerning Quakerism and War see *ante*, pp. 108 note, 130–33, 214.

This statement is in accord with what has been already said concerning the testimony for Peace as rooted in the central teaching of Quakerism. The conviction of "that of God in every man" involves the obligation to make appeal to this principle, avoiding everything calculated to violate it, and this to some extent determines the way that Friends, in their work for Peace, will take. The report of one of the American Commissions deals with this point.

> Our Quaker Peace message is not a detached programme of international comity, founded on economic or political expediency or idealism. It is one expression of our religious convictions and message. This makes it difficult for us to co-operate fully with other organizations and individuals engaged in Peace propaganda whose starting-point and goal are not exactly coincident with ours, and whose spirit and methods are often at variance with our own.[1]

This point is important inasmuch as Friends are sometimes called on to sink their Quakerism in a fellowship with all men of goodwill. To this demand the Council for International Service made answer:

> Friends are not better than other people, and they will co-operate with all religious and humane forces seeking the same ends. But they are under the special compulsion of a great idea. To *merge* their work in a general humanitarian activity would be to hinder themselves in setting forth the indwelling Spirit as the central and essential factor in the call to the humane life. To *merge* their work in a general Christian activity would be to weaken their testimony for the direct access of the spirit of man to God without priest, or outward sacrament, or set forms of worship.[2]

[1] All-Friends' Conference (1920), American Commission, vi. p. 11. Reports of the American and English Commissions are of permanent value in their treatment of Friends' testimony for Peace.

[2] *Quaker Thought in International Service*, a pamphlet issued by the Council for International Service in 1921, reissued in 1924.

The story of the Friends' Peace testimony from the beginning has been told by Margaret E. Hirst in her work, *The Quakers in Peace and War*.[1]

Five years after the All-Friends' Conference another new thing happened. For some time there had been a growing conviction that the headquarters of London Yearly Meeting situate in Bishopsgate were no longer adapted to the efficient carrying on of the work of the Society, but it was hard to leave the place which had, in part, belonged to Friends for two hundred and fifty years. Nevertheless, after much searching of heart, in the conviction that "men not walls make a city," the change was agreed to, and, in 1924, "Friends House," as it is called, began to arise in Euston Road. In the closing days of 1925 Friends left Devonshire House.[2]

A few months after this another work, likely to have far-reaching effects, opened out before Friends, In 1926 a dispute in the coal mining industry, involving a stoppage of work, caused widespread acute distress and the Meeting for Sufferings set up a watching committee to endeavour to bring together employers and employed and to pay visits to the distressed areas in order to arrange for relief. In South Wales the work at first consisted in the supplying of clothes and in the gathering of women into groups for sewing meetings and of men for the repairing of boots, the committee arranging for a supply of leather. In 1928 a Lord Mayor's Fund was raised and a large part of it was handed over to Friends inasmuch as they had well-established workers in the field. By one committee and

---

[1] It is in this work that there is made the statement mentioned in the footnote on p. 328.

[2] Part of the ground on which the premises stood was bought from the Earl of Devonshire in 1676, Friends having occupied it since 1666 (the year of the Fire of London). See *Old Devonshire House by Bishopsgate*, by Margaret Sefton-Jones. The new house is opposite Euston Station.

another, different forms of relief were organized and finally the work passed into the care of the Allotments Committee set up by the Meeting for Sufferings. From Friends and others it receives large sums of money to provide land for allotments on which the unemployed may raise vegetables for the use of themselves and their families and to buy at wholesale prices seeds, fertilizers and tools. The unemployed are organized in groups, each with its own secretary and treasurer, who forward to the committee such sums of money as the men are able to raise. The group formation is a corrective of the isolation and estrangement from others which is a serious effect of prolonged unemployment; and men and their families have found courage and hope renewed by participation in the scheme which, by giving them an interest in life, saves them from a deadening idleness. In a recent report issued before the writing (in 1938) of this account, it was stated that in the preceding twelve months to which it refers the sum of over £58,000 had been raised, that the participants in the benefit had numbered more than 135,000 in all parts of England and Wales, and that they themselves had paid in to the scheme more than £33,000. From the Government, grants are now received for the furtherance of the work.

It is, of course, not contended that this is a complete or final settlement of the problem of unemployment, but temporarily it is uplifting and saving many from material and spiritual despair.

The Land Settlement Association is perhaps the most striking outcome of the work: it has no official connection with the Society although several Friends are members of it. It deals with holdings larger than allotments and owing to the extent of its operations and the large sum of money involved in its working, perhaps half a million a year, the

Quakers, when the charge of the work was offered to them, felt it unwise to undertake the new responsibility in addition to that which they already had in hand.

In the earlier stages of the work in Wales there were set up under the care of Friends educational and social service settlements at Maes-yr-Haf, Brynmawr, Dowlais and elsewhere: these have all now become independent under committees of their own. In the distressed area of West Cumberland and in many other parts work for the benefit of the unemployed is being undertaken by Friends on their own initiative.

The concern of Friends for the unemployed was a pioneer work and it was taking effect before the Government was engaged in any kind of special relief measures.

I have now brought the history of English Quakerism down to the great Conference of 1920, to the Young Friends' Conference that followed it, to the work of the Friends' Service Council, and to the removal from Devonshire House, close upon two hundred and eighty years after Fox first "convinced" his hearers at Manchester. Of the world conference of 1937 mention has been made. I have recorded success and failure, strength and weakness, brightness and shade; and I can assert that to-day, learning the lessons taught by past and present, the Society of Friends looks forward with good hope. It can honestly and thankfully take to itself the words, "Thou hast a little strength, and hast not denied My name." It has rediscovered, neither easily nor quickly, the truth that it exists not for itself, but for the world's healing. With increasing boldness, its timidity not all cast aside, it ventures along new paths which lead to strange places. Confident in having a message for its generation, the Quaker Church seeks to send forth men and women strong to proclaim it, realizing that enthusiasm, and even sacrifice, for works of outward well-being, necessary as these are, do not absolve the Church or any member of it from the task of giving forth a definite message of God. And it may even be that Quakerism, which for so great a part of its history has turned aside from art, may yet achieve the synthesis of the aesthetic and spiritual sides of man's being, so that they shall work together for the harmonious and complete life, neither of them looking with suspicion on the other, and neither of them fastidiously shrinking away from the world of suffering humanity.

The message emphasized by the Society of Friends in the seventeenth century, and maintained (not always with clearness) throughout its history, is of special importance in this day of realization that the observance of religious practices, and the very profession of religion itself, must no longer depend ultimately on the support of authority or convention or public opinion. Not even in the name of loyalty or of gratitude to the Church are they to be *exacted*, however blameworthy failure of loyalty and gratitude may be. The spiritual life, and all that accompanies it, must, without aid of weapon or of defence, contend in the arena with the world's demands, making its own appeal to that of God in each human soul, in this way, and in no other, gaining its victory and winning a sure place for itself. That it may thus triumph is the very object of the association of individuals in a Christian society, each of them gaining ever greater skill worthily to enhearten his fellows. The wise teacher of music or art or literature does not press on his pupils his own mind or the minds of others, however eminent; but in showing them how to gain instruction from the past, even as he is himself doing, he seeks to attract them to the place where, by reason of *their own* perception of the highest, *their nature* is to move toward it. Even so must there be training in appreciation of spiritual values; the deeper this appreciation, the more evident the worth of every other good thing. But a nemesis, which is not yet worked out, has overtaken those Churches which have failed to give this teaching. To temptation in this way, the Society of Friends has, as we have seen, lain peculiarly open, by reason of imperfect understanding of its own message.

This historical sketch, designed to give understanding of present-day conditions, may now conclude by setting forth the strength of Quakerism which has overcome tendencies or influences apparently destined to destroy it. Although it is not difficult to set down in words the principles and practices for which the Society of Friends stands, a true comprehension of them, not lending itself to explicit description, can be reached only through experience. They are both the outcome and the cause of a certain way of looking at things, a method of approach to questions, a manner and attitude of life. Differing among themselves as Friends have done, they have at all times laid stress on individual Divine guidance, their quiet waiting in worship affording peculiar opportunity for its realization. This principle has, as we have seen, not always been fully understood in all its implications, but it has never been abandoned. Even in dark days it is this that has coloured the thoughts of countless men and women, often leading them in the way of hurt to their reputation or their profit, but also in the way of peace. It has produced a certain depth and calmness of mind especially marked in times of outward tumult. There has never failed a measure of the spirit commended and exemplified by Fox:

> Friends, go not into the aggravating part to strive with it, lest ye do hurt to your souls and run into the same nature, for patience must get the victory, and [it] answers to that of God in everyone, which will bring everyone from the contrary. . . . That which joins to the aggravating part sets up the aggravating part and breeds confusion, and reaches not to the witness of God in everyone.[1]

The truth of this has been manifested by the courageously patient bearing of Friends in the presence of the mob breaking up their meetings.[2] In times of Indian raids and of war in America and of disturbance in Ireland the quietness and confidence of lives lived in the secret place of the Most High have brought about wonderful results.[3] On the moss-troopers, murderers and robbers of the Scottish border, the influence of Friends was at one time so great that "the Earl of Carlisle told King Charles the Second, *That the Quakers had done more to suppress them than all his troops could do.*"[4]

In the following passage the Quaker attitude of mind is well described:

---

[1] *Epistles*, p. 87. See pp. 88, 211, 235 (*ante*, p. 107), 488. Compare the saying of St. Bernard: "When only one is angry something may still be done; when both wax angry, there is no further profit." Taken from G. G. Coulton's *Five Centuries of Religion*, p. 299.

[2] *Ante*, p. 106.

[3] See "Fierce Feathers," in L. Violet Hodgkin's *Quaker Saints*, also *Southern Heroes*, by Cartland (Stories of the Civil War in America), "American Friends in War Time" in Report of American Commission I, prepared for the Conference of all Friends, 1920; *Friends in Ireland*, a pamphlet by A. M. Hodgkin, *The Principles of Peace Exemplified by Friends in Ireland During the Rebellion of 1798*, by Dr. Thomas Hancock; and Braithwaite, *Second Period*, pp. 624–29.

[4] From *An Epistle to Friends*, etc., written by John Bellers in 1724, the *Epistle* is set out in *John Bellers (1654–1725)*, by A. Ruth Fry, p. 159; see also *First Publishers of Truth*, p. 63.

The condition of spiritual responsiveness has greatly varied, the place given to the intellect in the apprehension of guidance has altered, the recognition of the human fallibility of the saint has been made, and the area of life which the Society has left free for individual guidance has at one time been circumscribed and at another enlarged. But some of the deepest factors have been nearly constant. The Society from first to last has affirmed that the Spirit of man is the place of all others in which the Spirit of God can shine. . . . And, throughout a chequered history of strength and weakness, it has promoted retirement of heart and waiting upon the Lord as among the surest means for renewing spiritual strength.

The result has been to produce a type of character which is probably the chief enrichment of Christianity hitherto made by Quakerism—the man or woman who goes through life endeavouring to decide every question as it arises, not by passion or prejudice, nor mainly by the conclusions of human reason, but chiefly by reference to the light of God that shines in the prepared soul.[1]

It was the writer of these words who was almost wholly responsible for the exposition of the Quaker faith officially put forth by London Yearly Meeting in 1921. At various times that meeting has issued statements of doctrine coloured by the prevailing thought of the day, but that of 1921 differed from its predecessors. Laying the emphasis on vital experience, it did not set forth an ordered statement of belief, but under different headings it arranged the expressions or records of the experiences of Friends in all times of the Society's history. The collection includes passages taken from official documents. The extracts that are quoted are not in perfect accord among themselves but, as the Preface states:

The attempt has been made throughout to state truth, not by formulating it, but by expressing it through the

[1] Braithwaite, *Spiritual Guidance in Quaker Experience*, pp. 81–82, see *ante*, pp. 169–70.

vital personal and corporate experience of Friends. Life itself, with its variety of outlook and condition, seems to us the way by which God has spoken to men through the prophets and supremely through Jesus Christ, and by which His living Spirit has spoken and is still speaking to man.[1]

In similar strain a report presented to the Yearly Meeting of 1920 defines the Quaker standpoint. It was drawn up in accordance with a request made by the promoters of a movement directed toward a union of the Christian Churches throughout the world.

The main difference between ourselves and most other bodies of Christians arise from the emphasis we place on the Light of God's Holy Spirit in the human soul—potentially in all human souls, and known in actual experience as these are turned towards the Light and are obedient to it. This direct contact between the Spirit of Christ and the human spirit we are prepared to trust to, as the basis of our individual and corporate life.

From this source all our special "testimonies" flow. In our Church meetings, and in our Meetings for Worship, we seek to rely entirely upon the actual presence and leadership of the Holy Spirit. We do not make arrangements for a "service" which will preclude the immediate guidance of the Spirit—nor do we leave the public service in the hands of those ordained or set apart for it. Our experience, which we hold in trust for the whole Church, is that, in meetings so held, the Holy Spirit does guide frequently in unexpected ways, and to unexpected conclusions, and that such meetings can be held in an orderly way, under His leadership, to the profit of all, and to the furtherance of the work of the Church.

We are thus compelled at times to stand apart from other communions in such matters as a separated Ministry, forms in public worship, and the use of outward Sacraments. We

[1] The work is entitled *Christian Life, Faith and ¦Thought in the Society of Friends*. In 1925 another volume entitled *Christian Practice* was officially issued, and in 1931 a third volume which was entitled *Church Government* (this has undergone slight revision later). Concerning the movement leading up to this revision see Mekeel, *Quakerism and a Creed*, c. xi.

z

feel that we must maintain our practice in these things as a vital part of our belief—as our testimony to the reality of the Spirit's presence with, and guidance of, our individual and corporate life. We do not make use of the outward rites of Baptism and the Lord's Supper, but we do believe in the inward experiences they symbolize. Our testimony is to the actuality of this experience even without the external rite.[1]

So, also, the conviction that the Spirit of Christ dwells, potentially at least, in the souls of all men is the source of our refusal to take part in war, and of our opposition to slavery and oppression in every form. We believe that the primary Christian duty in relation to others is to appeal to "that of God" in them, and, therefore, any method of oppression or violence that renders such an appeal impossible must be set on one side.[2]

The history of the Society of Friends does not show them as making any marked contribution to speculative theology, but rather as specializing in a type of conduct and corporate witness that they believe to be in harmony with the inward experience of God in the soul.[3] It has been generally recognized by those who have observed the Society of Friends from without, even by many who feel they are doctrinally in error, that honesty in business, a truthfulness that refused to admit the double standard by the taking of oaths, simplicity and purity of life, work for the weak and downtrodden, slaves and prisoners, a witness for truth whatever the consequences, have, broadly speaking, characterized the Quaker community, while, of course, we should be the first to admit there have been lapses, and much blindness to the full implication of the faith. What Friends hold however, is that the type of life and the inward experience are indissolubly connected, that the experience without the life is sentimentalism, that life without the experience is barren. We believe that further applications of our belief to life and conduct will be revealed as we are loyal to Jesus Christ, and obedient to His Light in our souls.

[1] *Ante*, p. 67 note 2.   [2] *Ante*, pp. 130–133, 214–15.
[3] See Grubb, *Thoughts on the Divine in Man* (a pamphlet), pp. 14–16.

INDEX

Access to Royalty, ease of, 59 n., 90 n.
Ackworth, 184 n., 187, 193 n., 210, 212, 214 n., 223, 224, 225 n., 227, 264, 269, 285, 293 n., 294 n., 295, 306, 318 n.
Addison, 122
Adult Schools, 279, 308, 318
Affirmation, 189. *See* Oaths
After Bunyan, 271
Aldam, Thomas, 175
Algiers, prisoners, 46
Aliens, enemy, 331, 332
Allegiance, oath of, 153, 154
Allegorical preaching, 258
Allen, Wm., 229, 265, 266 n., 329
All-Friends' Conference (1920), 343, 345 n; (1937) 47, 341
Allotments, 347
Ambulance Unit, Friends', 328
America(n), 36, 87 ff., 175, 185 n., 207, 317, 331, 351
Ames, William, 176
Amsterdam, 341
Anabaptists, 20
Anarchy of the Ranters, 172
Anatomy of Melancholy, 21, 25 n.
Andrews, Lancelot, 31
"Answering that of God," 53-55; *see* "That of God"
Antinomianism, 136
Apology. See Barclay
Appleby, 153
Archdale, John, 189 n.
Armada, Spanish, 19
Arnold, Matthew, quoted, 301-2
Ash, Edward, 262 n.
Askew, Ann, 16
Atonement, 48
"Attenders," 297 n.
Audland, Ann, 156
Audland, Jno., 71, 110, 156, 176
Austin, Ann, 88
Authority, 45, 228, 233, 349
Authority, corporate, 122, 173

Awful, ministry, 244, 261, 265, 266 n., 270, 318 n.

Backhouse, James, 258
Bacon, Christopher, 132 n.
Bacon, Francis, 24
Baddesley, 75
Balkan wars, 329
Ball, William, 272 n.
Banks, John, 119
Banks, Quaker, 204
Baptist(s), 24, 32 n., 103, 111, 116, 143, 144 n., 145, 146 n., 182 n., 226 n.
Barbados, 80, 88, 92, 233 n.
Barber, W., 157
"Barclay of Ury," 177
Barclay, John, 223 n.
Barclay, Lydia Ann, 266
Barclay, Robert, 43, 52, 56, 61, 62, 105, 106, 119, 130, 143, 166, 167 n., 172, 177, 227, 238, 243, 245, 246, 249 n., 251, 283
Bargaining, 86, 137-8
Bartlet and Carlyle, quoted, 112 n., 113 n., 173 n.
Baxter, Richard, 26 n., 29, 30, 31, 45 n., 49, 56, 59, 95, 136, 144, 158
Beacon, The, 230, 232, 233
"Being" (= "house"), 64 n., 79 n., 89 n.
Belasco, P. S., 165, 204 n.
Belgium, 339
Bell, John, 276 n.
Bellers, John, 183 n., 197 n., 203-04, 351 n.
Benezet, Anthony, 99, 207, 208
Bennett, Arnold, 129 n.
Bennett, Justice, 42
Berlin, 332
Bernard, St., quoted, 351 n.
Besse, Joseph, 276 n.
Bevan, Jos. G., 196
Beverley, 117

GEORGE ALLEN & UNWIN LTD
LONDON: 40 MUSEUM STREET, W.C.1
LEIPZIG: (F. VOLCKMAR) HOSPITALSTR. 10
CAPE TOWN: 73 ST. GEORGE'S STREET
TORONTO: 91 WELLINGTON STREET, WEST
BOMBAY: 15 GRAHAM ROAD, BALLARD ESTATE
WELLINGTON, N.Z.: 8 KINGS CRESCENT, LOWER HUTT
SYDNEY, N.S.W.: AUSTRALIA HOUSE, WYNYARD SQUARE

THE SWARTHMORE LECTURES

Cr. 8vo, Cloth, 2s. 6d. net each

(Please see overleaf)

THE SWARTHMORE LECTURES

Cr. 8vo, Cloth, 2s. 6d. net each

* These are also available in Paper, 1s. 6d. net

GEORGE ALLEN & UNWIN LTD., Museum Street, W.C.1

Printed in the United Kingdom
by Lightning Source UK Ltd.
132590UK00001B/117/A